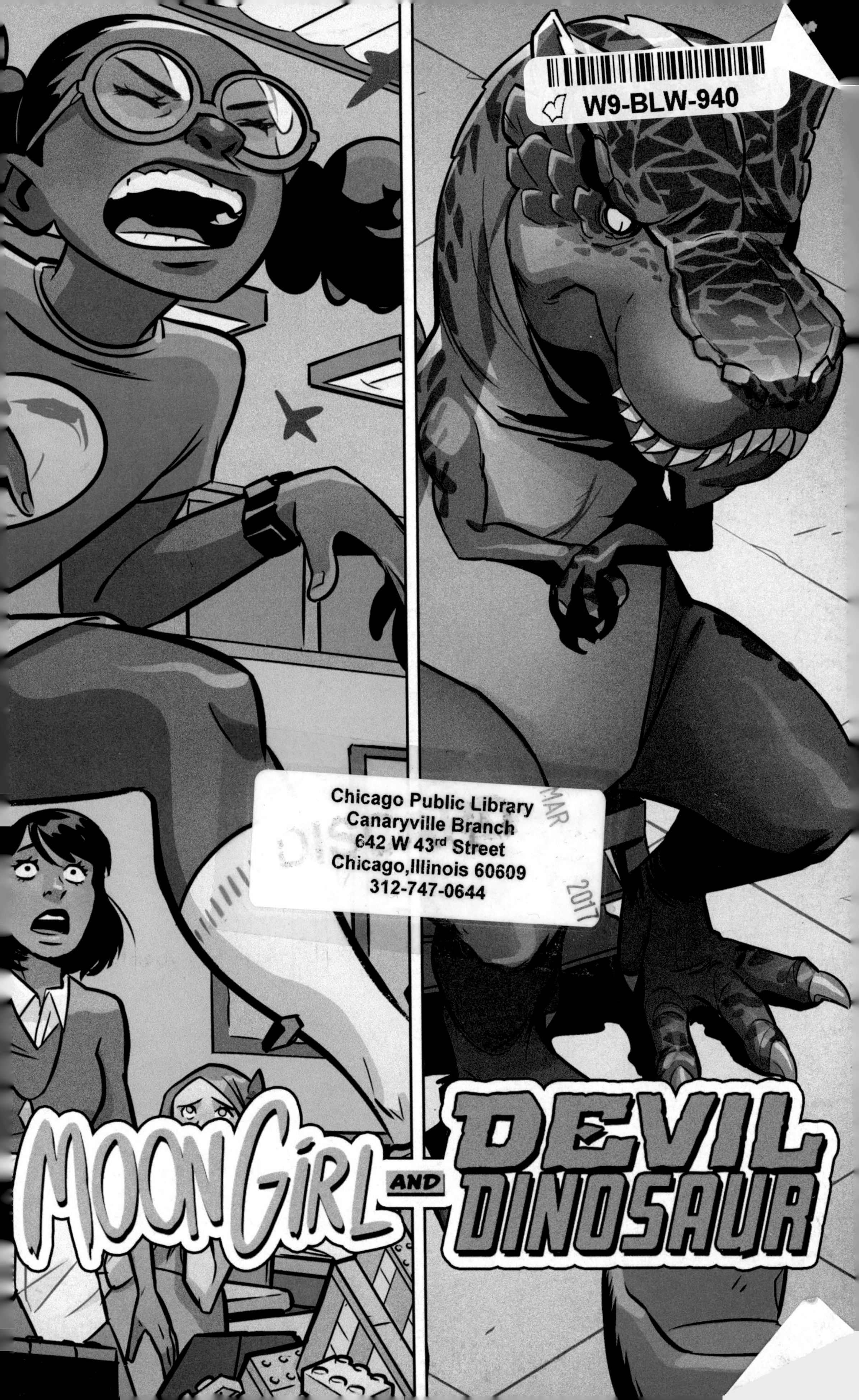
MOON GIRL
AND
DEVIL DINOSAUR

LUNELLA LAFAYETTE GETS TEASED BY THE KIDS IN HER CLASS. THEY CALL HER "MOON GIRL" AND LAUGH AT HER INVENTIONS. BUT WHO NEEDS FRIENDS WHEN YOU HAVE COOL GIZMOS AND BOOKS? SHE'S JUST BIDING HER TIME UNTIL SHE CAN GET INTO A REAL SCHOOL FOR GENIUS KIDS LIKE HER.

THERE'S ONLY ONE PROBLEM: LUNELLA HAS THE INHUMAN GENE. WHICH MEANS IF SHE ENCOUNTERS THE DEADLY TERRIGEN MISTS, SHE COULD TRANSFORM INTO A FREAK WITH POWERS AT ANY MOMENT!

SHE HAS FOUND A DEVICE THAT COULD STOP IT — A PIECE OF KREE TECHNOLOGY, THE OMNI-WAVE PROJECTOR.

ITS ACTIVATION CREATED A TIME PORTAL THAT BROUGHT FORTH A BIG, RED T. REX NAMED DEVIL DINOSAUR!

LUNELLA AND DEVIL DINO LEARNED HOW TO WORK TOGETHER TO BECOME A TEAM. THEY TOOK ON A STREET GANG CALLED THE KILLER FOLK AND WERE CELEBRATING THEIR VICTORY WHEN LUNELLA'S WORST NIGHTMARE OCCURRED...

...SHE WAS ENVELOPED BY THE TERRIGEN MISTS! LUNELLA BEGAN THE FIRST PHASE OF BECOMING AN INHUMAN — THE COCOON. WHAT WILL HAPPEN WHEN SHE EMERGES? ONLY TIME WILL TELL...

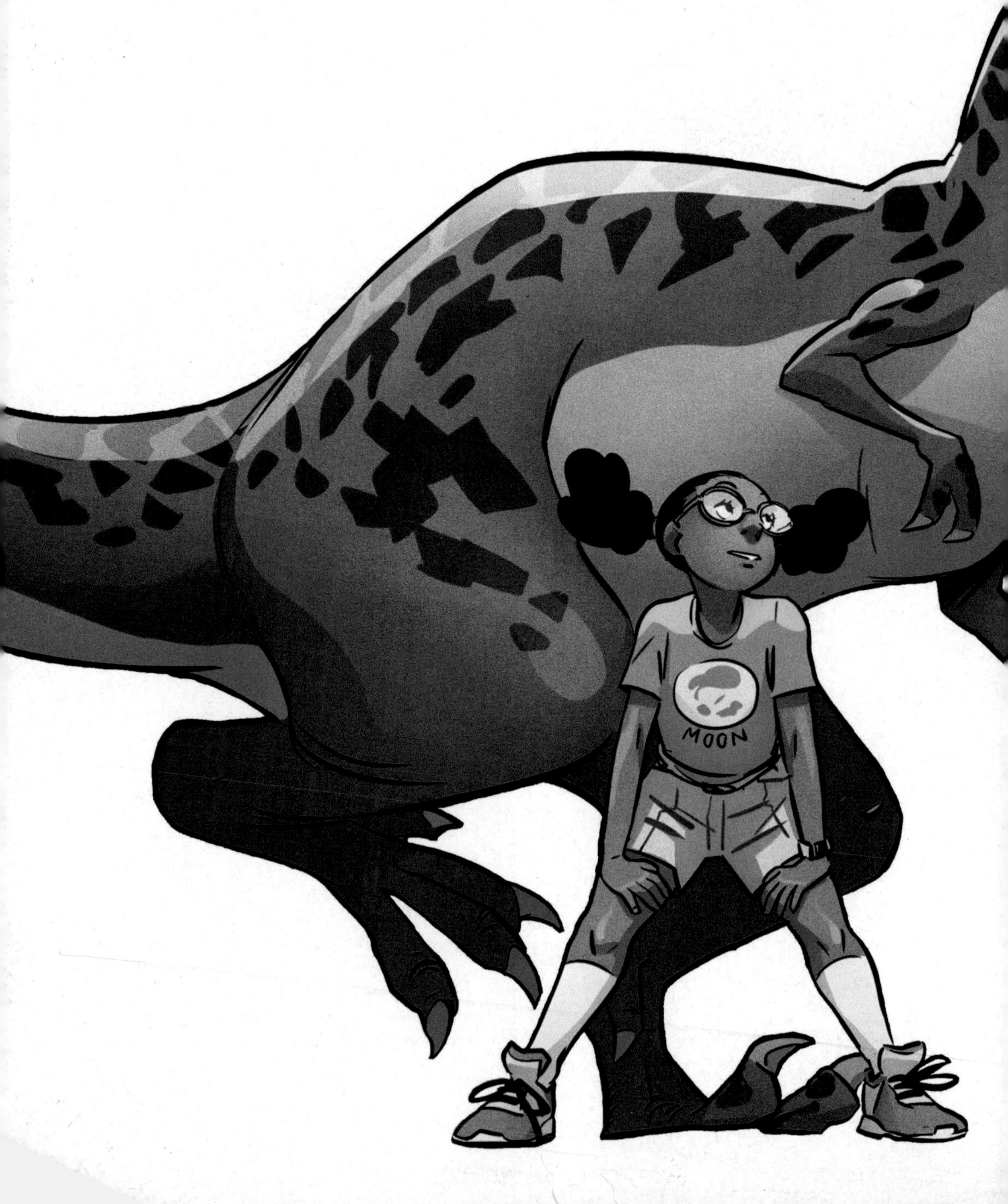
MOON

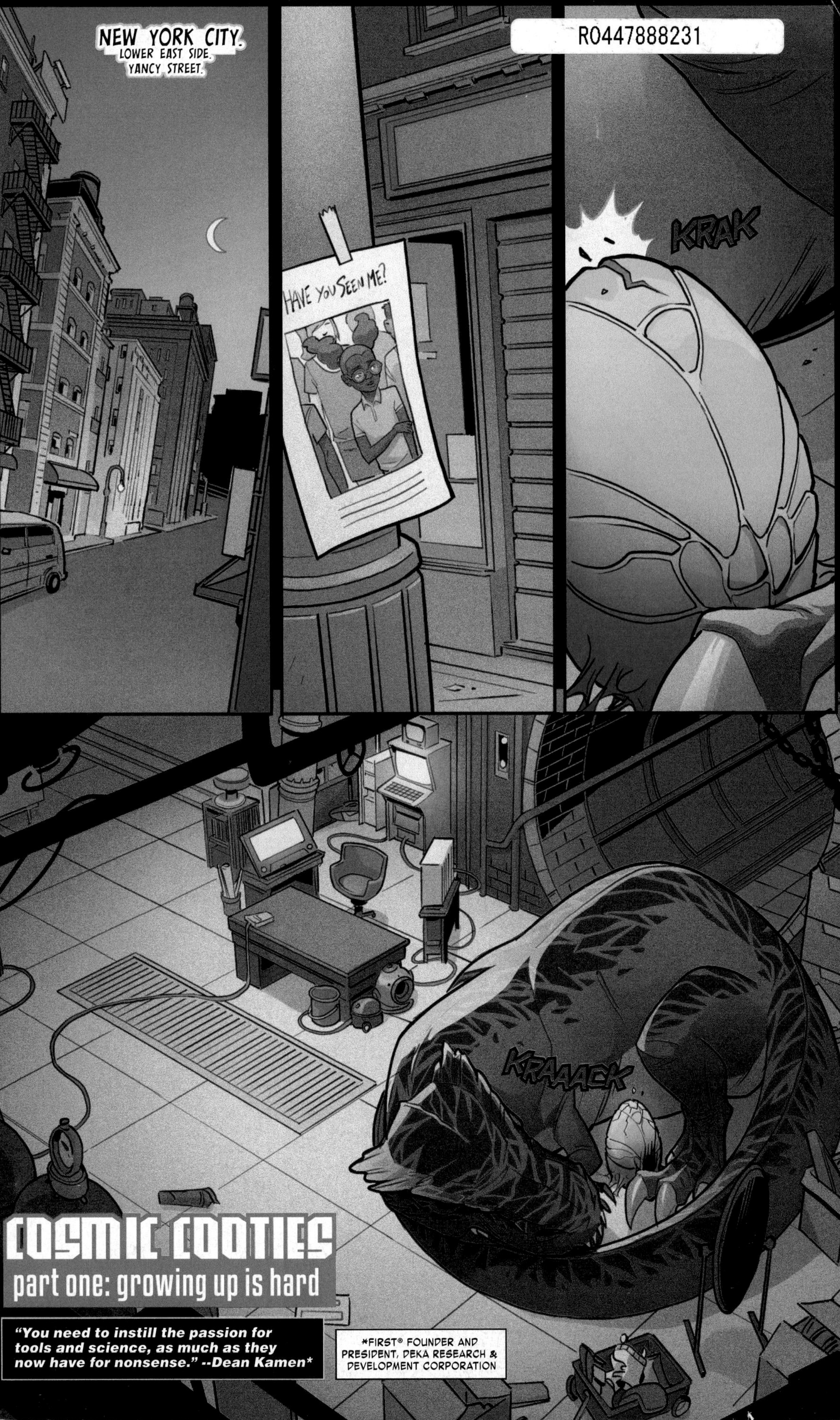
NEW YORK CITY.
LOWER EAST SIDE.
YANCY STREET.
HAVE YOU SEEN ME?
KRAK
KRAAACK
COSMIC COOTIES
part one: growing up is hard
"You need to instill the passion for tools and science, as much as they now have for nonsense." --Dean Kamen*
*FIRST® FOUNDER AND PRESIDENT, DEKA RESEARCH & DEVELOPMENT CORPORATION

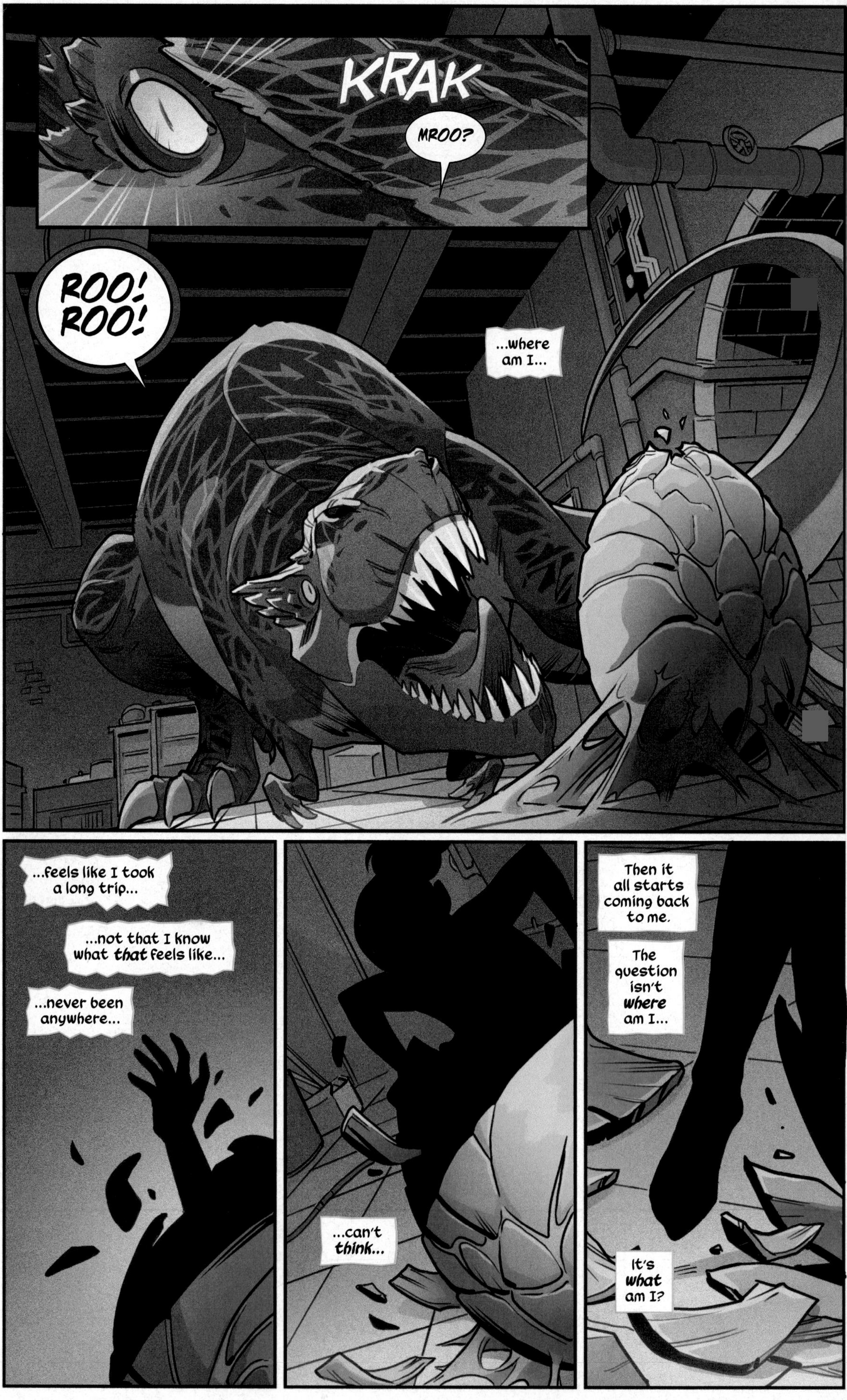
KRAK
MROO?
ROO! ROO!
...where am I...
...feels like I took a long trip...
...not that I know what *that* feels like...
...never been anywhere...
...can't *think*...
Then it all starts coming back to me.
The question isn't *where* am I...
It's *what* am I?

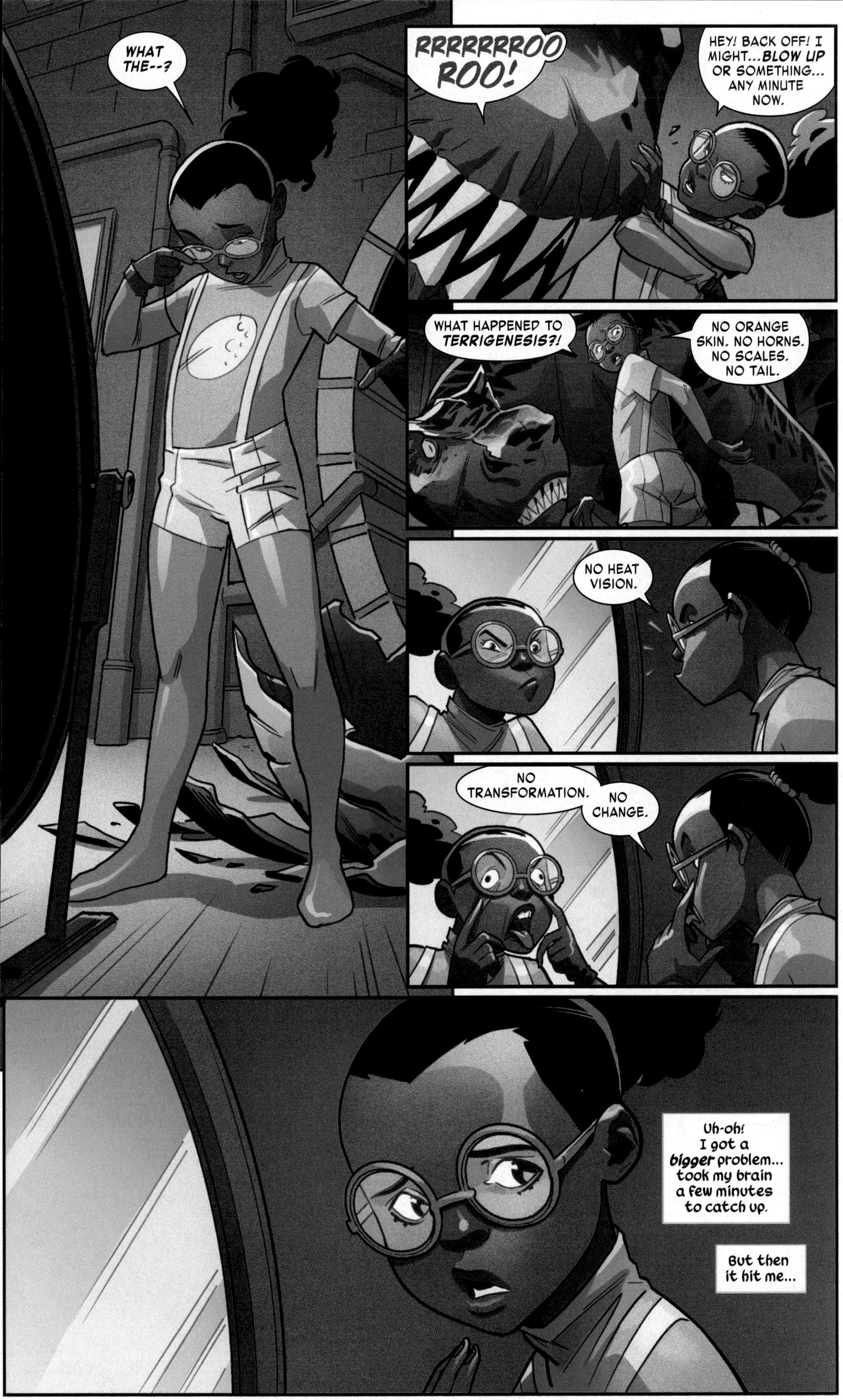
WHAT THE--?
RRRRRRROO ROO!
HEY! BACK OFF! I MIGHT...BLOW UP OR SOMETHING... ANY MINUTE NOW.
WHAT HAPPENED TO TERRIGENESIS?!
NO ORANGE SKIN. NO HORNS. NO SCALES. NO TAIL.
NO HEAT VISION.
NO TRANSFORMATION.
NO CHANGE.
Uh-oh! I got a bigger problem... took my brain a few minutes to catch up.
But then it hit me...

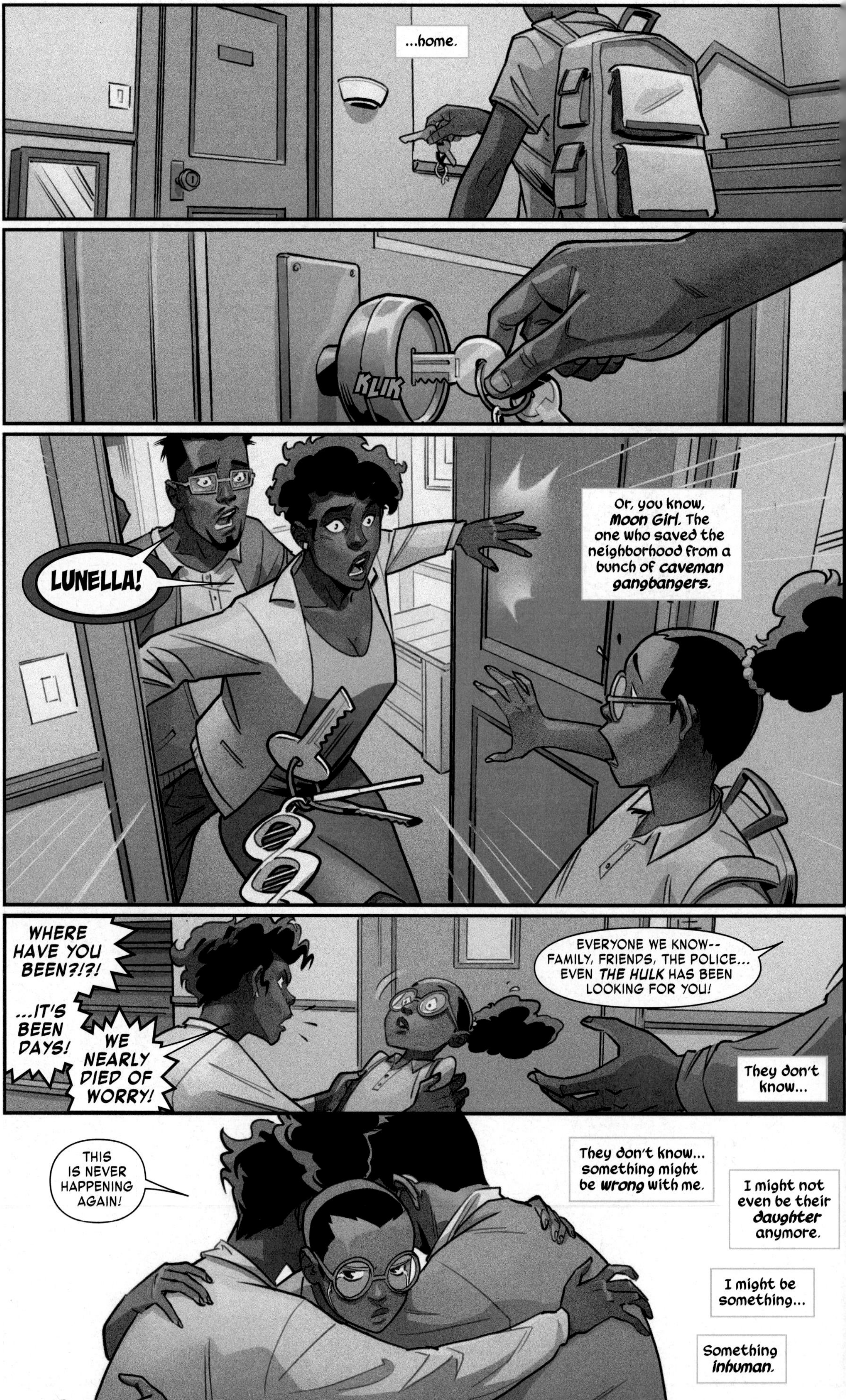

...home.
KLIK
LUNELLA!
Or, you know, Moon Girl. The one who saved the neighborhood from a bunch of caveman gangbangers.
WHERE HAVE YOU BEEN?!?!
...IT'S BEEN DAYS!
WE NEARLY DIED OF WORRY!
EVERYONE WE KNOW-- FAMILY, FRIENDS, THE POLICE... EVEN THE HULK HAS BEEN LOOKING FOR YOU!
They don't know...
THIS IS NEVER HAPPENING AGAIN!
They don't know... something might be wrong with me.
I might not even be their daughter anymore.
I might be something...
Something inhuman.

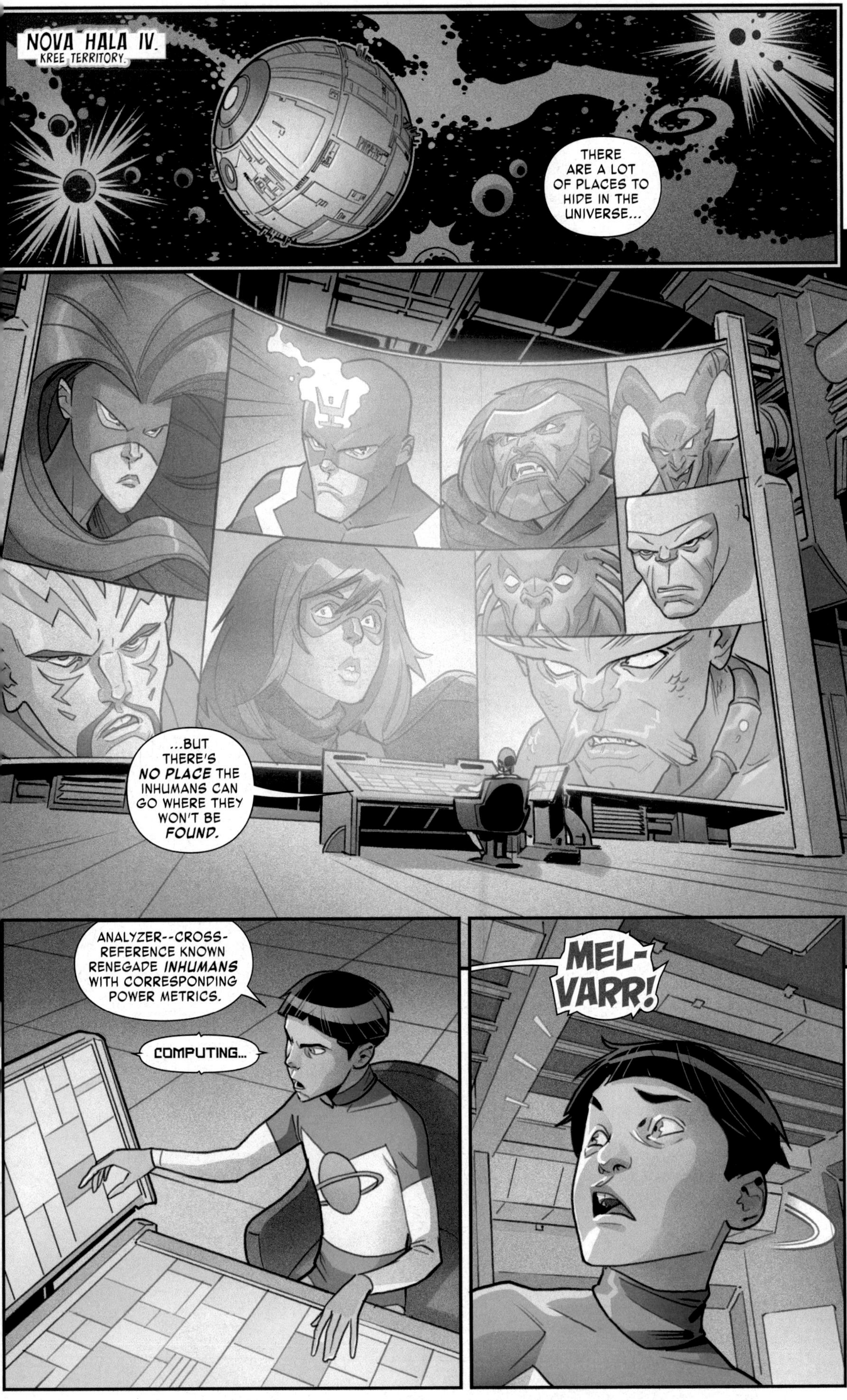
NOVA HALA IV.
KREE TERRITORY.
THERE ARE A LOT OF PLACES TO HIDE IN THE UNIVERSE...
...BUT THERE'S NO PLACE THE INHUMANS CAN GO WHERE THEY WON'T BE FOUND.
ANALYZER--CROSS-REFERENCE KNOWN RENEGADE INHUMANS WITH CORRESPONDING POWER METRICS.
COMPUTING...
MEL-VARR!

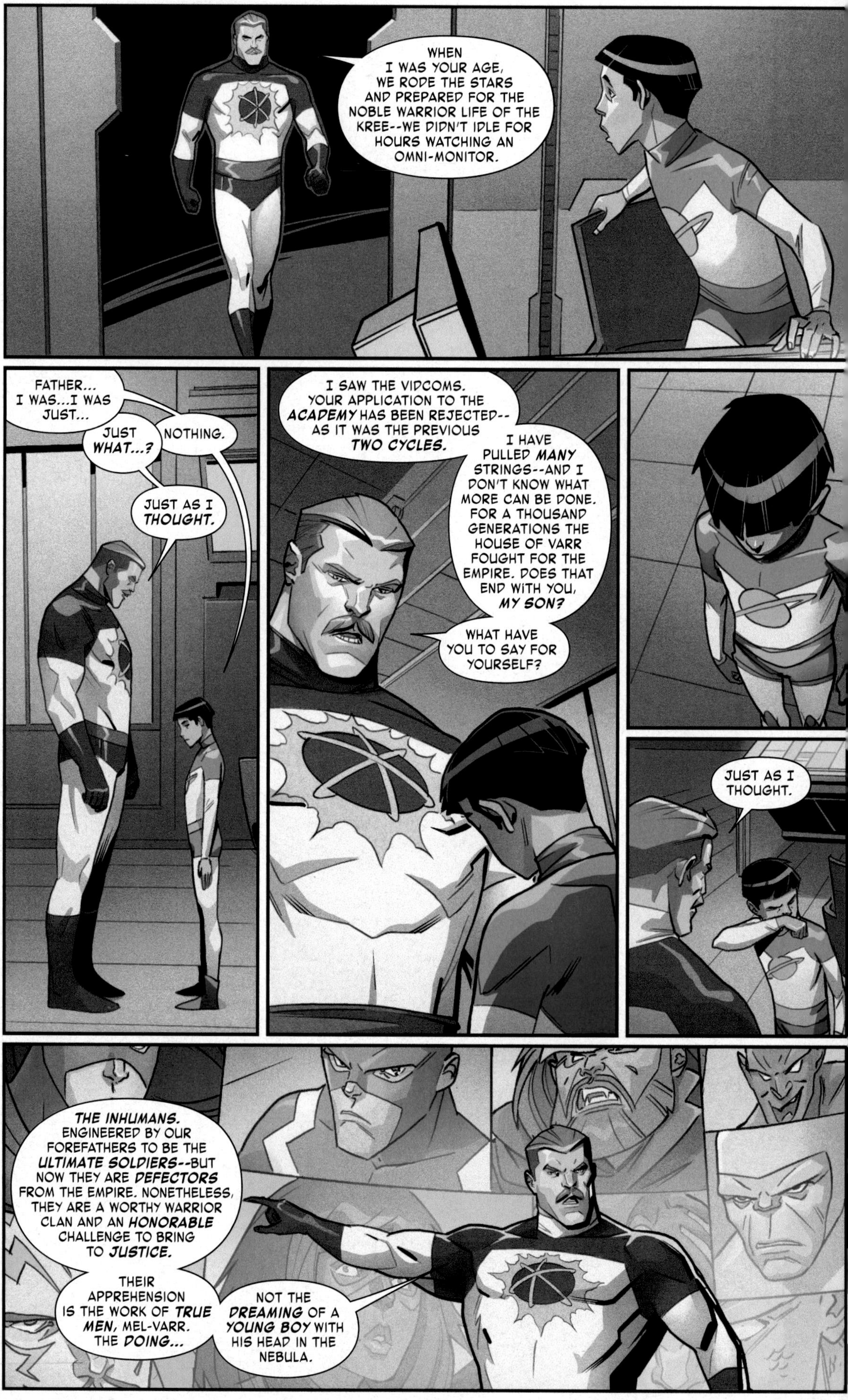
WHEN I WAS YOUR AGE, WE RODE THE STARS AND PREPARED FOR THE NOBLE WARRIOR LIFE OF THE KREE--WE DIDN'T IDLE FOR HOURS WATCHING AN OMNI-MONITOR.
FATHER... I WAS...I WAS JUST...
JUST *WHAT...?*
NOTHING.
JUST AS I *THOUGHT.*
I SAW THE VIDCOMS. YOUR APPLICATION TO THE *ACADEMY* HAS BEEN REJECTED-- AS IT WAS THE PREVIOUS *TWO CYCLES.*
I HAVE PULLED *MANY* STRINGS--AND I DON'T KNOW WHAT MORE CAN BE DONE. FOR A THOUSAND GENERATIONS THE HOUSE OF VARR FOUGHT FOR THE EMPIRE. DOES THAT END WITH YOU, *MY SON?*
WHAT HAVE YOU TO SAY FOR YOURSELF?
JUST AS I THOUGHT.
THE INHUMANS. ENGINEERED BY OUR FOREFATHERS TO BE THE *ULTIMATE SOLDIERS*--BUT NOW THEY ARE *DEFECTORS* FROM THE EMPIRE. NONETHELESS, THEY ARE A WORTHY WARRIOR CLAN AND AN *HONORABLE* CHALLENGE TO BRING TO *JUSTICE.*
THEIR APPREHENSION IS THE WORK OF *TRUE MEN,* MEL-VARR. THE *DOING...*
NOT THE *DREAMING* OF A *YOUNG BOY* WITH HIS HEAD IN THE NEBULA.

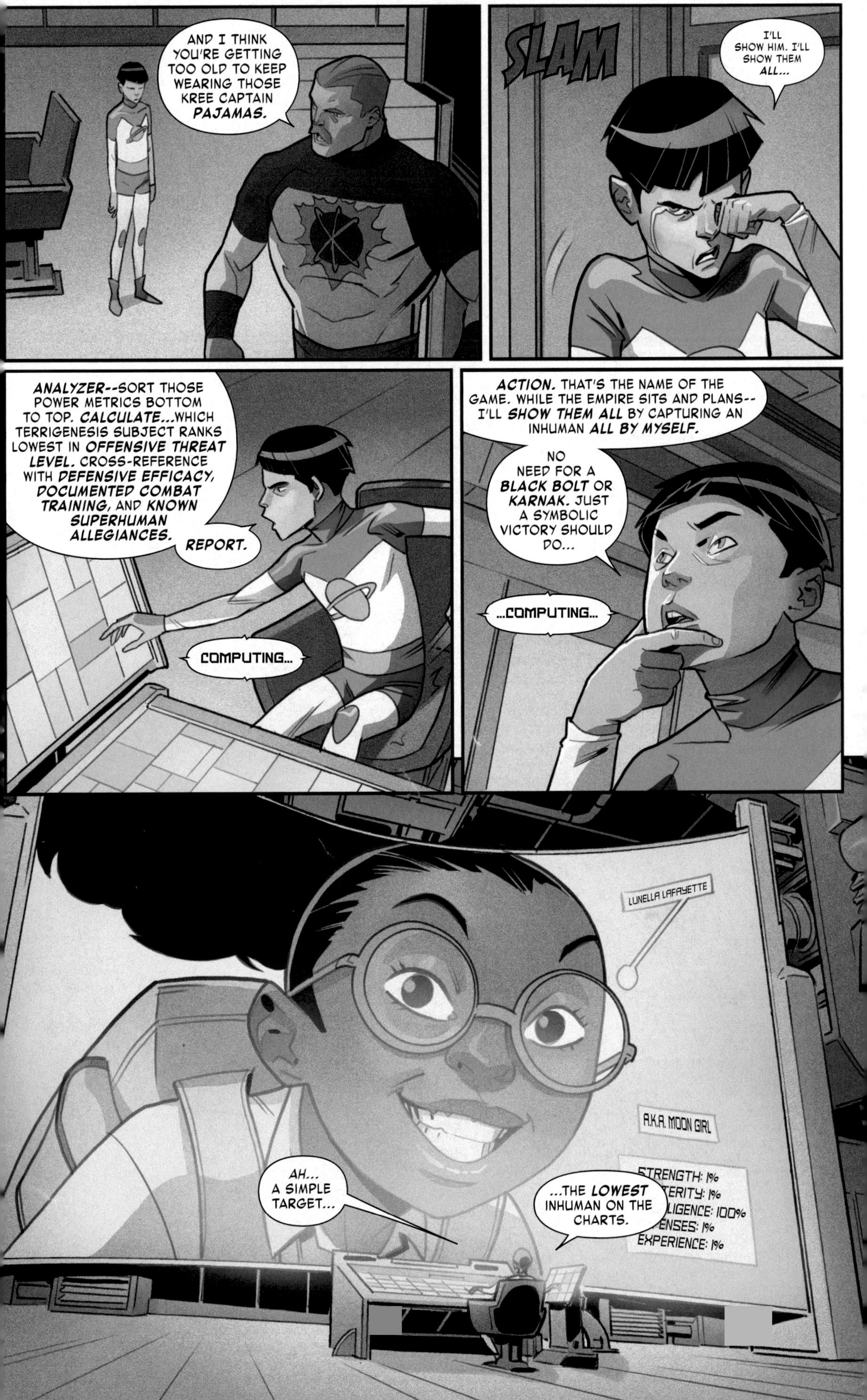
AND I THINK YOU'RE GETTING TOO OLD TO KEEP WEARING THOSE KREE CAPTAIN PAJAMAS.
SLAM
I'LL SHOW HIM. I'LL SHOW THEM ALL...
ANALYZER--SORT THOSE POWER METRICS BOTTOM TO TOP. CALCULATE...WHICH TERRIGENESIS SUBJECT RANKS LOWEST IN OFFENSIVE THREAT LEVEL. CROSS-REFERENCE WITH DEFENSIVE EFFICACY, DOCUMENTED COMBAT TRAINING, AND KNOWN SUPERHUMAN ALLEGIANCES.
REPORT.
COMPUTING...
ACTION. THAT'S THE NAME OF THE GAME. WHILE THE EMPIRE SITS AND PLANS-- I'LL SHOW THEM ALL BY CAPTURING AN INHUMAN ALL BY MYSELF.
NO NEED FOR A BLACK BOLT OR KARNAK. JUST A SYMBOLIC VICTORY SHOULD DO...
...COMPUTING...
LUNELLA LAFAYETTE
A.K.A. MOON GIRL
STRENGTH: 1%
EXPERIENCE: 1%
AH... A SIMPLE TARGET...
...THE LOWEST INHUMAN ON THE CHARTS.

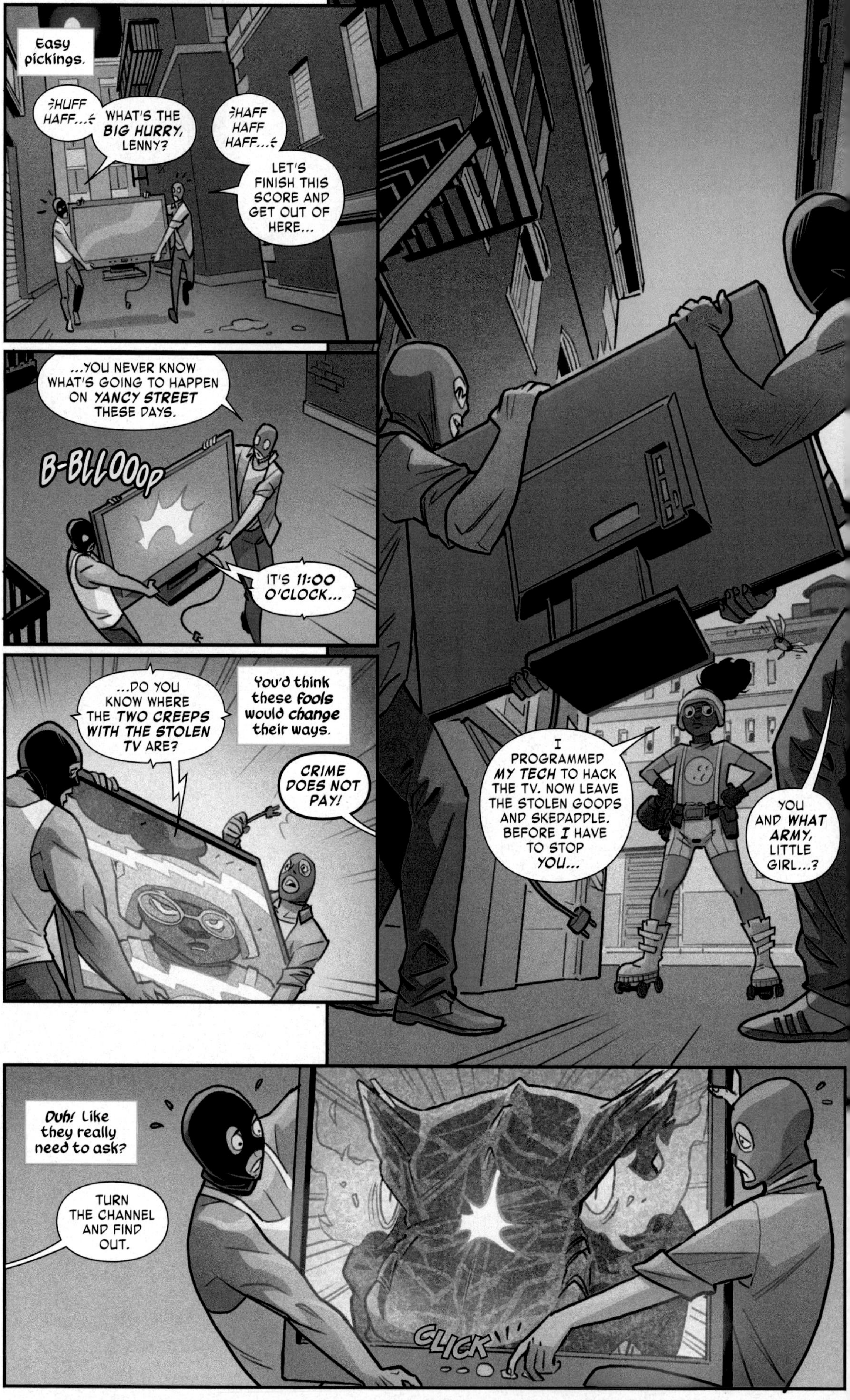
Easy pickings.
⸗HUFF HAFF...⸗
WHAT'S THE BIG HURRY, LENNY?
⸗HAFF HAFF HAFF...⸗
LET'S FINISH THIS SCORE AND GET OUT OF HERE...
...YOU NEVER KNOW WHAT'S GOING TO HAPPEN ON YANCY STREET THESE DAYS.
B-BLLOOOP
IT'S 11:00 O'CLOCK...
...DO YOU KNOW WHERE THE TWO CREEPS WITH THE STOLEN TV ARE?
You'd think these fools would change their ways.
CRIME DOES NOT PAY!
I PROGRAMMED MY TECH TO HACK THE TV. NOW LEAVE THE STOLEN GOODS AND SKEDADDLE. BEFORE I HAVE TO STOP YOU...
YOU AND WHAT ARMY, LITTLE GIRL...?
Duh! Like they really need to ask?
TURN THE CHANNEL AND FIND OUT.
CLICK

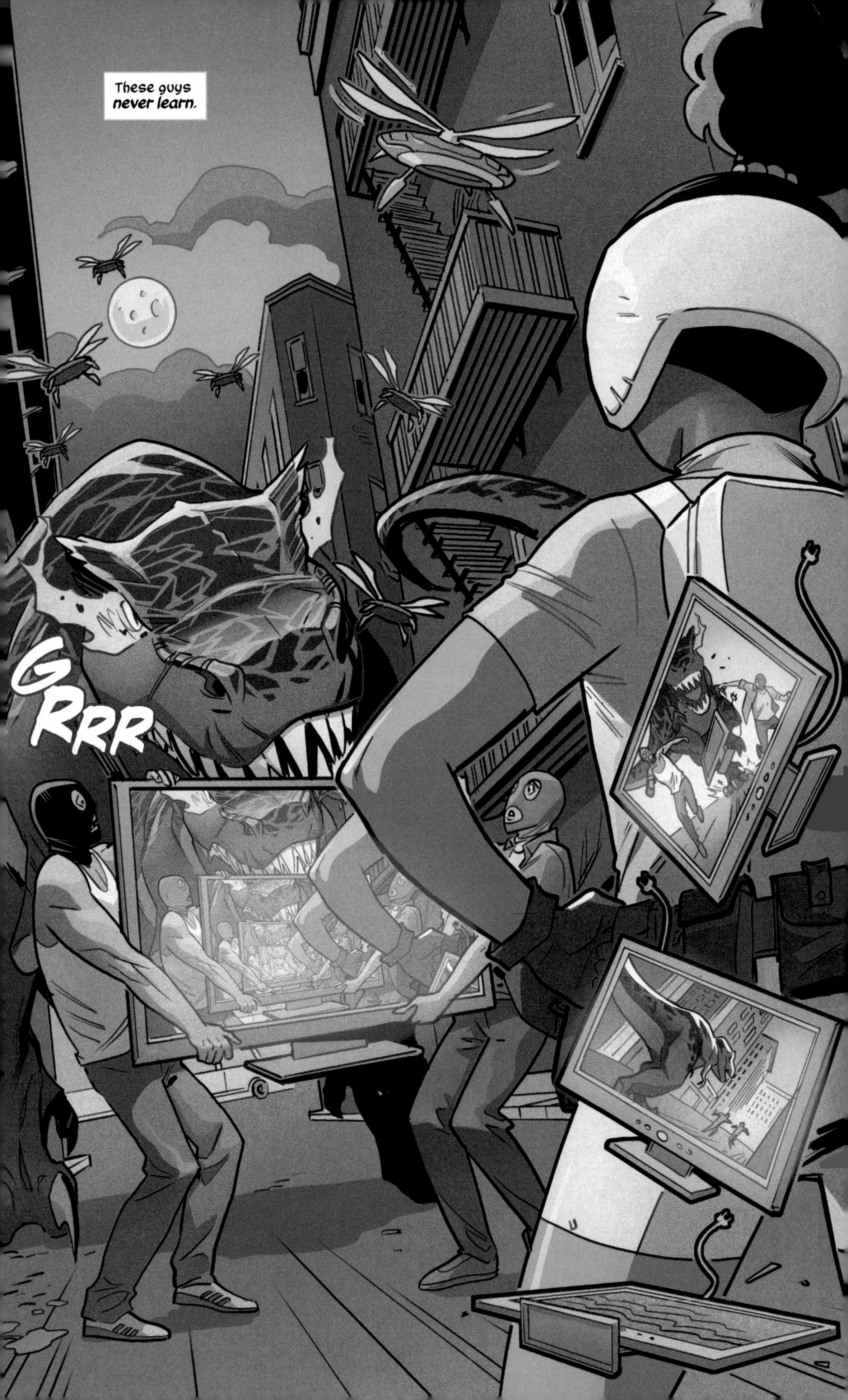
These guys never learn.
GRRR

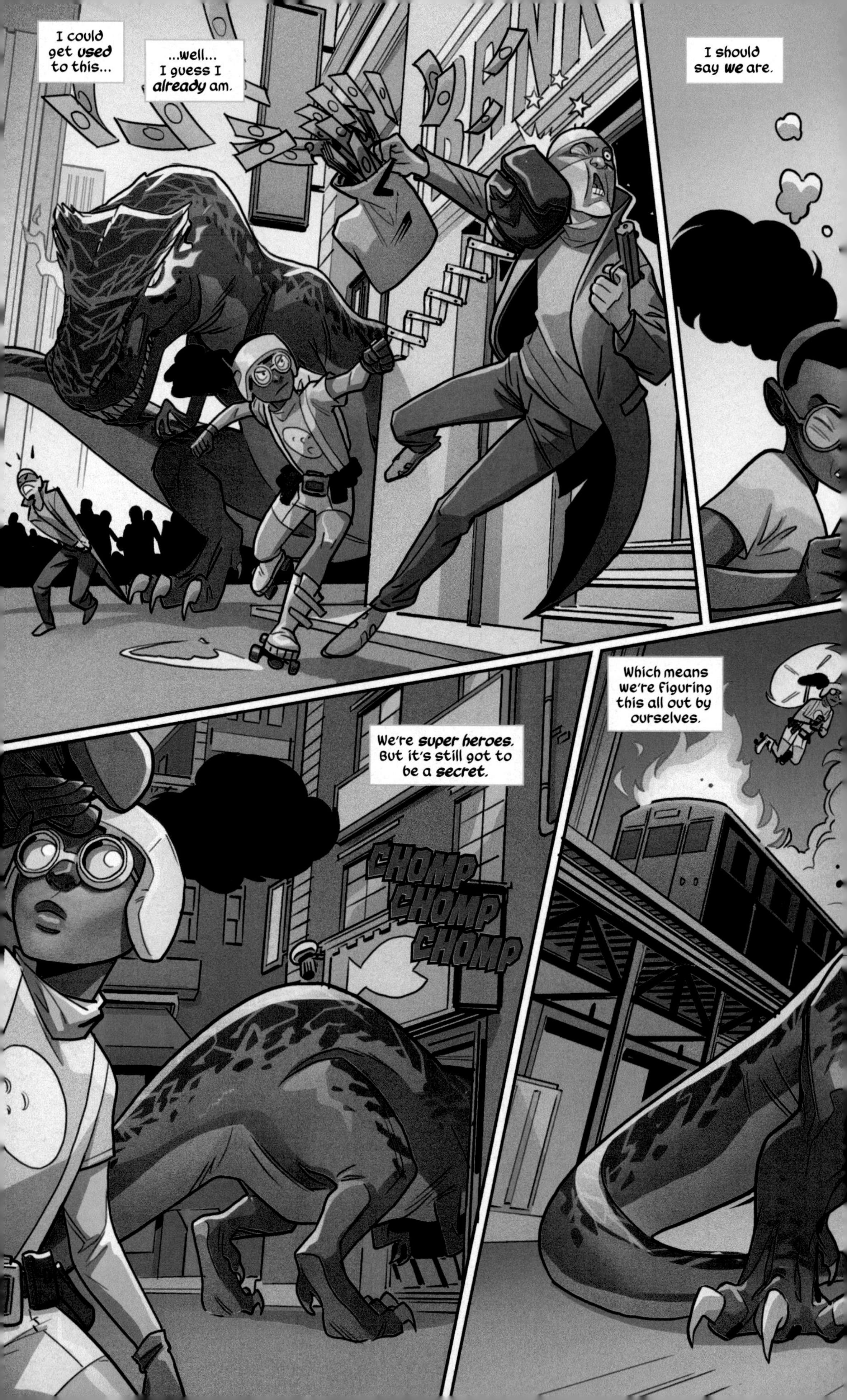
I could get used to this...
...well... I guess I already am.
I should say we are.
We're super heroes. But it's still got to be a secret.
Which means we're figuring this all out by ourselves.
CHOMP CHOMP CHOMP

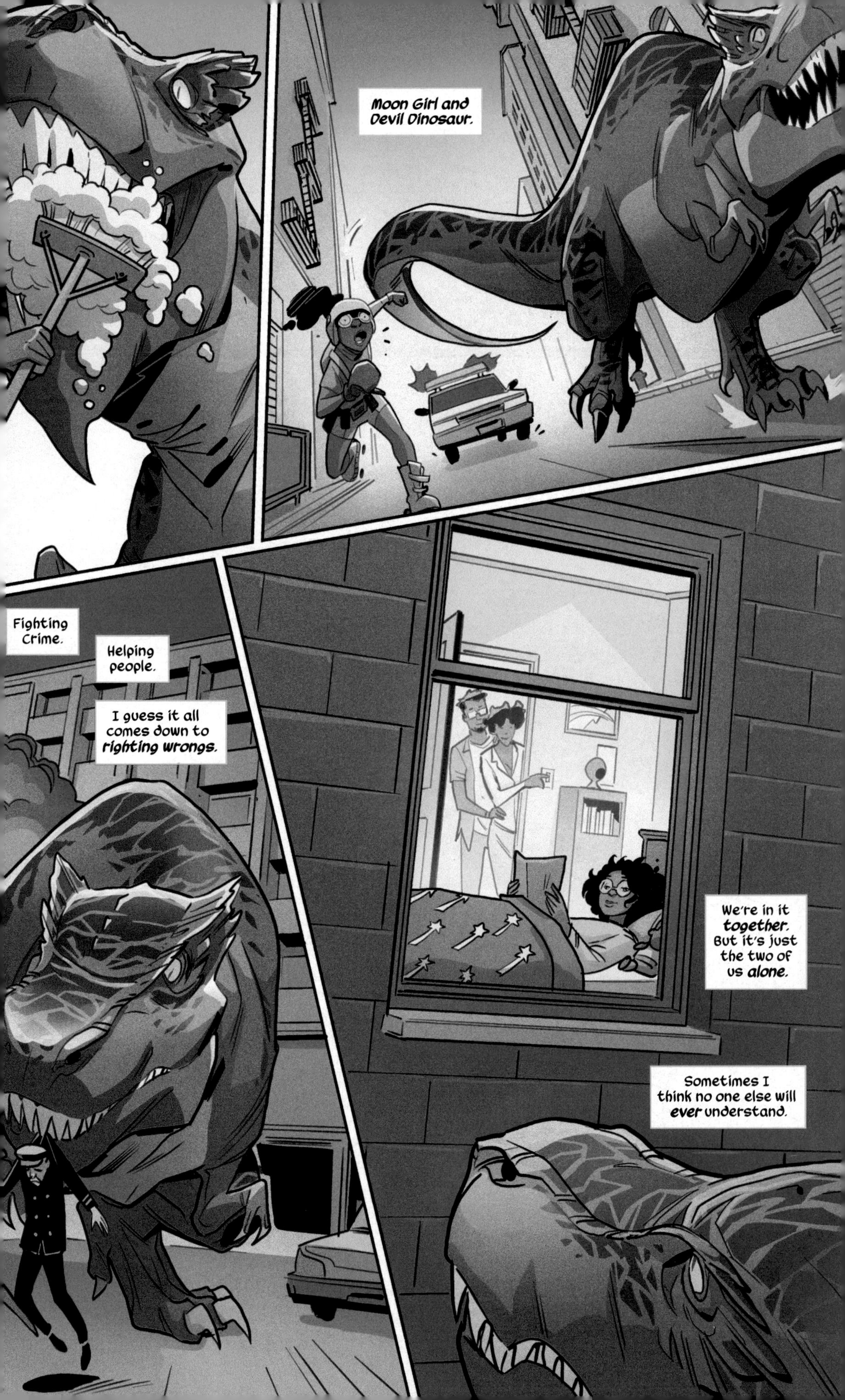
Moon Girl and Devil Dinosaur.
Fighting Crime.
Helping people.
I guess it all comes down to righting wrongs.
We're in it together. But it's just the two of us alone.
Sometimes I think no one else will ever understand.

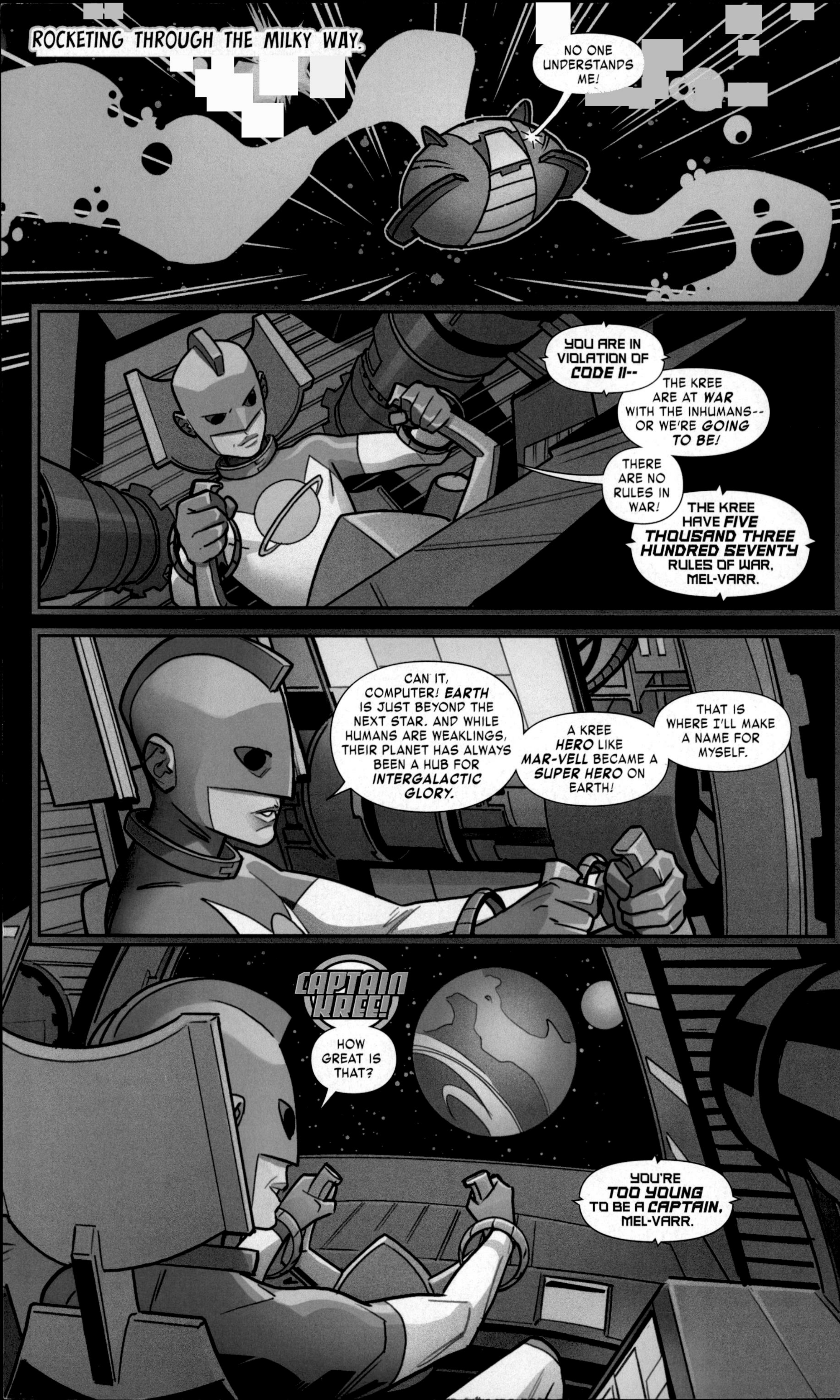
ROCKETING THROUGH THE MILKY WAY.
NO ONE UNDERSTANDS ME!
YOU ARE IN VIOLATION OF CODE 11--
THE KREE ARE AT WAR WITH THE INHUMANS-- OR WE'RE GOING TO BE!
THERE ARE NO RULES IN WAR!
THE KREE HAVE FIVE THOUSAND THREE HUNDRED SEVENTY RULES OF WAR, MEL-VARR.
CAN IT, COMPUTER! EARTH IS JUST BEYOND THE NEXT STAR. AND WHILE HUMANS ARE WEAKLINGS, THEIR PLANET HAS ALWAYS BEEN A HUB FOR INTERGALACTIC GLORY.
A KREE HERO LIKE MAR-VELL BECAME A SUPER HERO ON EARTH!
THAT IS WHERE I'LL MAKE A NAME FOR MYSELF.
CAPTAIN KREE!
HOW GREAT IS THAT?
YOU'RE TOO YOUNG TO BE A CAPTAIN, MEL-VARR.

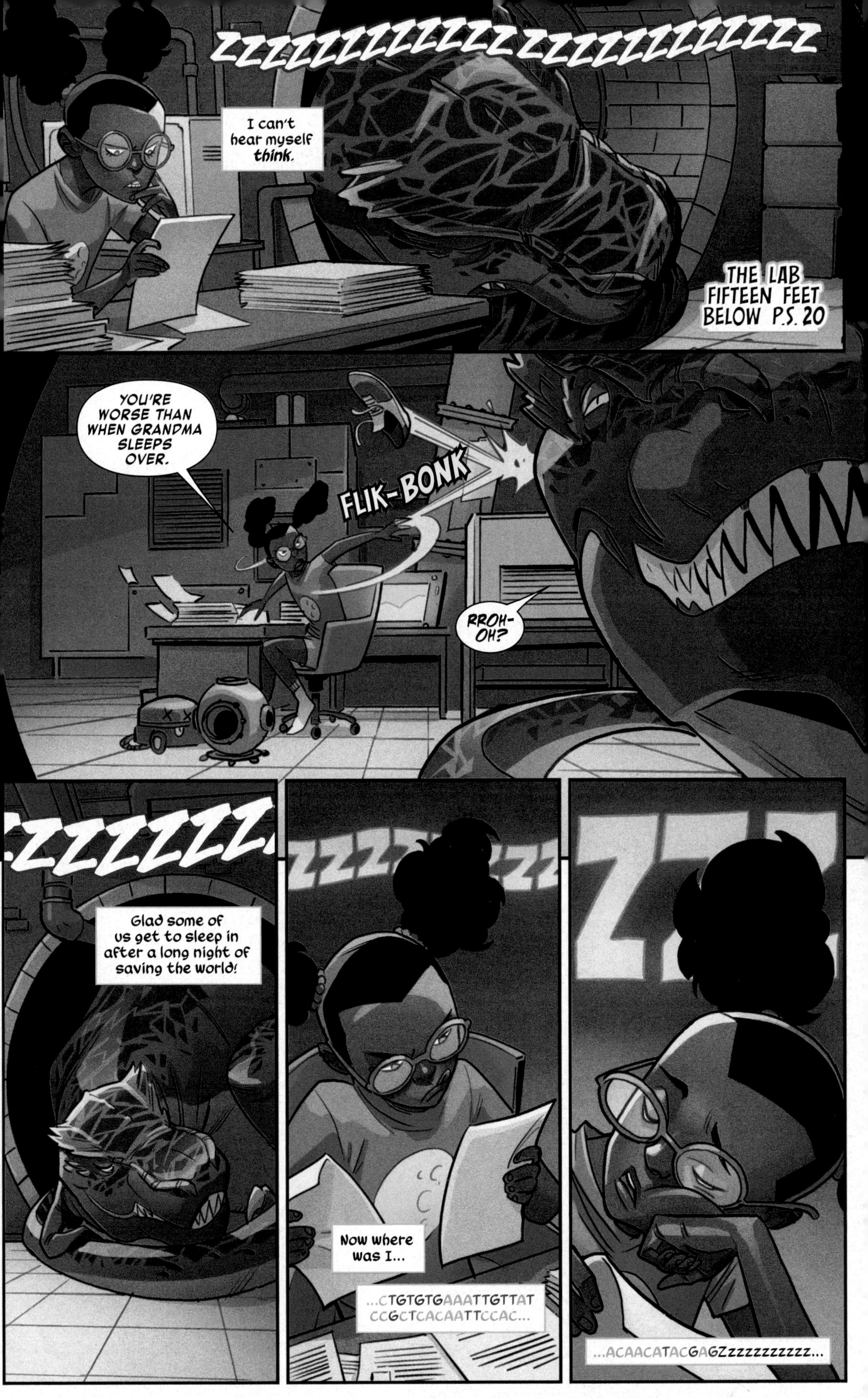
ZZZZZZZZZZZZZZZZZZZZZZZZZZZ
I can't hear myself think.
THE LAB FIFTEEN FEET BELOW P.S. 20
YOU'RE WORSE THAN WHEN GRANDMA SLEEPS OVER.
FLIK-BONK
RROH-OH?
ZZZZZZZ
Glad some of us get to sleep in after a long night of saving the world!
Now where was I...
...CTGTGTGAAATTGTTAT CCGCTCACAATTCCAC...
...ACAACATACGAGZzzzzzzzzz...

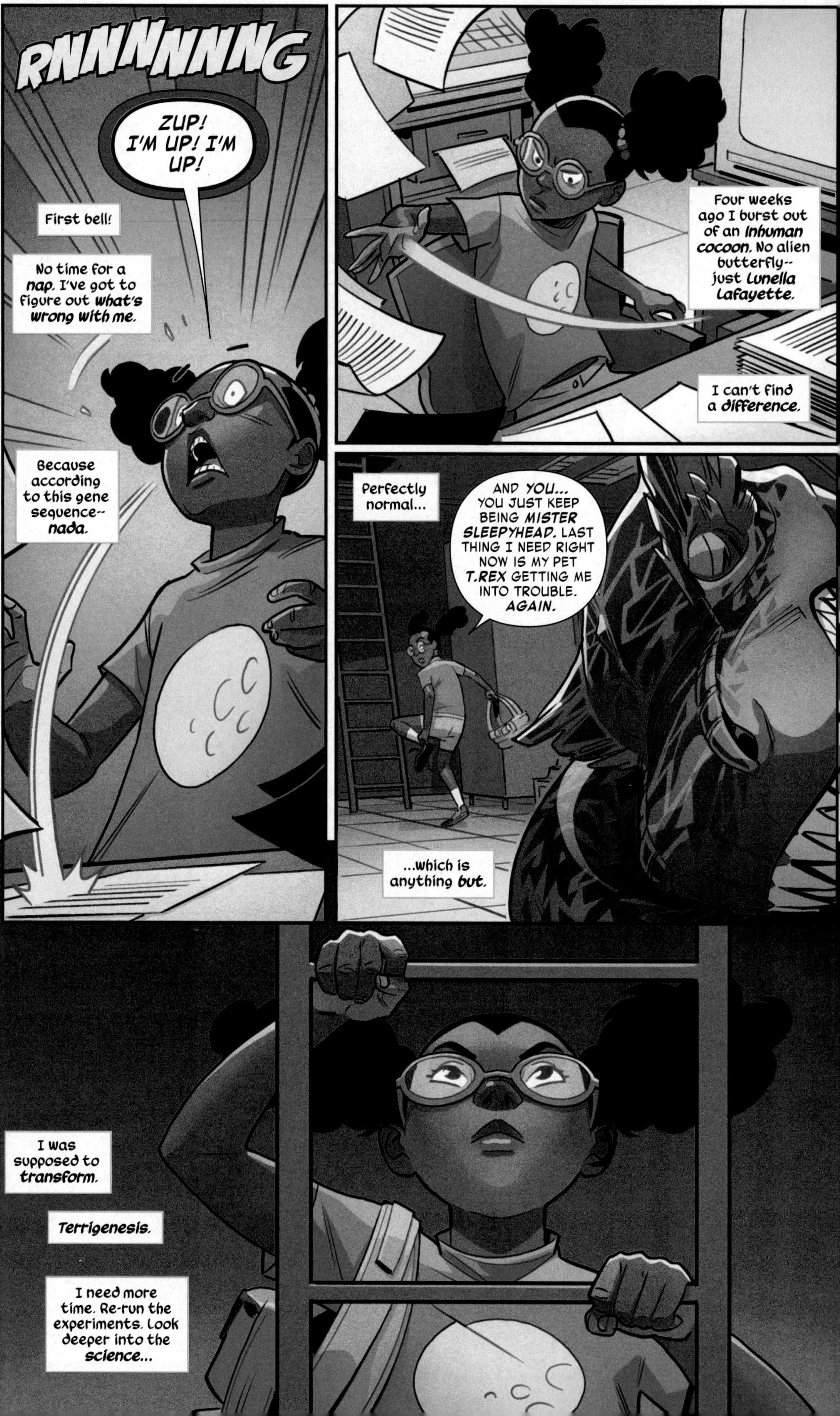
RNNNNNNG
ZUP! I'M UP! I'M UP!
First bell!
No time for a nap. I've got to figure out what's wrong with me.
Because according to this gene sequence-- nada.
Four weeks ago I burst out of an Inhuman cocoon. No alien butterfly-- just Lunella Lafayette.
I can't find a difference.
Perfectly normal...
AND YOU... YOU JUST KEEP BEING MISTER SLEEPYHEAD. LAST THING I NEED RIGHT NOW IS MY PET T.REX GETTING ME INTO TROUBLE. AGAIN.
...which is anything but.
I was supposed to transform.
Terrigenesis.
I need more time. Re-run the experiments. Look deeper into the science...

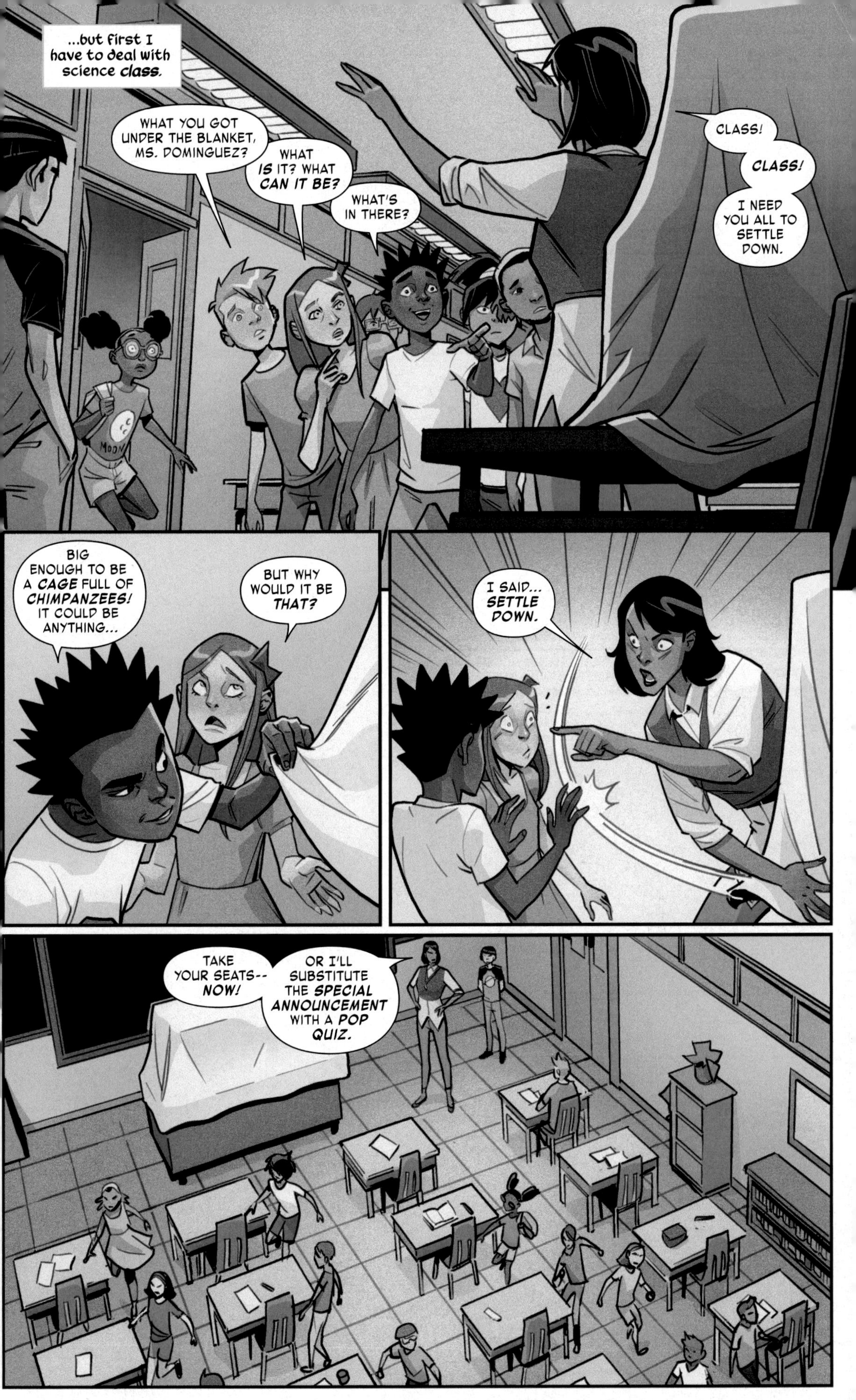
...but first I have to deal with science class.
WHAT YOU GOT UNDER THE BLANKET, MS. DOMINGUEZ?
WHAT IS IT? WHAT CAN IT BE?
WHAT'S IN THERE?
CLASS!
CLASS!
I NEED YOU ALL TO SETTLE DOWN.
MOON
BIG ENOUGH TO BE A CAGE FULL OF CHIMPANZEES! IT COULD BE ANYTHING...
BUT WHY WOULD IT BE THAT?
I SAID... SETTLE DOWN.
TAKE YOUR SEATS-- NOW!
OR I'LL SUBSTITUTE THE SPECIAL ANNOUNCEMENT WITH A POP QUIZ.

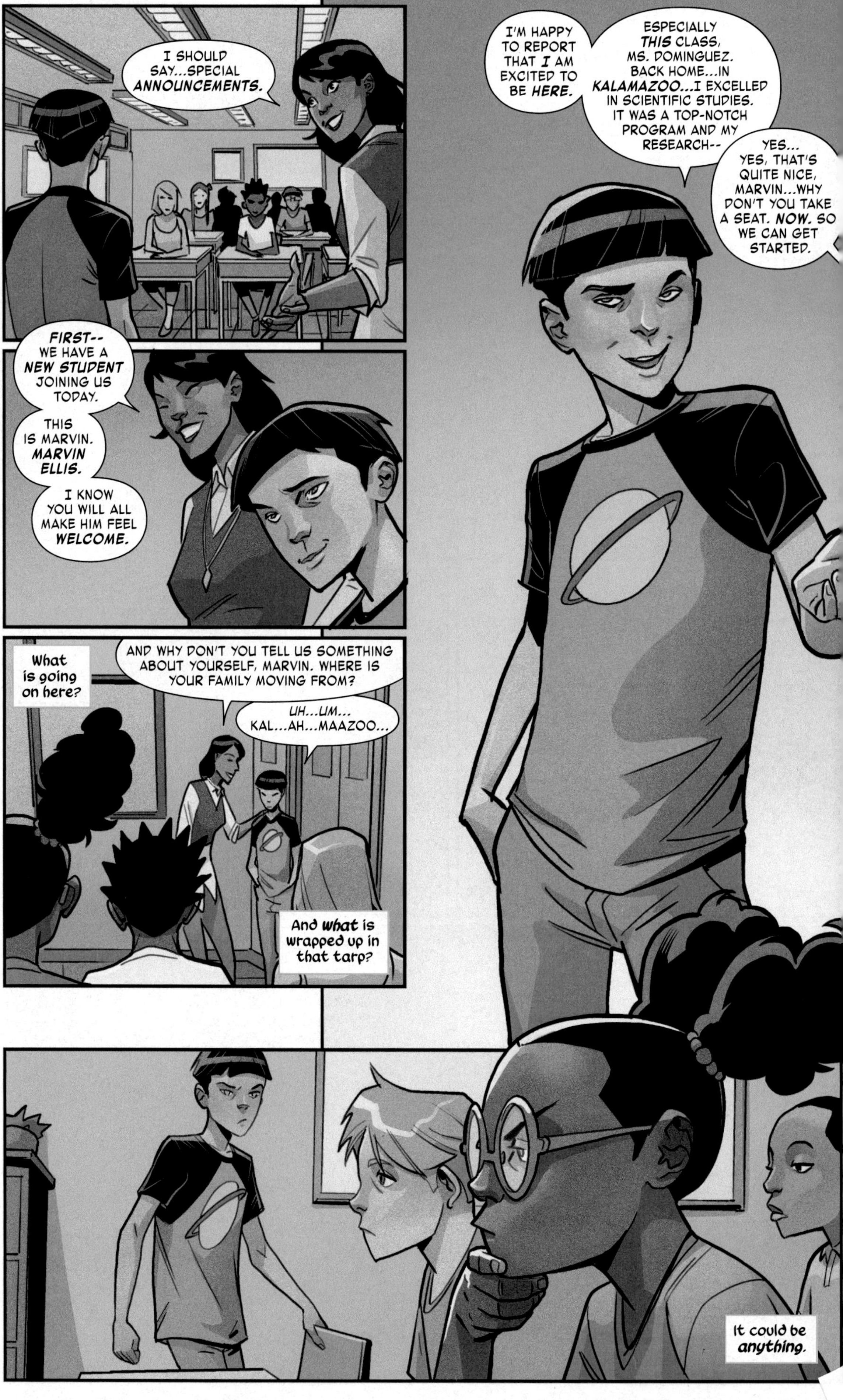
I SHOULD SAY...SPECIAL ANNOUNCEMENTS.
FIRST-- WE HAVE A NEW STUDENT JOINING US TODAY.
THIS IS MARVIN. MARVIN ELLIS.
I KNOW YOU WILL ALL MAKE HIM FEEL WELCOME.
What is going on here?
AND WHY DON'T YOU TELL US SOMETHING ABOUT YOURSELF, MARVIN. WHERE IS YOUR FAMILY MOVING FROM?
UH...UM... KAL...AH...MAAZOO...
And what is wrapped up in that tarp?
I'M HAPPY TO REPORT THAT I AM EXCITED TO BE HERE.
ESPECIALLY THIS CLASS, MS. DOMINGUEZ. BACK HOME...IN KALAMAZOO...I EXCELLED IN SCIENTIFIC STUDIES. IT WAS A TOP-NOTCH PROGRAM AND MY RESEARCH--
YES... YES, THAT'S QUITE NICE, MARVIN...WHY DON'T YOU TAKE A SEAT. NOW. SO WE CAN GET STARTED.
It could be anything.

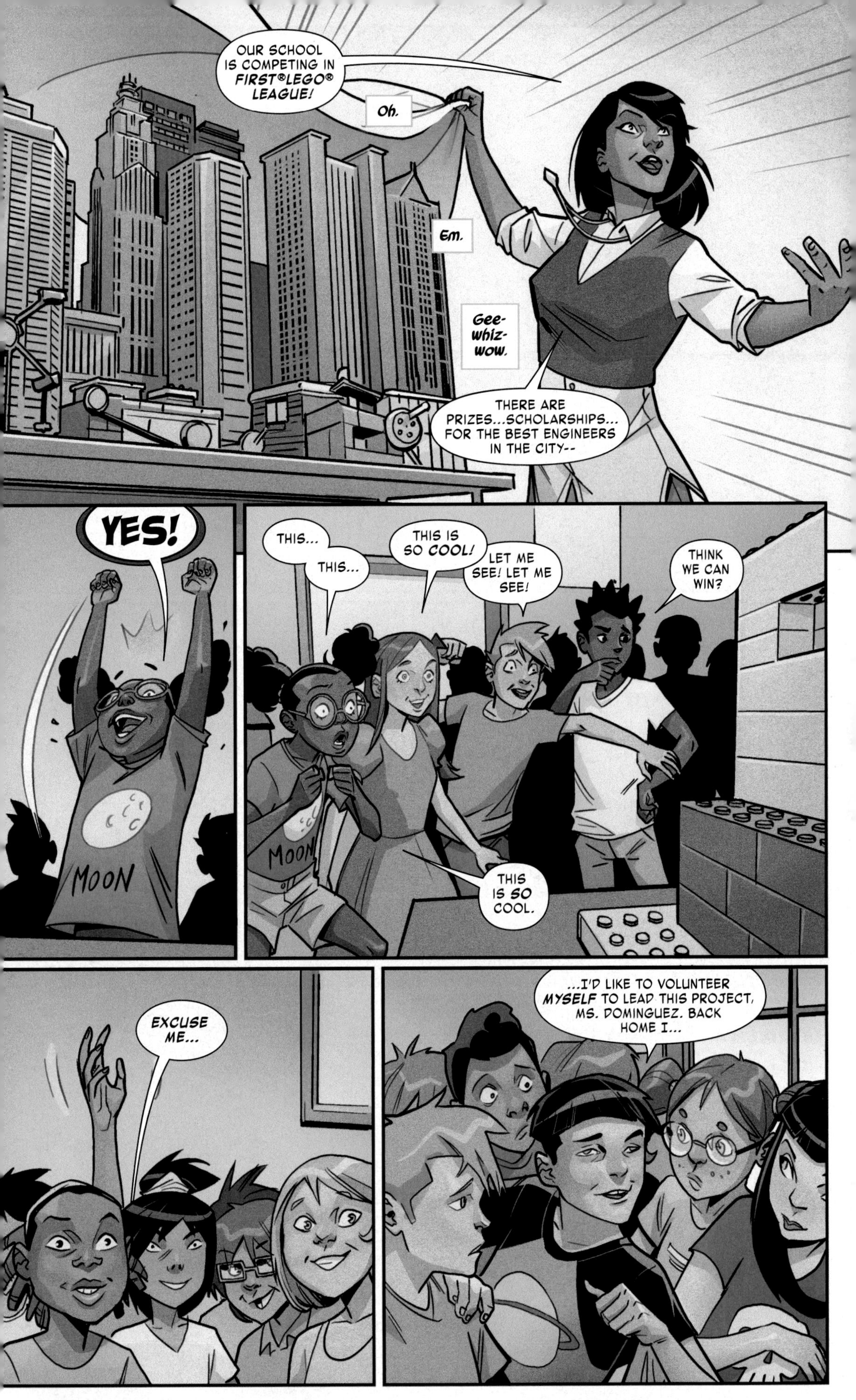
OUR SCHOOL IS COMPETING IN FIRST®LEGO® LEAGUE!
Oh.
Em.
Gee-whiz-wow.
THERE ARE PRIZES...SCHOLARSHIPS... FOR THE BEST ENGINEERS IN THE CITY--
YES!
MOON
THIS...
THIS...
THIS IS SO COOL!
LET ME SEE! LET ME SEE!
THINK WE CAN WIN?
MOON
THIS IS SO COOL.
EXCUSE ME...
...I'D LIKE TO VOLUNTEER MYSELF TO LEAD THIS PROJECT, MS. DOMINGUEZ. BACK HOME I...

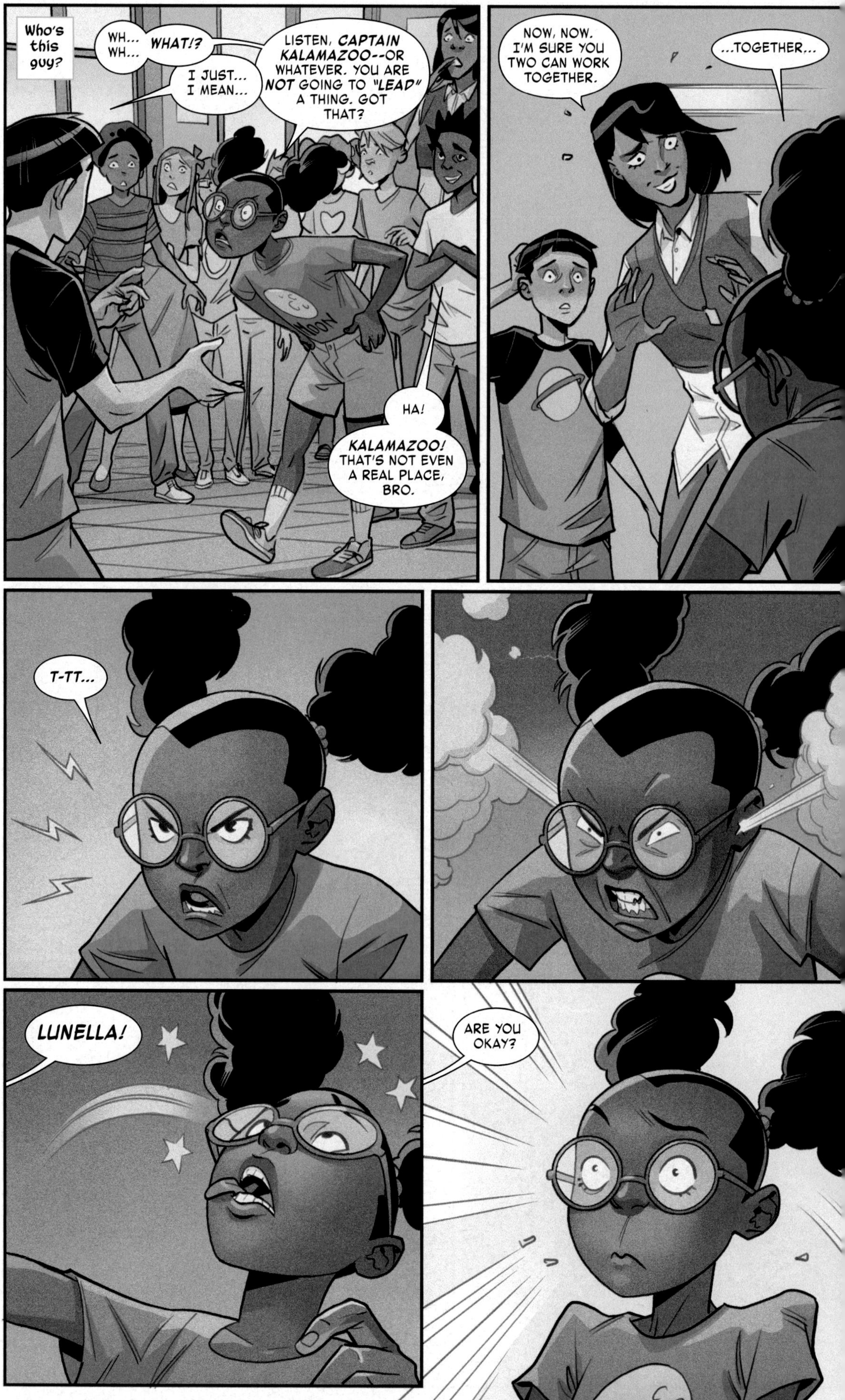
Who's this guy?
WH... WH...
WHAT!?
I JUST... I MEAN...
LISTEN, CAPTAIN KALAMAZOO--OR WHATEVER. YOU ARE NOT GOING TO "LEAD" A THING. GOT THAT?
HA!
KALAMAZOO! THAT'S NOT EVEN A REAL PLACE, BRO.
NOW, NOW. I'M SURE YOU TWO CAN WORK TOGETHER.
...TOGETHER...
T-TT...
LUNELLA!
ARE YOU OKAY?

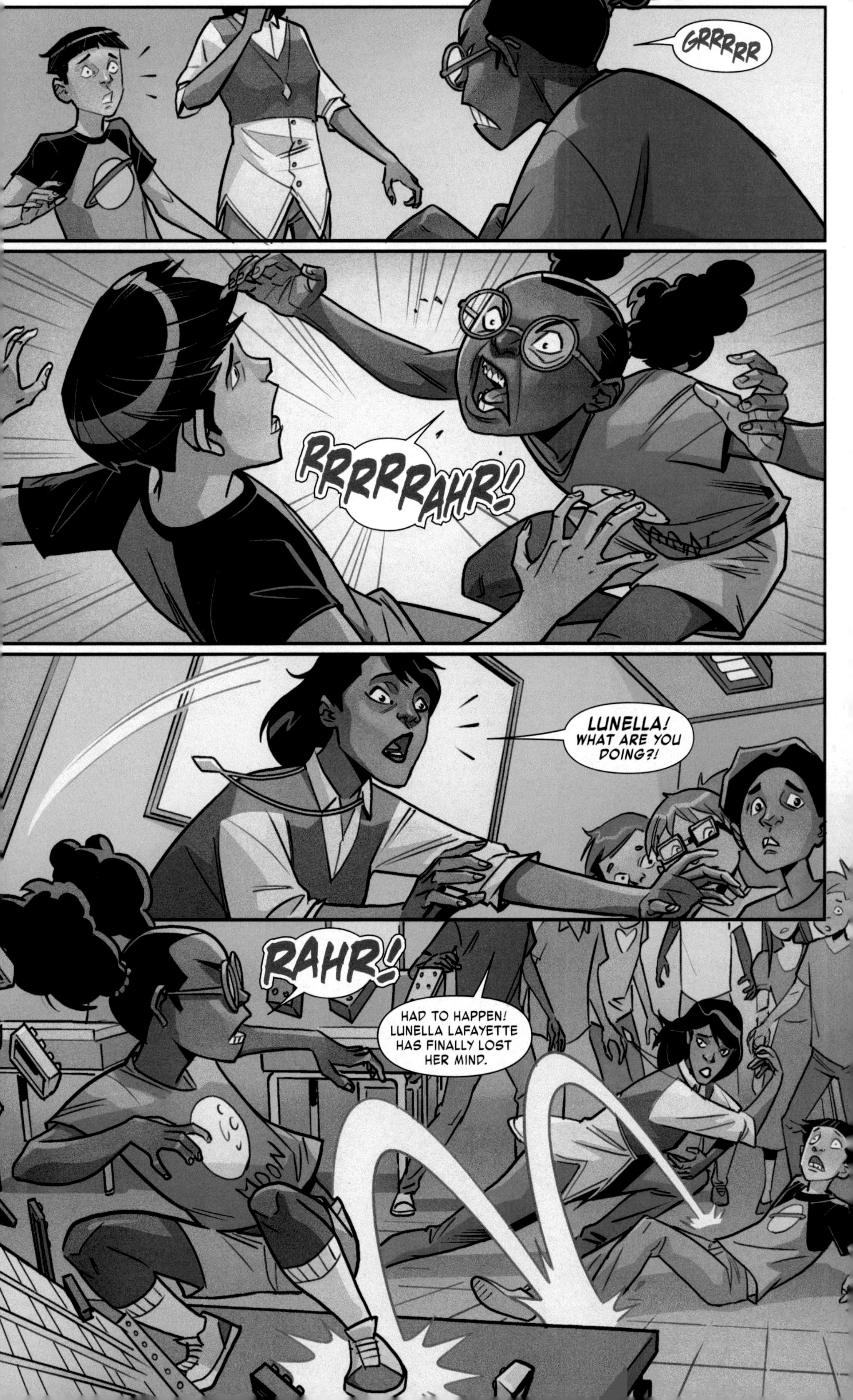
GRRRRR
RRRRRAHR!
LUNELLA! WHAT ARE YOU DOING?!
RAHR!
HAD TO HAPPEN! LUNELLA LAFAYETTE HAS FINALLY LOST HER MIND.

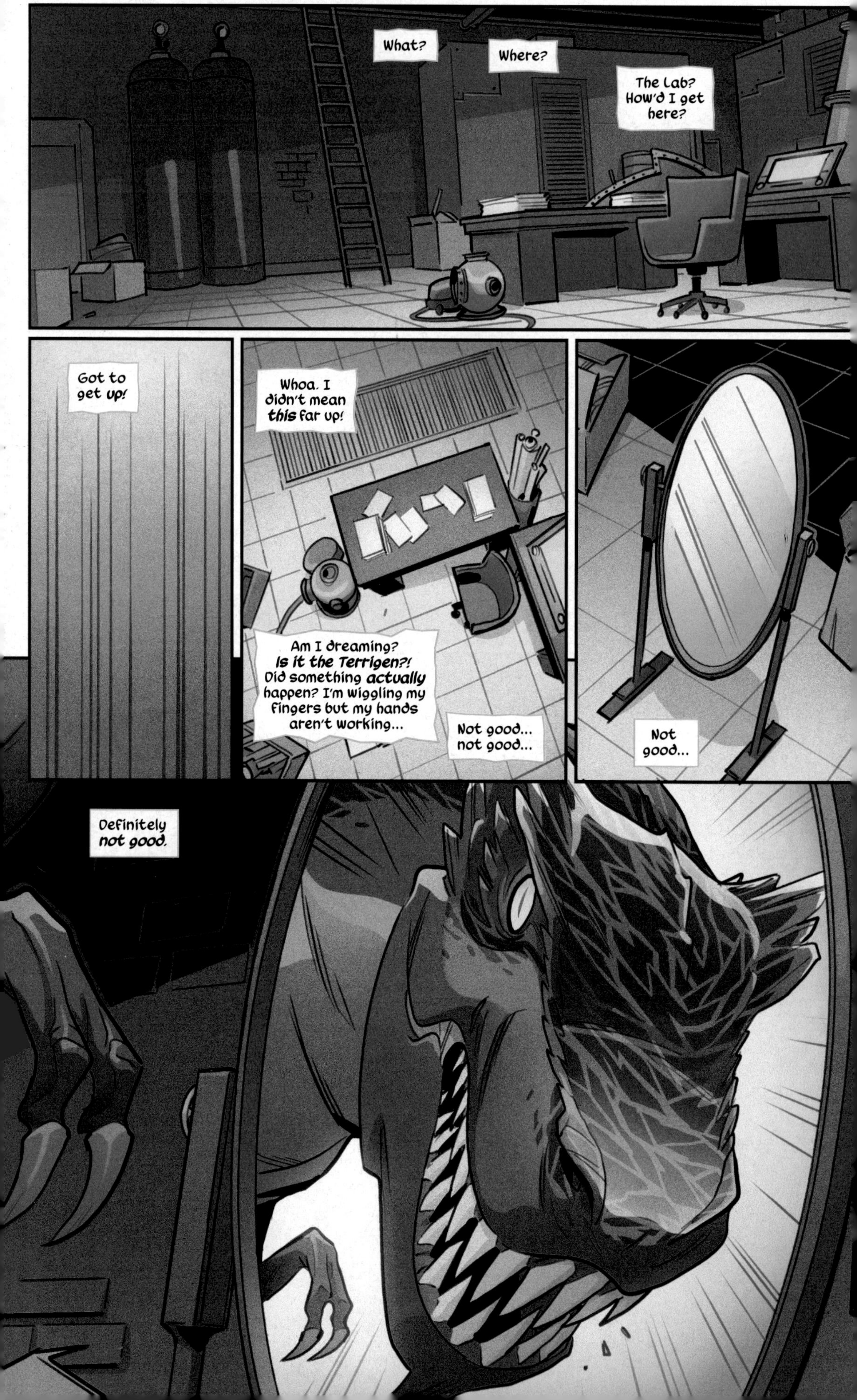
What?
Where?
The Lab? How'd I get here?
Got to get **up**!
Whoa. I didn't mean **this** far up!
Am I dreaming? **Is it the Terrigen?!** Did something **actually** happen? I'm wiggling my fingers but my hands aren't working...
Not good... not good...
Not good...
Definitely **not good**.

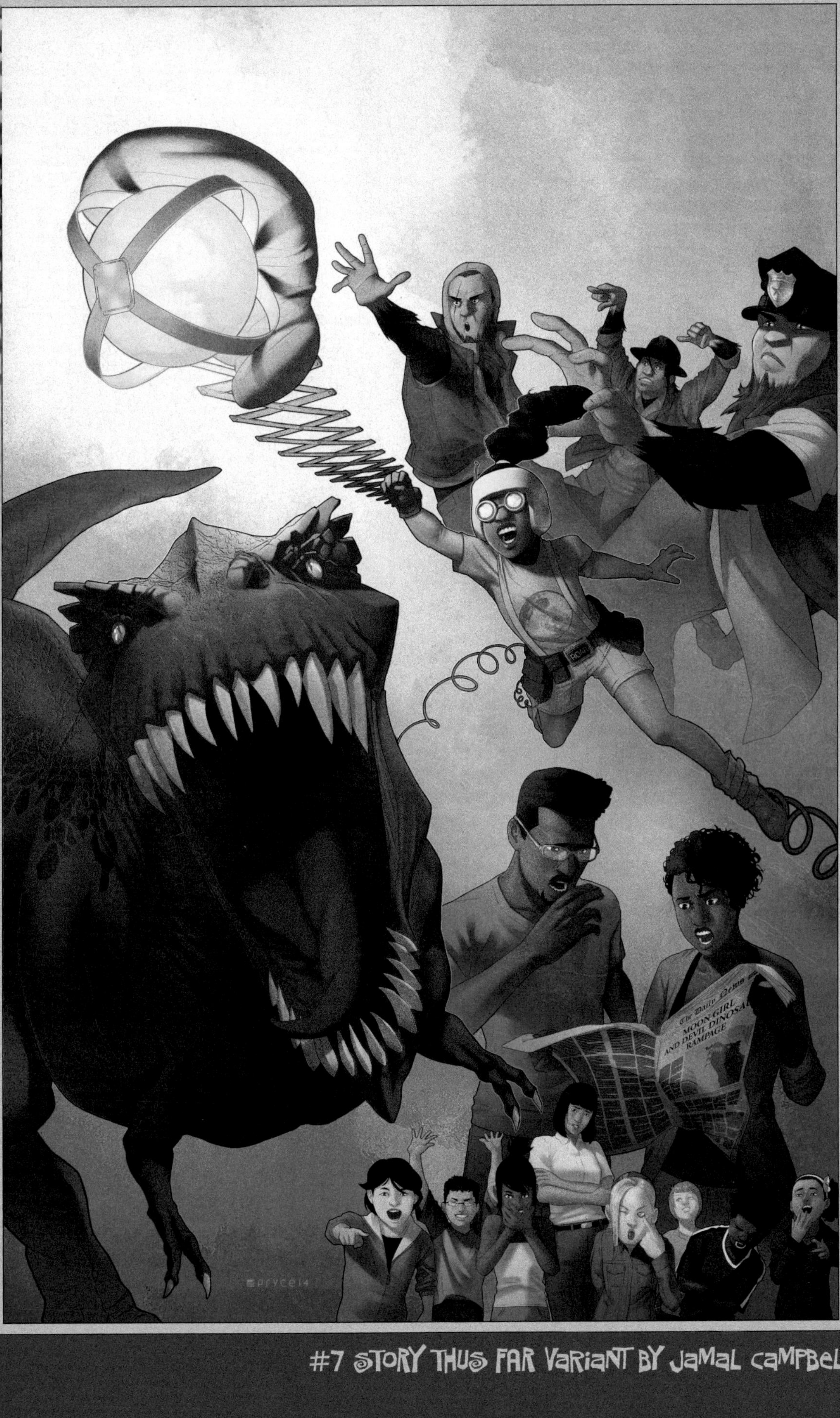
The Daily News
MOON GIRL
RAMPAGE

#7 STORY THUS FAR VARIANT BY JAMAL CAMPBELL

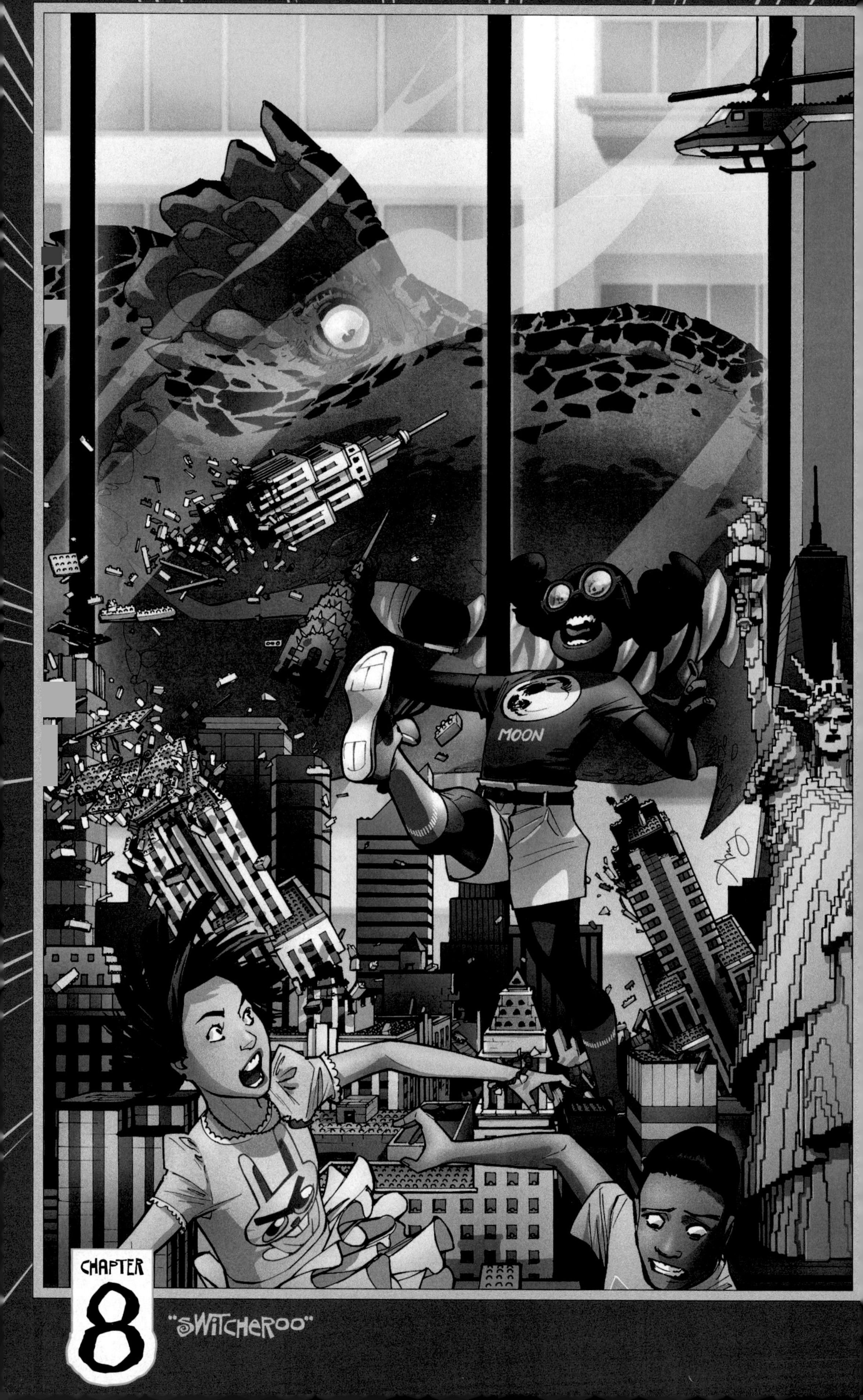
MOON

CHAPTER 8

"SWITCHEROO"

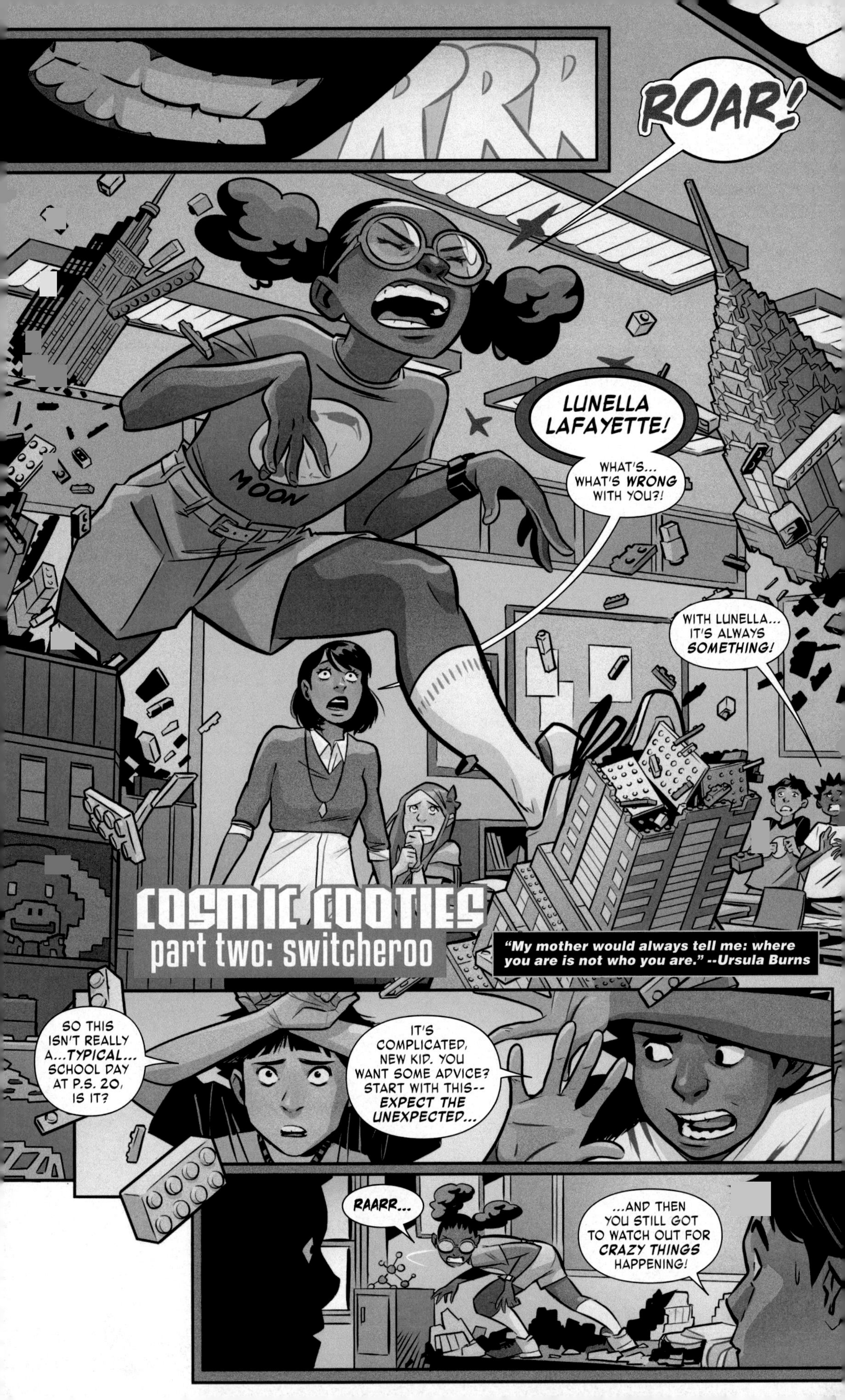
RRR
ROAR!
LUNELLA LAFAYETTE!
WHAT'S... WHAT'S WRONG WITH YOU?!
WITH LUNELLA... IT'S ALWAYS SOMETHING!
MOON
COSMIC COOTIES
part two: switcheroo
"My mother would always tell me: where you are is not who you are." --Ursula Burns
SO THIS ISN'T REALLY A...TYPICAL... SCHOOL DAY AT P.S. 20, IS IT?
IT'S COMPLICATED, NEW KID. YOU WANT SOME ADVICE? START WITH THIS-- EXPECT THE UNEXPECTED...
RAARR...
...AND THEN YOU STILL GOT TO WATCH OUT FOR CRAZY THINGS HAPPENING!

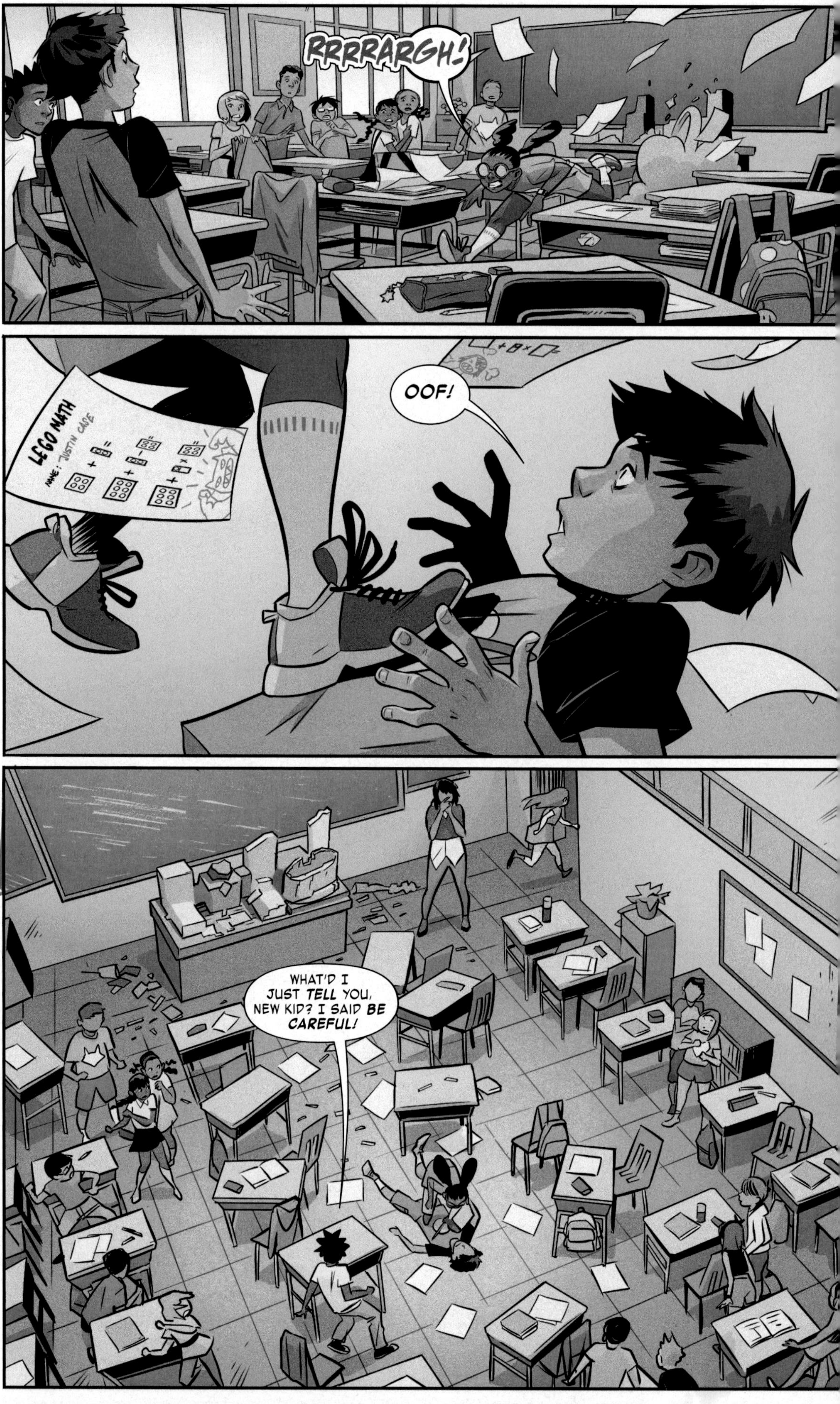
RRRRARGH!
LEGO MATH
NAME: JUSTIN CASE
OOF!
WHAT'D I JUST TELL YOU, NEW KID? I SAID BE CAREFUL!

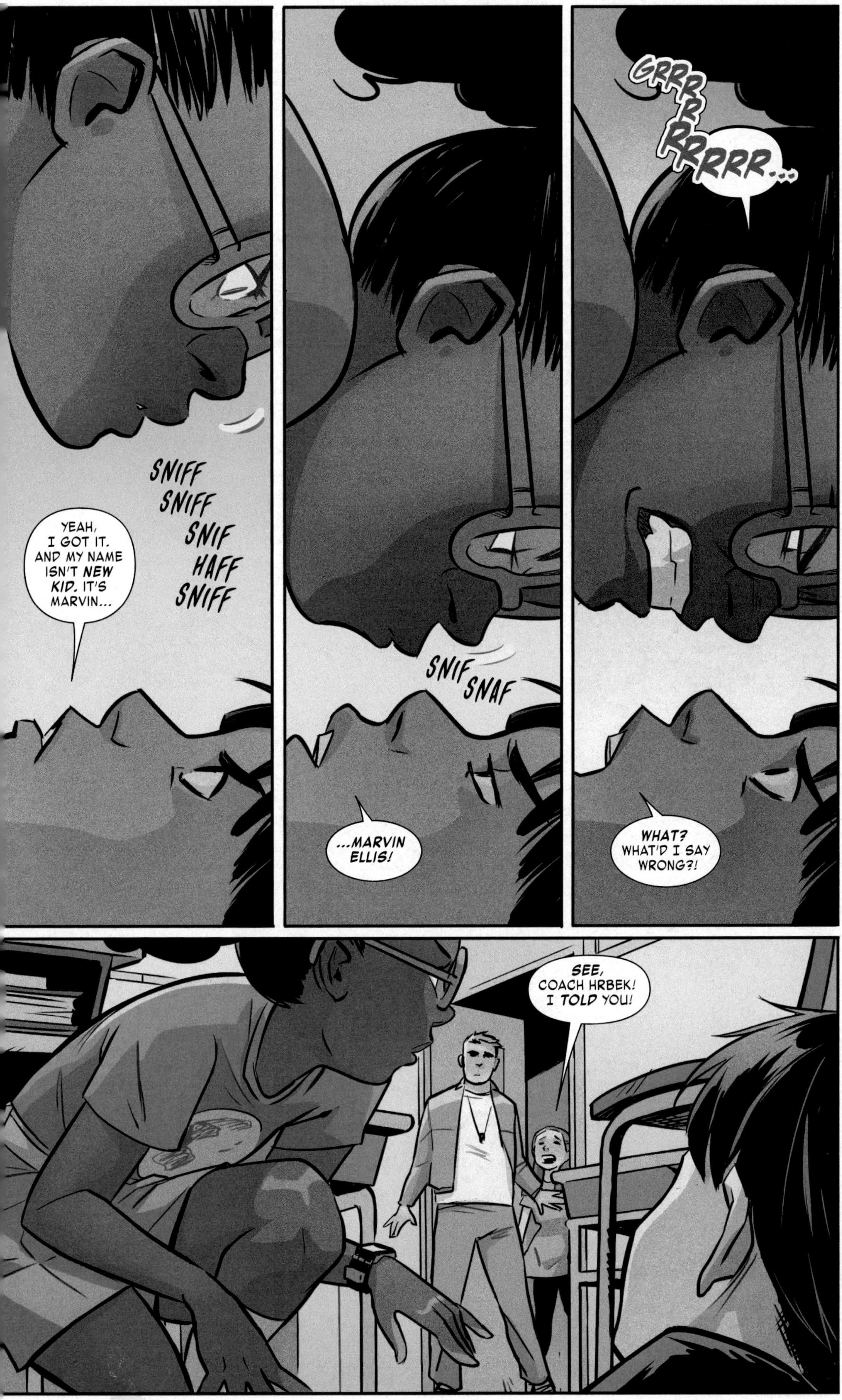
SNIFF
SNIFF
SNIF
HAFF
SNIFF
YEAH, I GOT IT. AND MY NAME ISN'T NEW KID. IT'S MARVIN...
SNIF SNAF
...MARVIN ELLIS!
GRRRR RRRRR...
WHAT? WHAT'D I SAY WRONG?!
SEE, COACH HRBEK! I TOLD YOU!

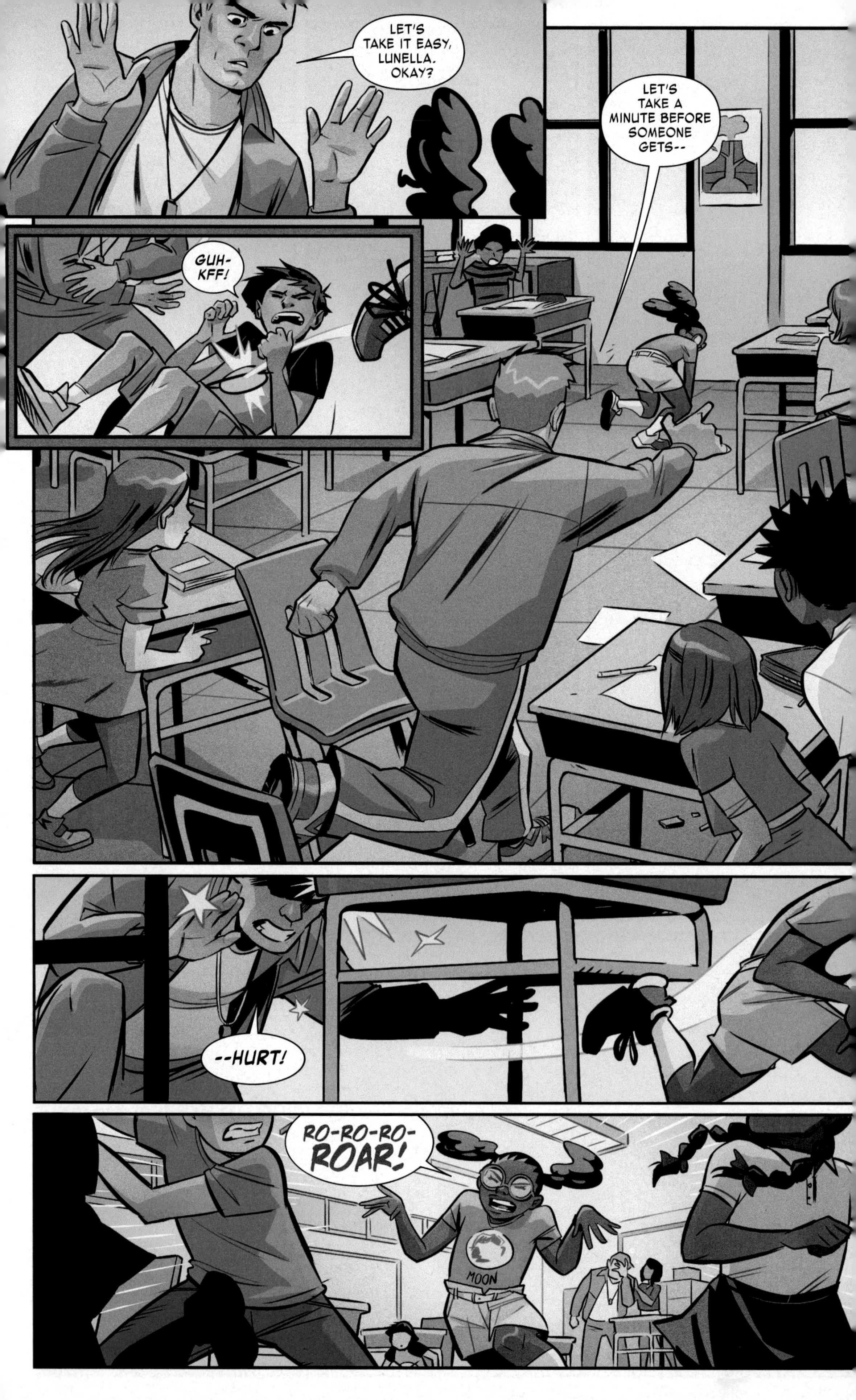
LET'S TAKE IT EASY, LUNELLA. OKAY?
LET'S TAKE A MINUTE BEFORE SOMEONE GETS--
GUH-KFF!
--HURT!
RO-RO-RO-ROAR!
MOON

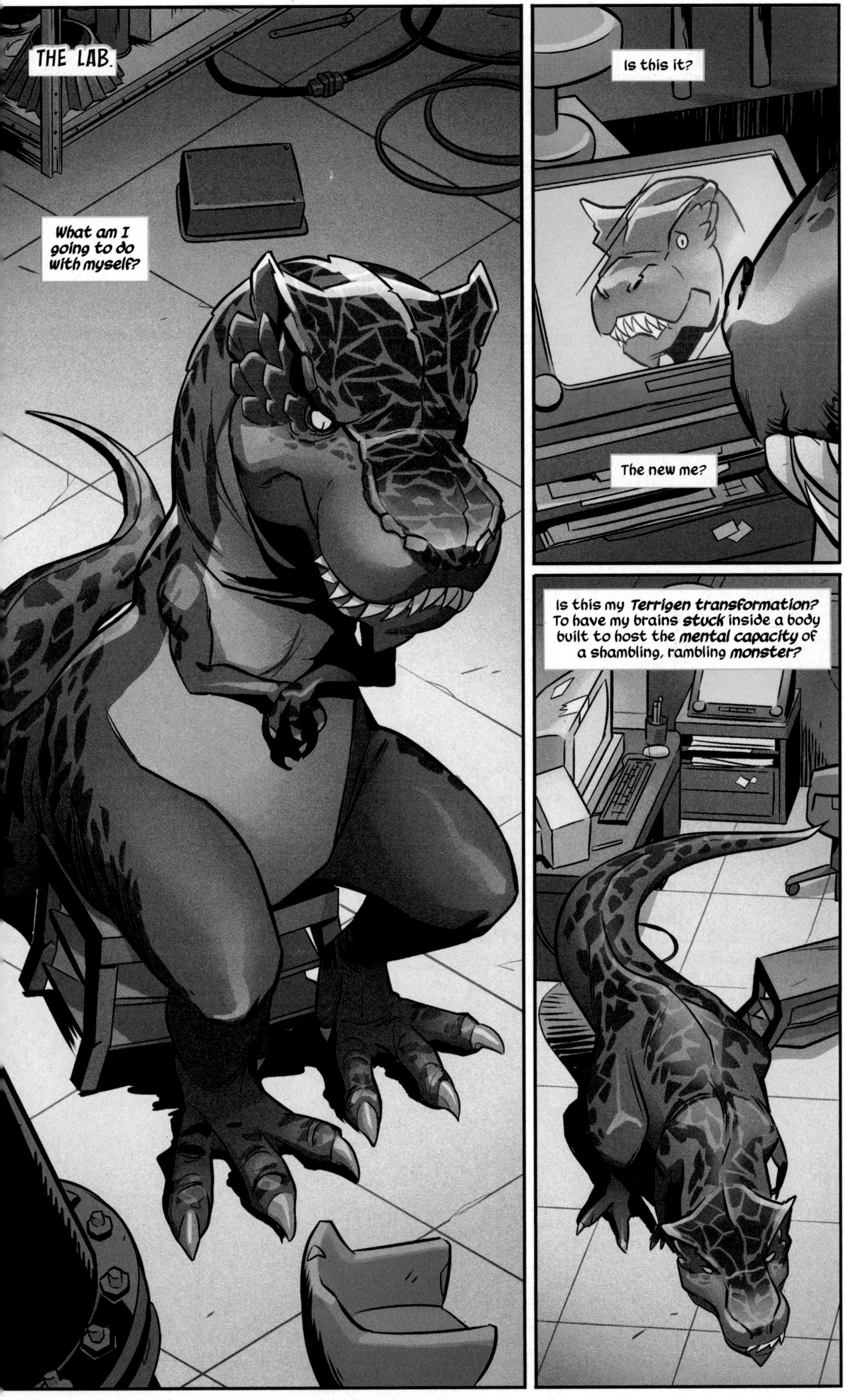
THE LAB.
What am I going to do with myself?
Is this it?
The new me?
Is this my *Terrigen transformation?* To have my brains *stuck* inside a body built to host the *mental capacity* of a shambling, rambling *monster?*

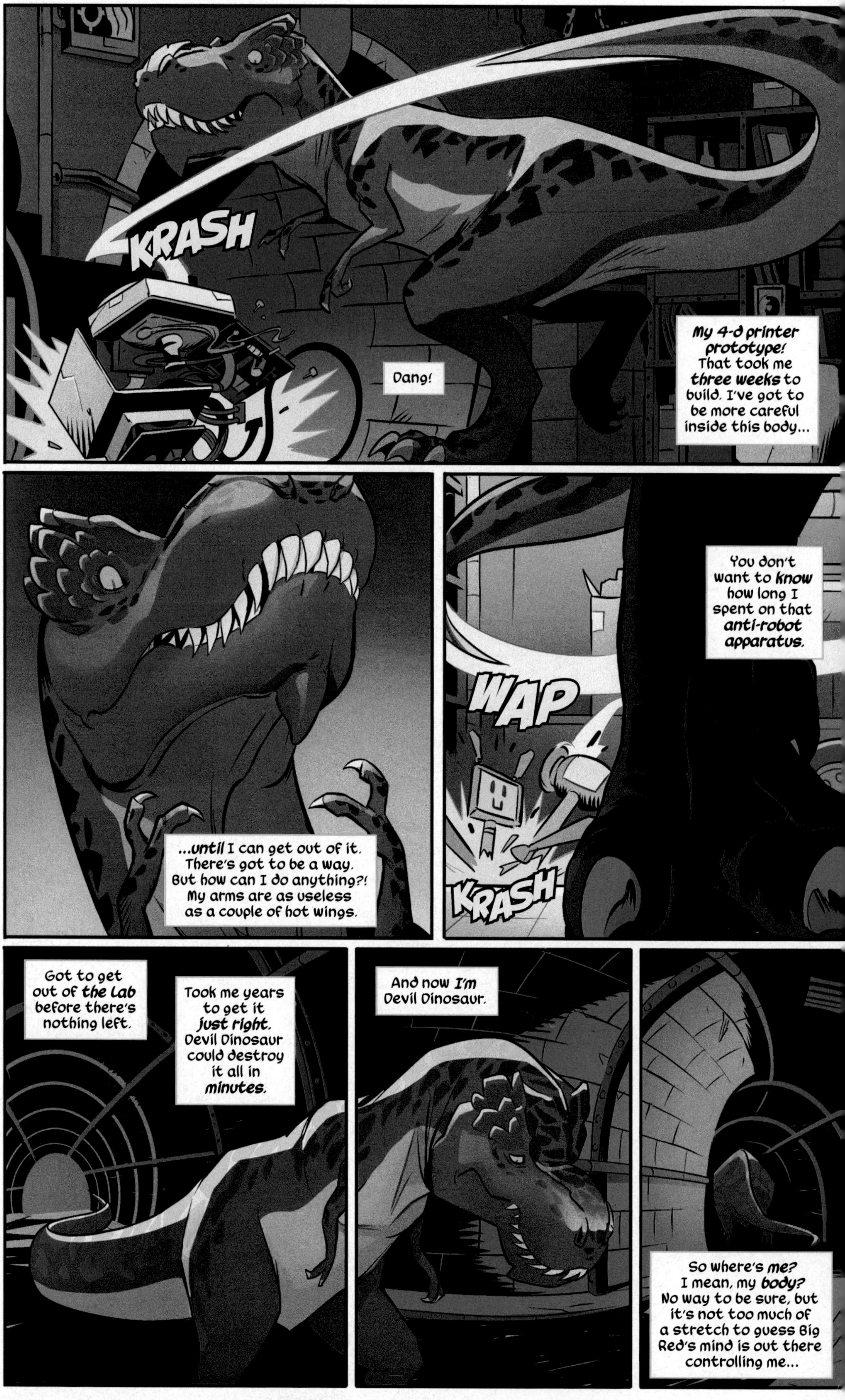
KRASH
Dang!
My 4-D printer prototype! That took me ***three weeks*** to build. I've got to be more careful inside this body...
...until I can get out of it. There's got to be a way. But how can I do anything?! My arms are as useless as a couple of hot wings.
You don't want to ***know*** how long I spent on that ***anti-robot apparatus.***
WAP
KRASH
Got to get out of ***the Lab*** before there's nothing left.
Took me years to get it ***just right.*** Devil Dinosaur could destroy it all in ***minutes.***
And now *I'm* Devil Dinosaur.
So where's ***me?*** I mean, my ***body?*** No way to be sure, but it's not too much of a stretch to guess Big Red's mind is out there controlling me...

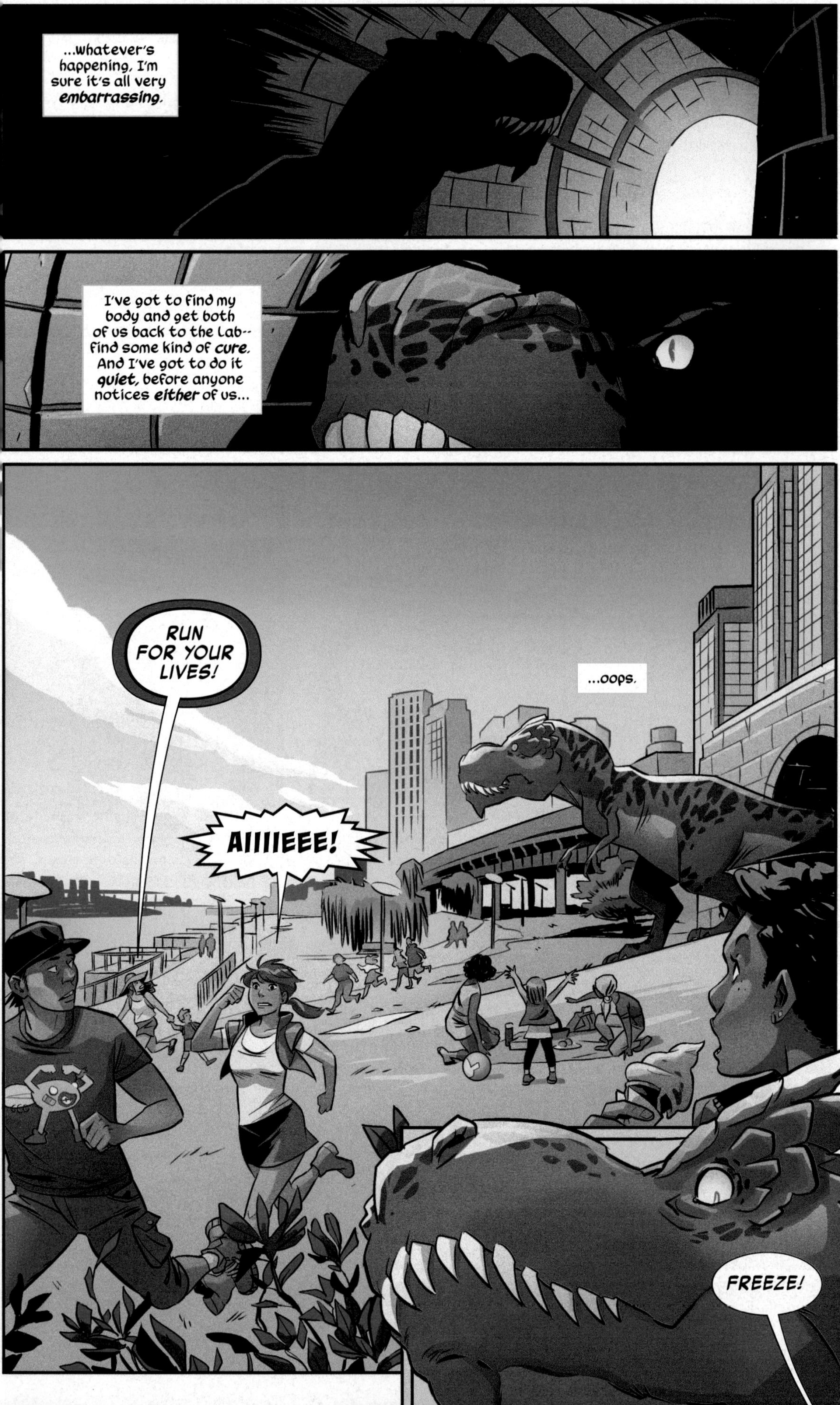
...whatever's happening, I'm sure it's all very *embarrassing*.
I've got to find my body and get both of us back to the Lab-- find some kind of *cure*. And I've got to do it *quiet*, before anyone notices *either* of us...
RUN FOR YOUR LIVES!
AIIIIEEE!
...oops.
FREEZE!

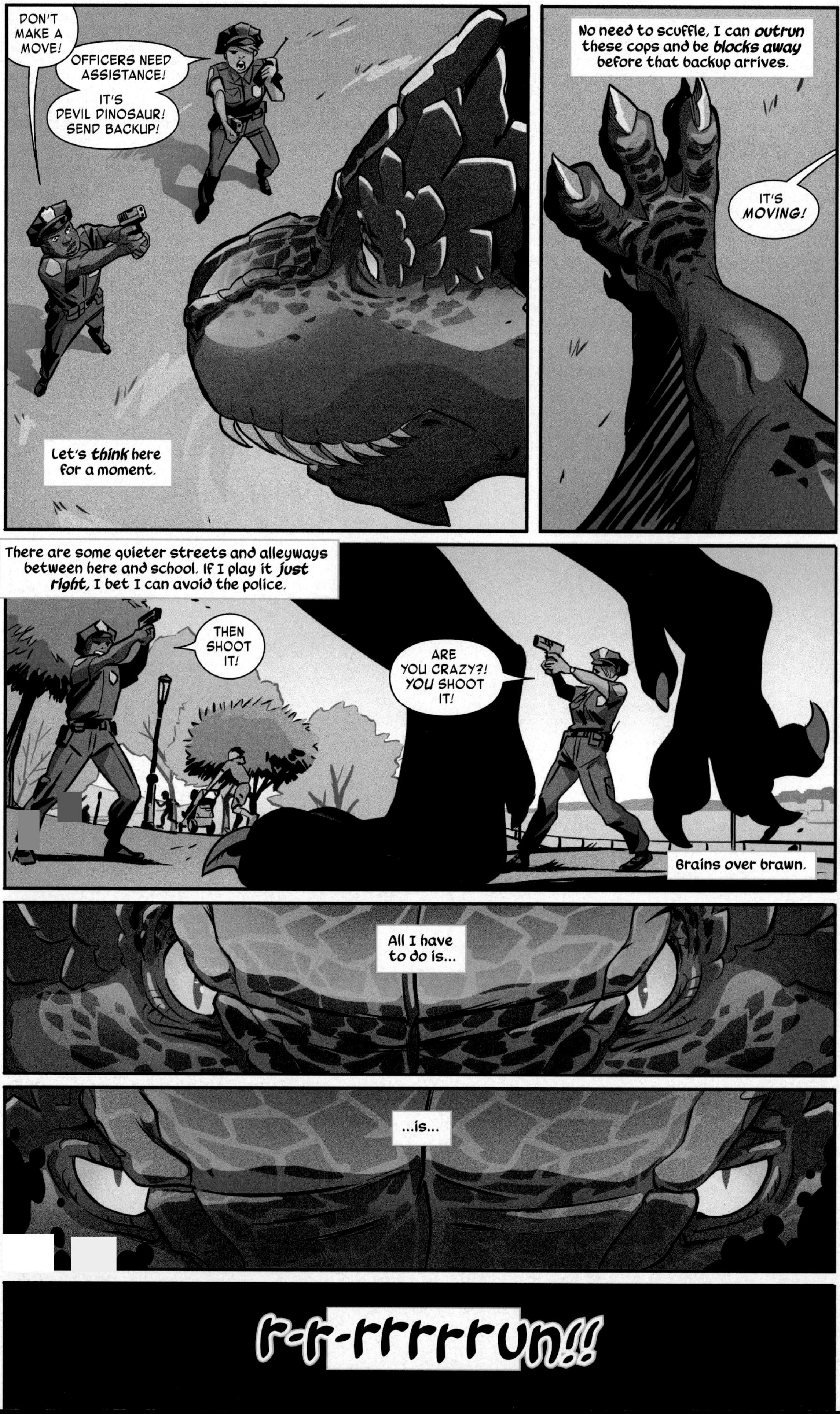

DON'T MAKE A MOVE!
OFFICERS NEED ASSISTANCE!
IT'S DEVIL DINOSAUR! SEND BACKUP!
Let's think here for a moment.
No need to scuffle, I can outrun these cops and be blocks away before that backup arrives.
IT'S MOVING!
There are some quieter streets and alleyways between here and school. If I play it just right, I bet I can avoid the police.
THEN SHOOT IT!
ARE YOU CRAZY?! YOU SHOOT IT!
Brains over brawn.
All I have to do is...
...is...
R-R-RRRRRUN!!

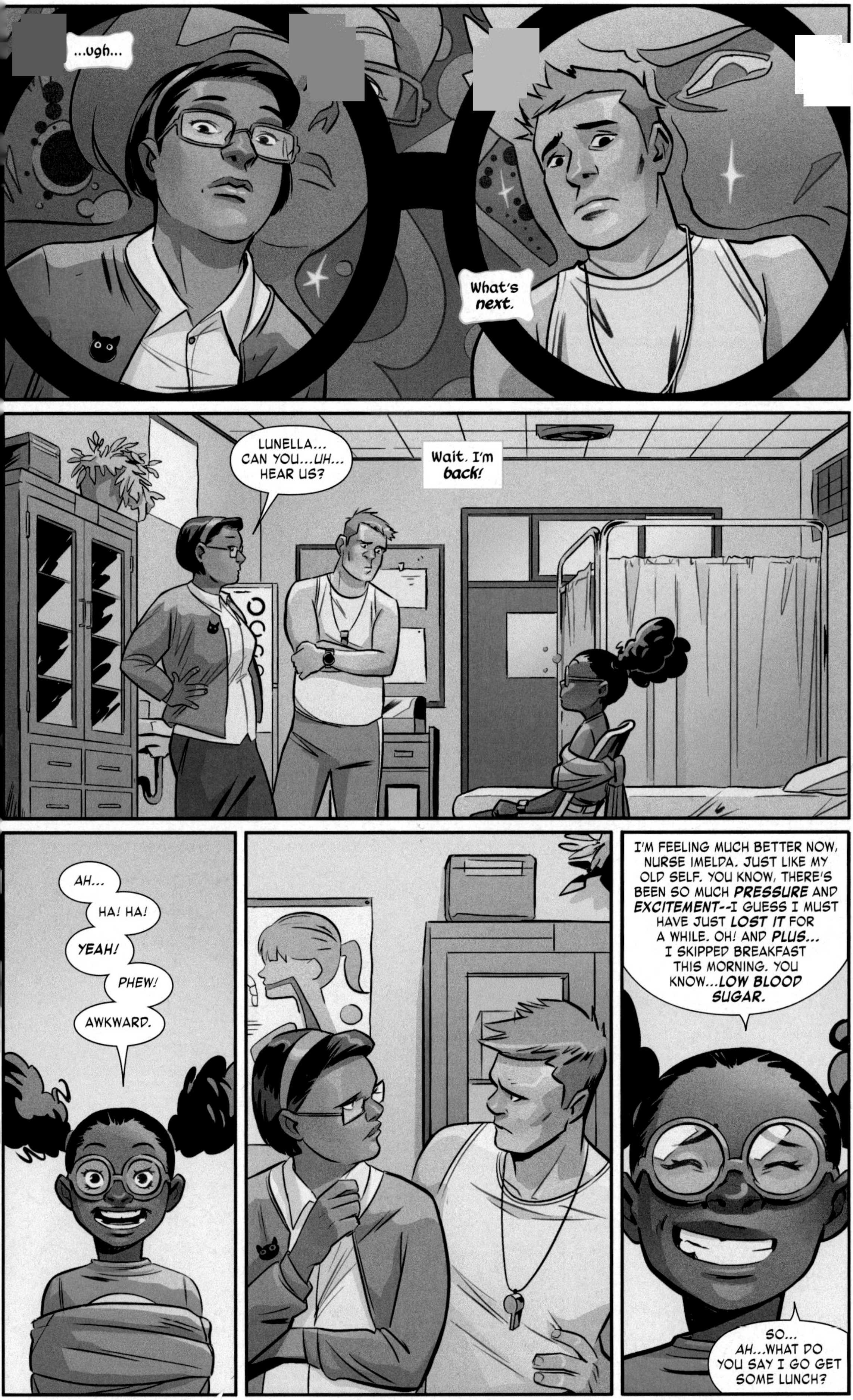
...ugh...
What's next.
LUNELLA... CAN YOU...UH... HEAR US?
Wait. I'm back!
AH...
HA! HA!
YEAH!
PHEW!
AWKWARD.
I'M FEELING MUCH BETTER NOW, NURSE IMELDA. JUST LIKE MY OLD SELF. YOU KNOW, THERE'S BEEN SO MUCH PRESSURE AND EXCITEMENT--I GUESS I MUST HAVE JUST LOST IT FOR A WHILE. OH! AND PLUS... I SKIPPED BREAKFAST THIS MORNING. YOU KNOW...LOW BLOOD SUGAR.
SO... AH...WHAT DO YOU SAY I GO GET SOME LUNCH?

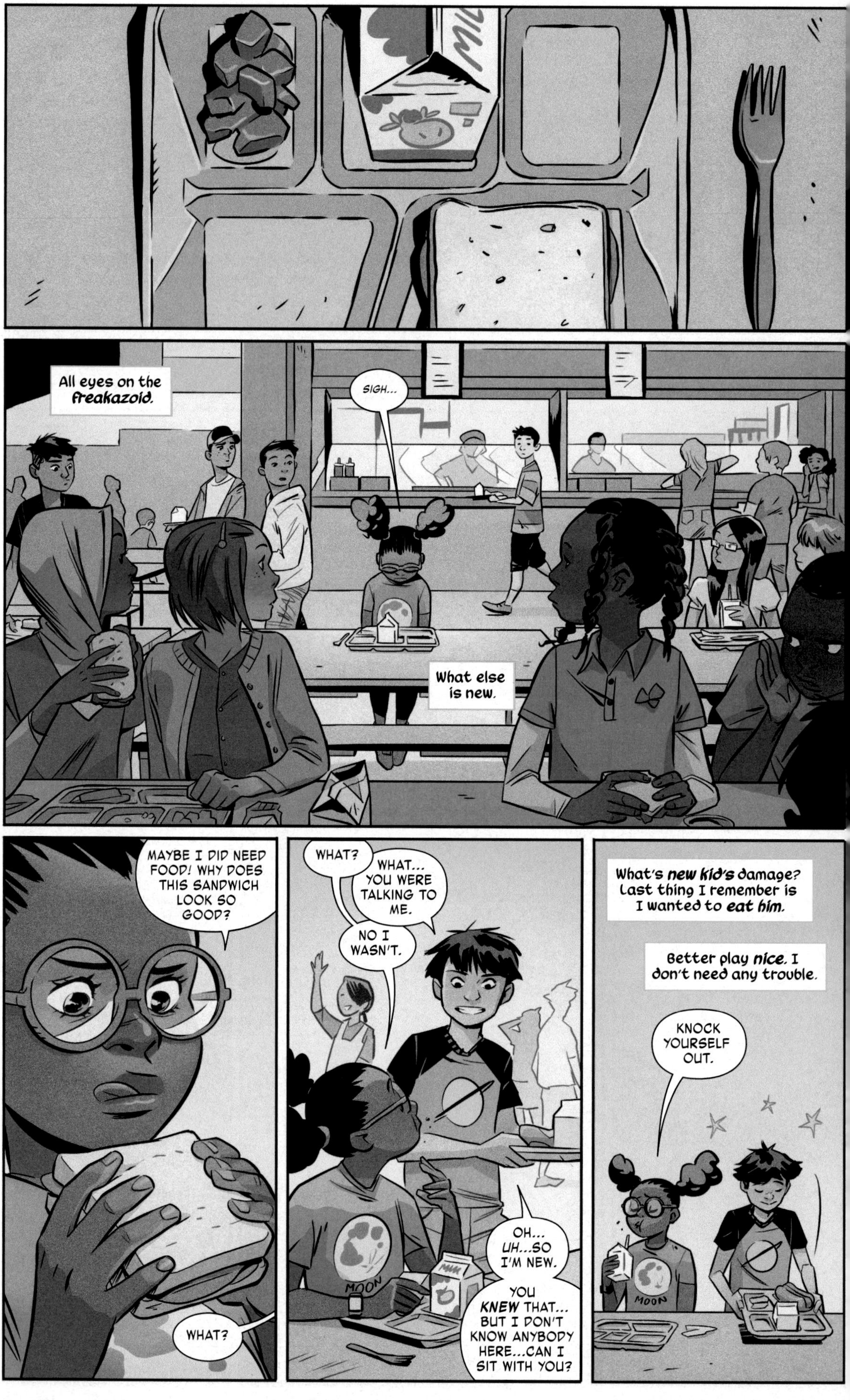
MILK
All eyes on the freakazoid.
SIGH...
What else is new.
MAYBE I DID NEED FOOD! WHY DOES THIS SANDWICH LOOK SO GOOD?
WHAT?
WHAT?
WHAT... YOU WERE TALKING TO ME.
NO I WASN'T.
OH... UH...SO I'M NEW.
YOU KNEW THAT... BUT I DON'T KNOW ANYBODY HERE...CAN I SIT WITH YOU?
MOON
What's new kid's damage? Last thing I remember is I wanted to eat him.
Better play nice. I don't need any trouble.
KNOCK YOURSELF OUT.
MOON

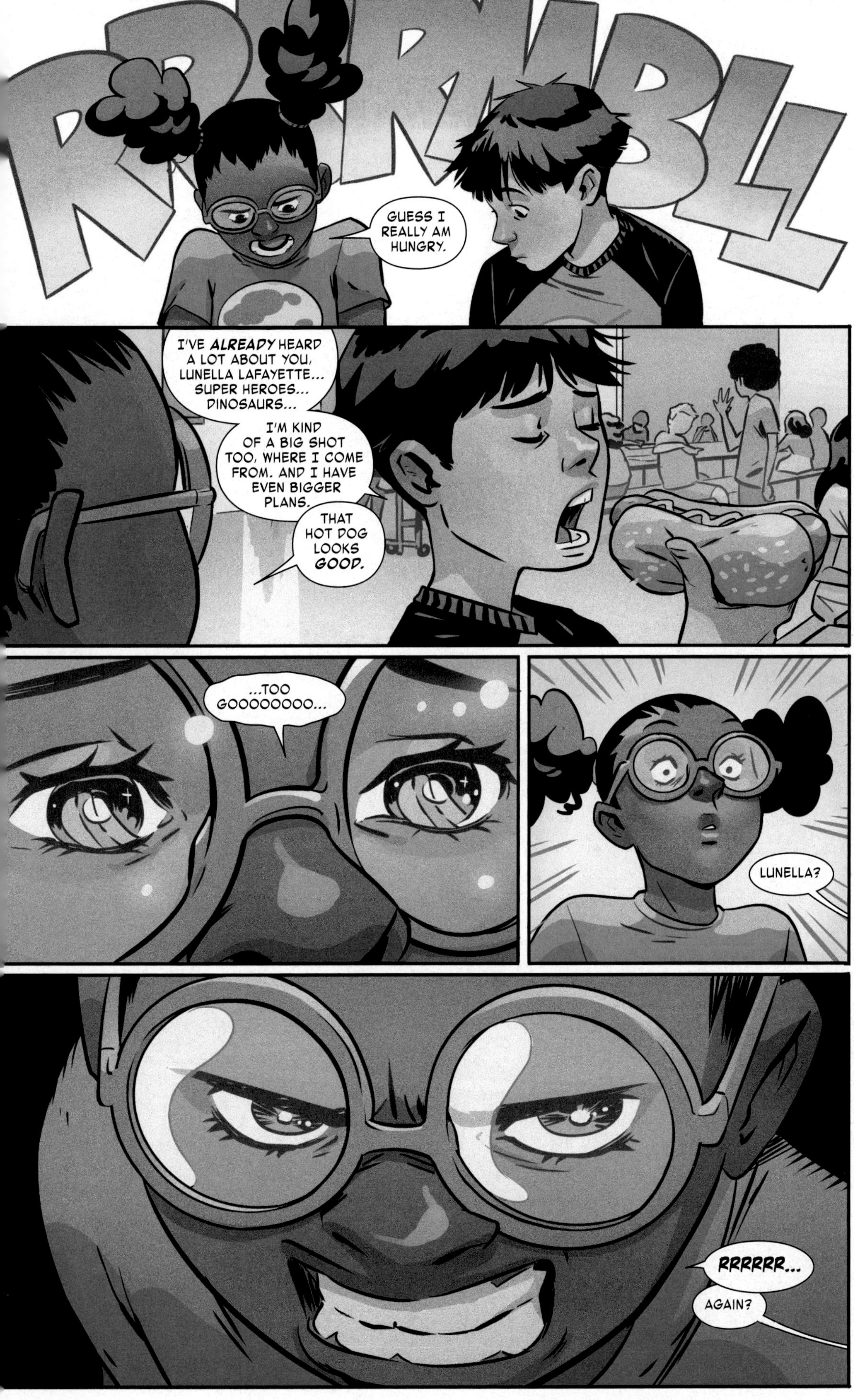
RRRRUMBLLL
GUESS I REALLY AM HUNGRY.
I'VE ALREADY HEARD A LOT ABOUT YOU, LUNELLA LAFAYETTE... SUPER HEROES... DINOSAURS...
I'M KIND OF A BIG SHOT TOO, WHERE I COME FROM. AND I HAVE EVEN BIGGER PLANS.
THAT HOT DOG LOOKS GOOD.
...TOO GOOOOOOOO...
LUNELLA?
RRRRRR...
AGAIN?

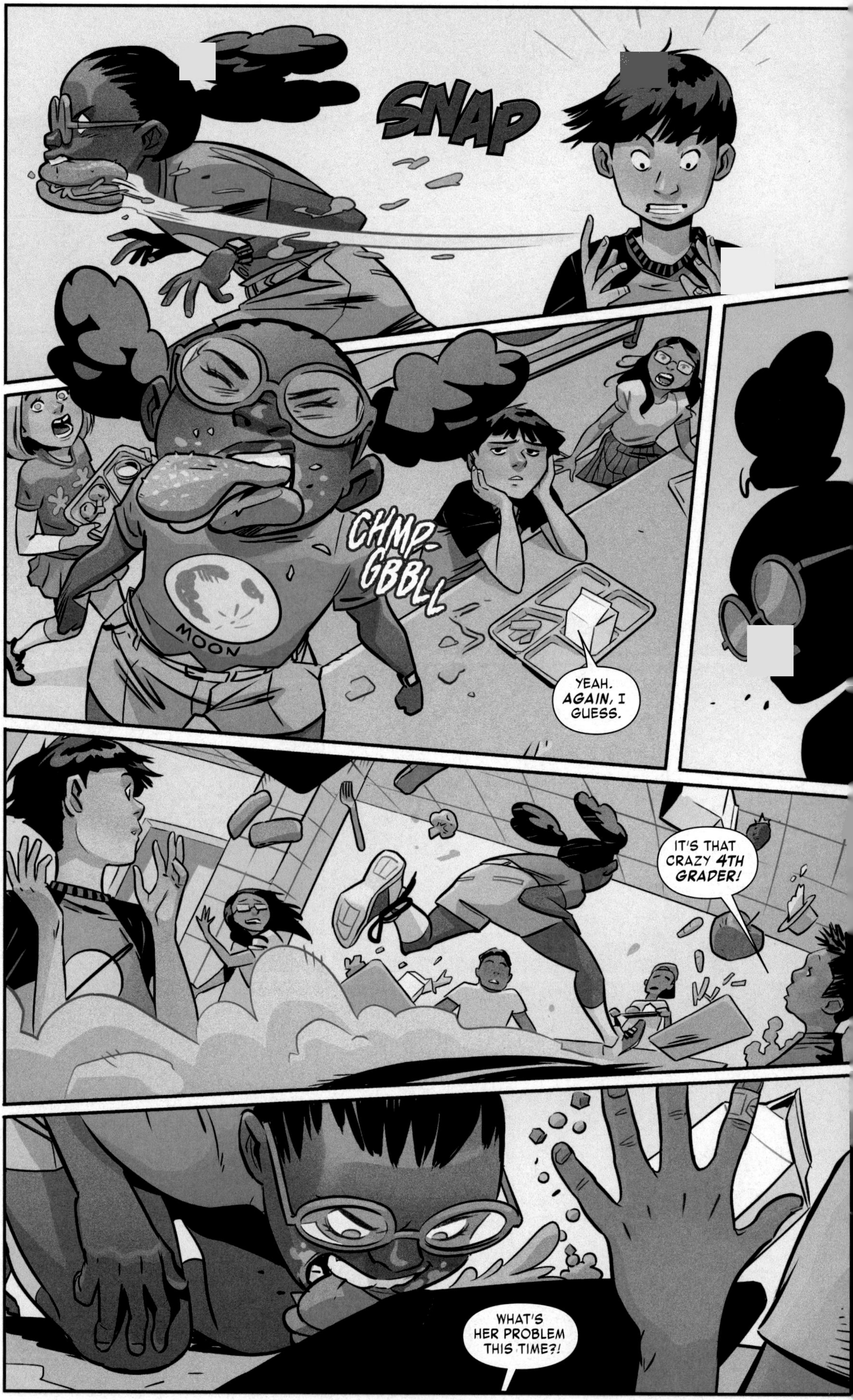
SNAP
CHMP-GBBLL
MOON
YEAH. AGAIN, I GUESS.
IT'S THAT CRAZY 4TH GRADER!
WHAT'S HER PROBLEM THIS TIME?!

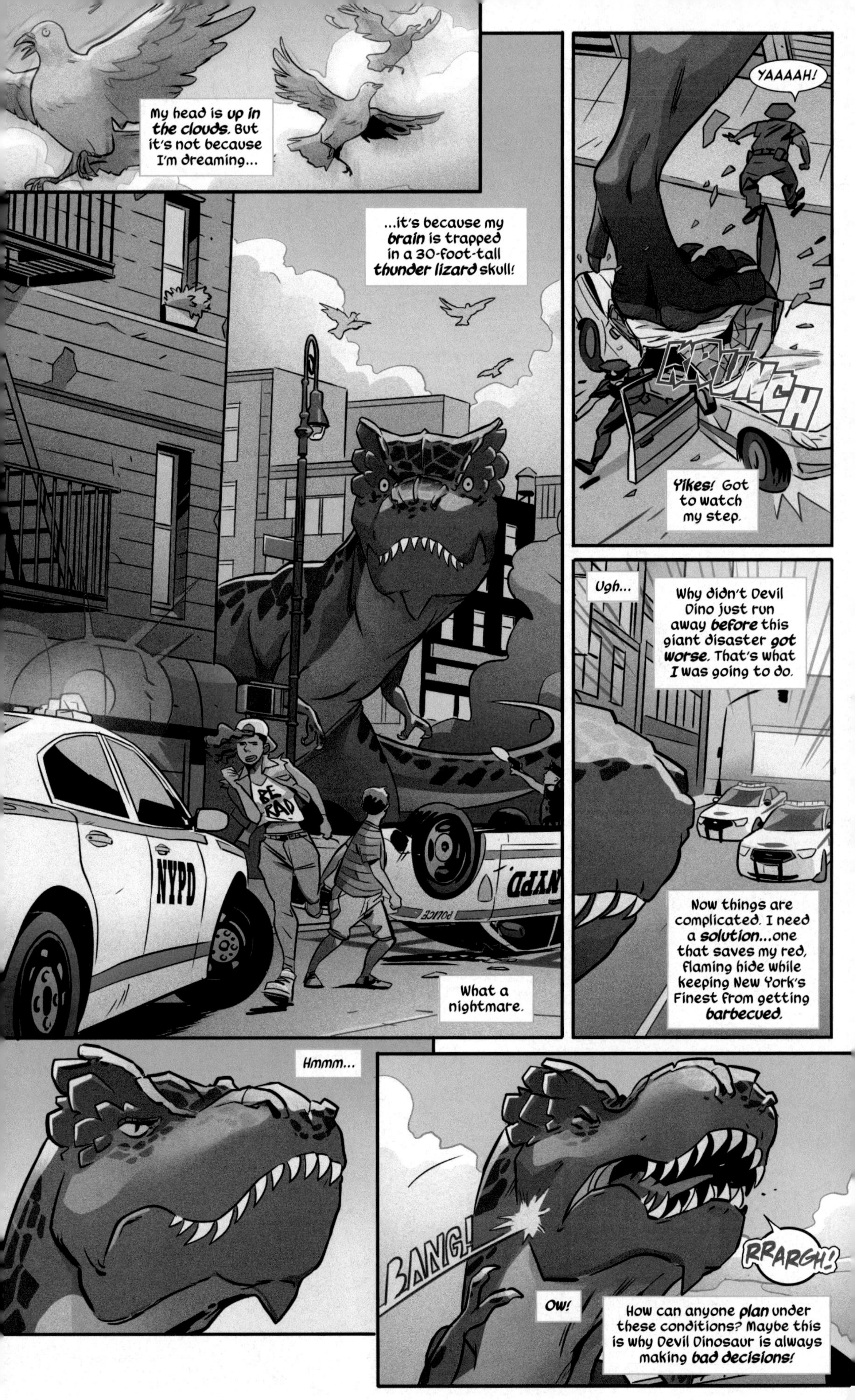

My head is up in the clouds. But it's not because I'm dreaming...
...it's because my brain is trapped in a 30-foot-tall thunder lizard skull!
BE RAD
NYPD
NYPD
POLICE
What a nightmare.
YAAAAH!
KRUNCH
Yikes! Got to watch my step.
Ugh...
Why didn't Devil Dino just run away before this giant disaster got worse. That's what I was going to do.
Now things are complicated. I need a solution...one that saves my red, flaming hide while keeping New York's Finest from getting barbecued.
Hmmm...
BANG!
RRARGH!
OW!
How can anyone plan under these conditions? Maybe this is why Devil Dinosaur is always making bad decisions!

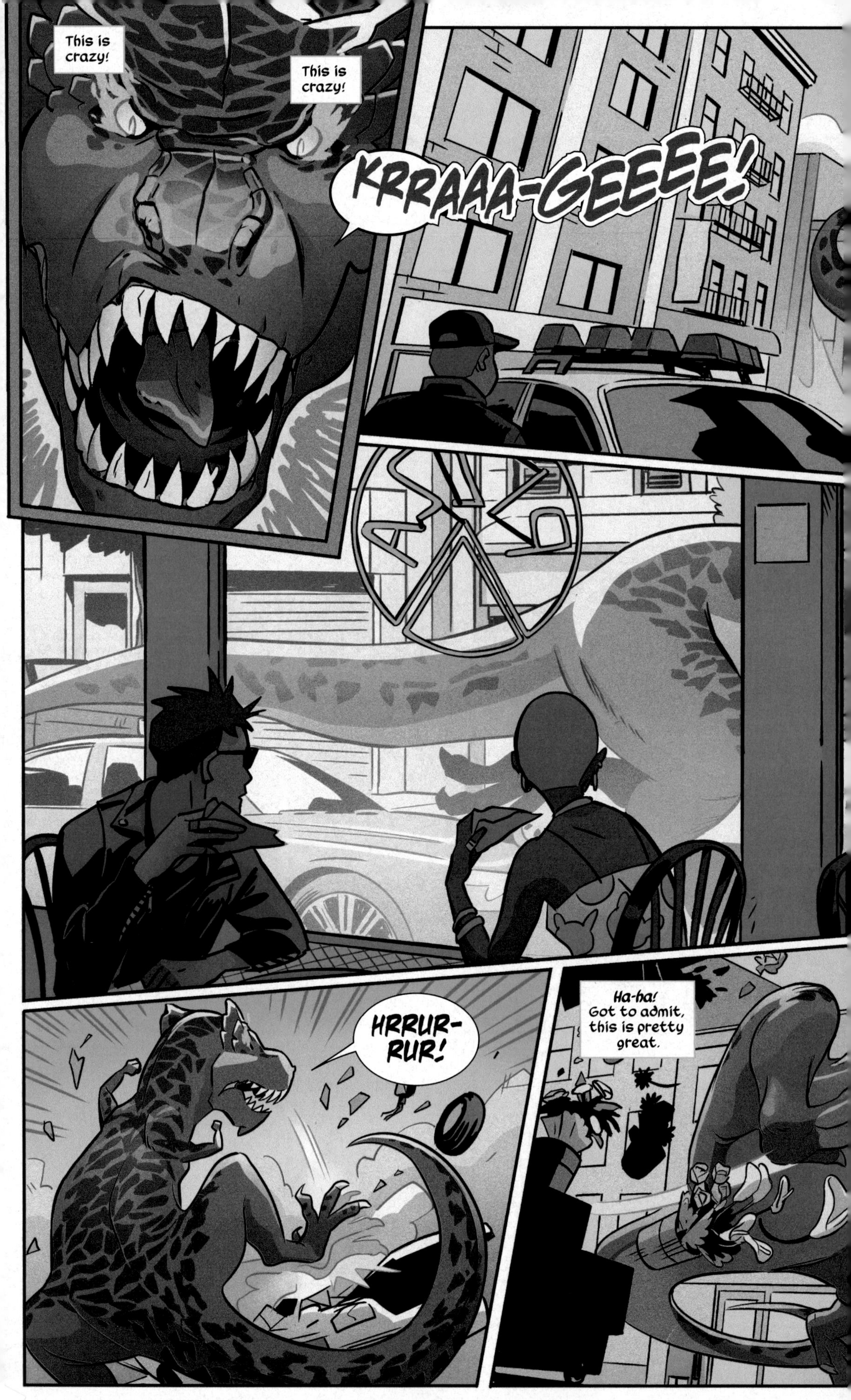
This is crazy!
This is crazy!
KRRAAA-GEEEE!
HRRUR-RUR!
Ha-ha! Got to admit, this is pretty great.

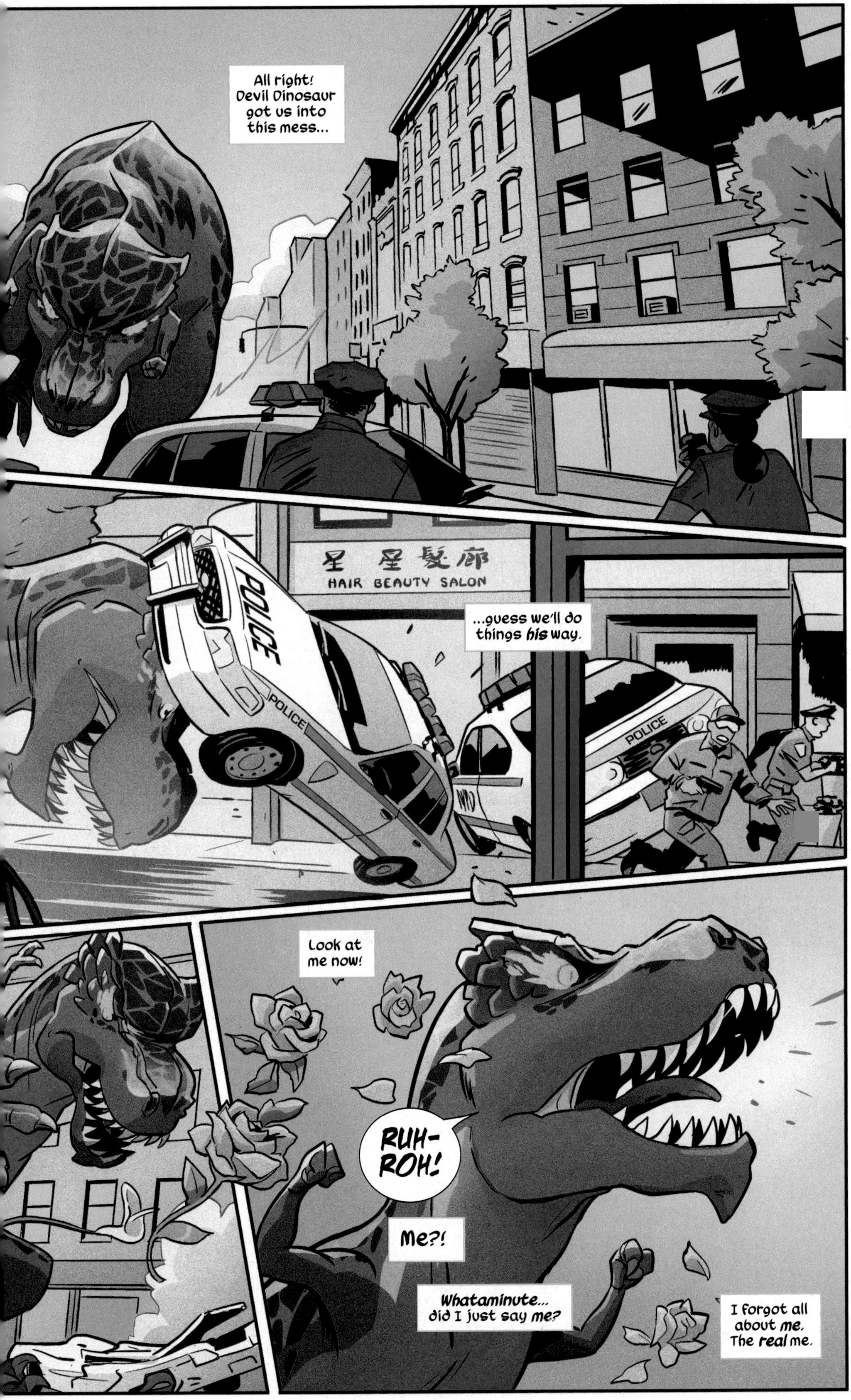
All right! Devil Dinosaur got us into this mess...
星 屋髮廊
HAIR BEAUTY SALON
...guess we'll do things his way.
POLICE
Look at me now!
RUH-ROH!
Me?!
Whataminute... did I just say me?
I forgot all about me. The real me.

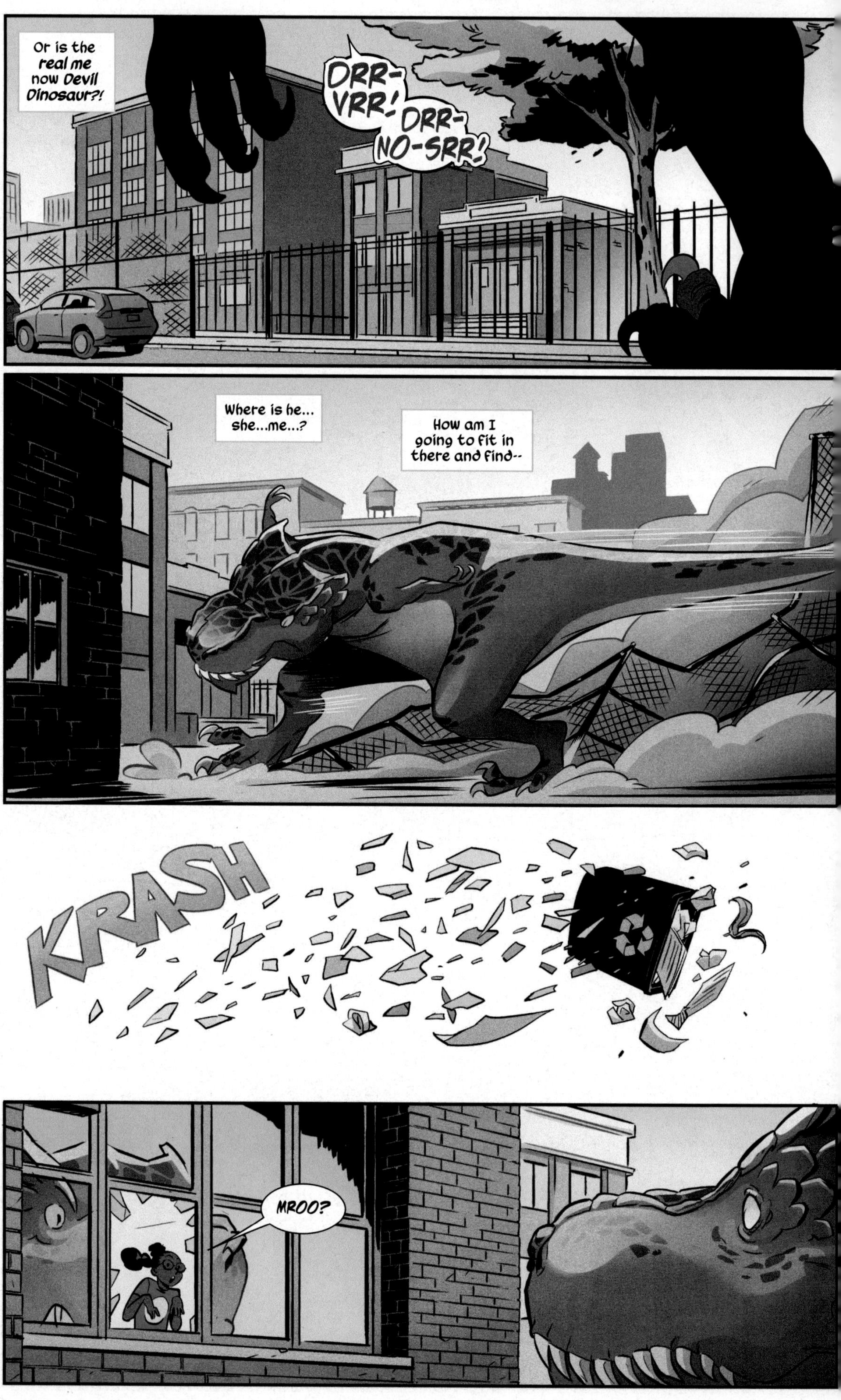
Or is the real me now Devil Dinosaur?!
ORR-VRR! ORR-NO-SRR!
Where is he... she...me...?
How am I going to fit in there and find--
KRASH
MROO?

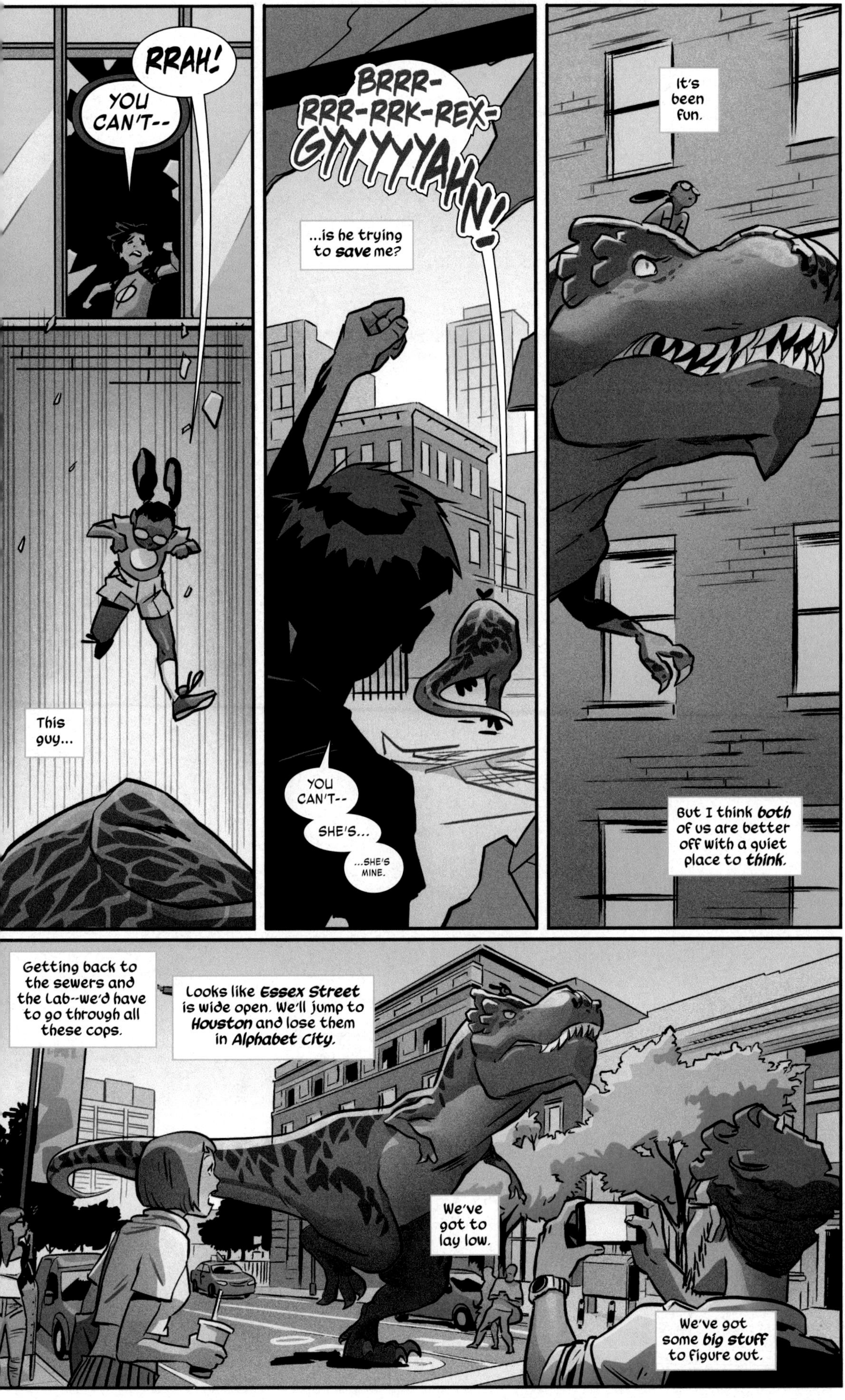

YOU CAN'T--
RRAH!
This guy...
BRRRR-RRR-RRK-REX-GYYYYYAHN!
...is he trying to save me?
YOU CAN'T--
SHE'S...
...SHE'S MINE.
It's been fun.
But I think both of us are better off with a quiet place to think.
Getting back to the sewers and the Lab--we'd have to go through all these cops.
Looks like Essex Street is wide open. We'll jump to Houston and lose them in Alphabet City.
We've got to lay low.
We've got some big stuff to figure out.

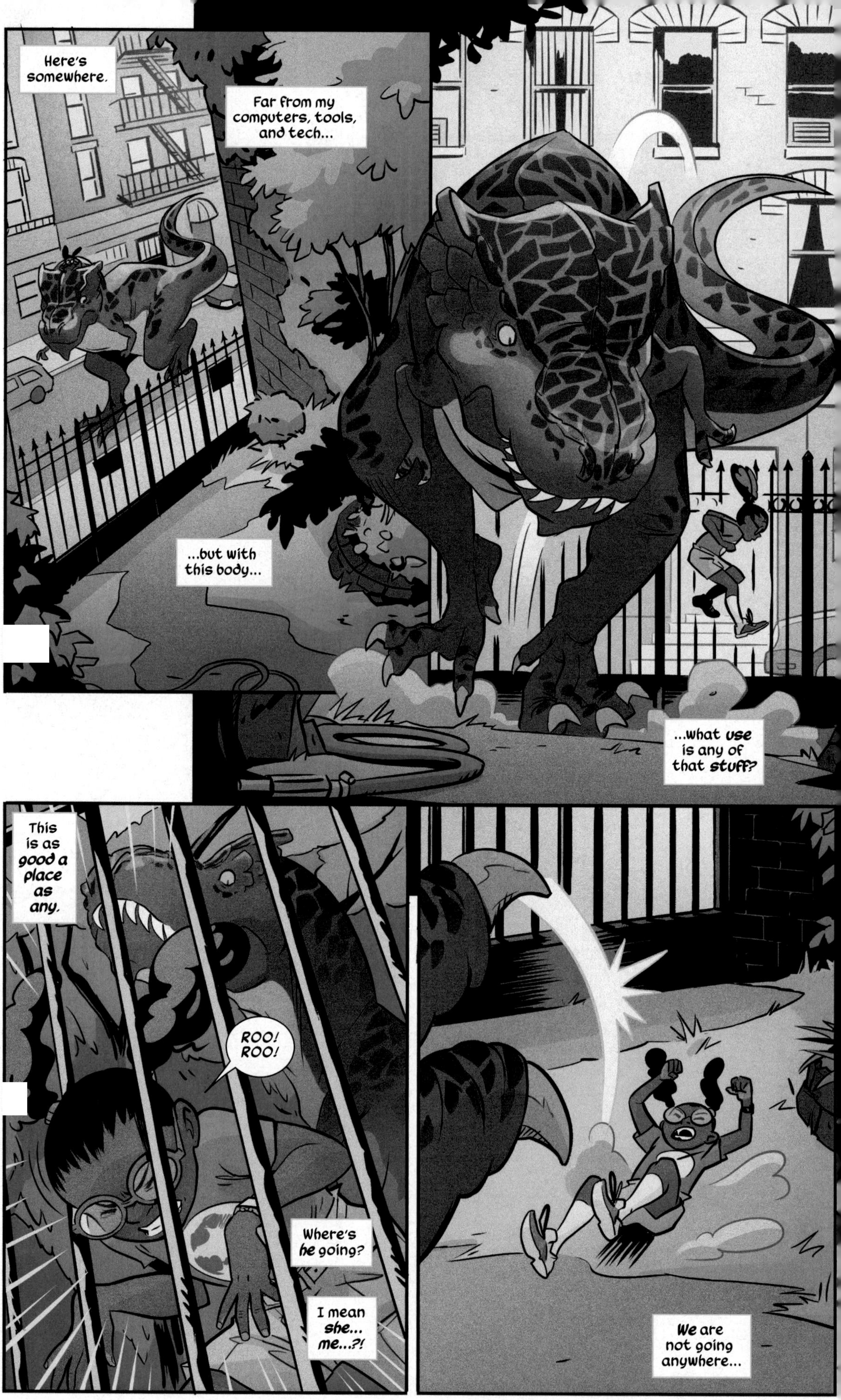
Here's somewhere.
Far from my computers, tools, and tech...
...but with this body...
...what use is any of that stuff?
This is as good a place as any.
ROO! ROO!
Where's he going?
I mean she... me...?!
We are not going anywhere...

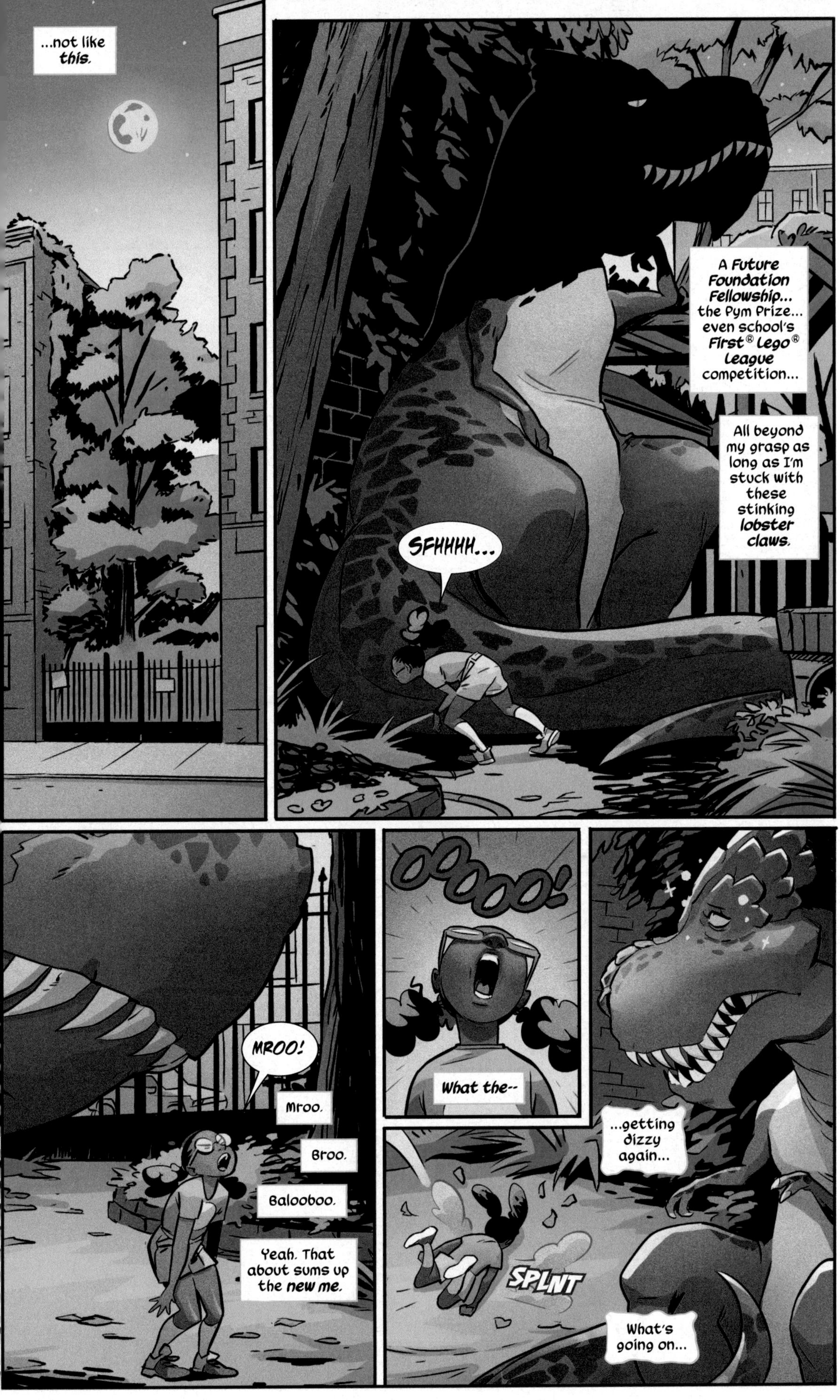
...not like this.
A Future Foundation Fellowship... the Pym Prize... even school's First® Lego® League competition...
All beyond my grasp as long as I'm stuck with these stinking lobster claws.
SFHHHH...
MROO!
Mroo.
Broo.
Balooboo.
Yeah. That about sums up the new me.
OOOOOO!
What the--
...getting dizzy again...
SPLNT
What's going on...

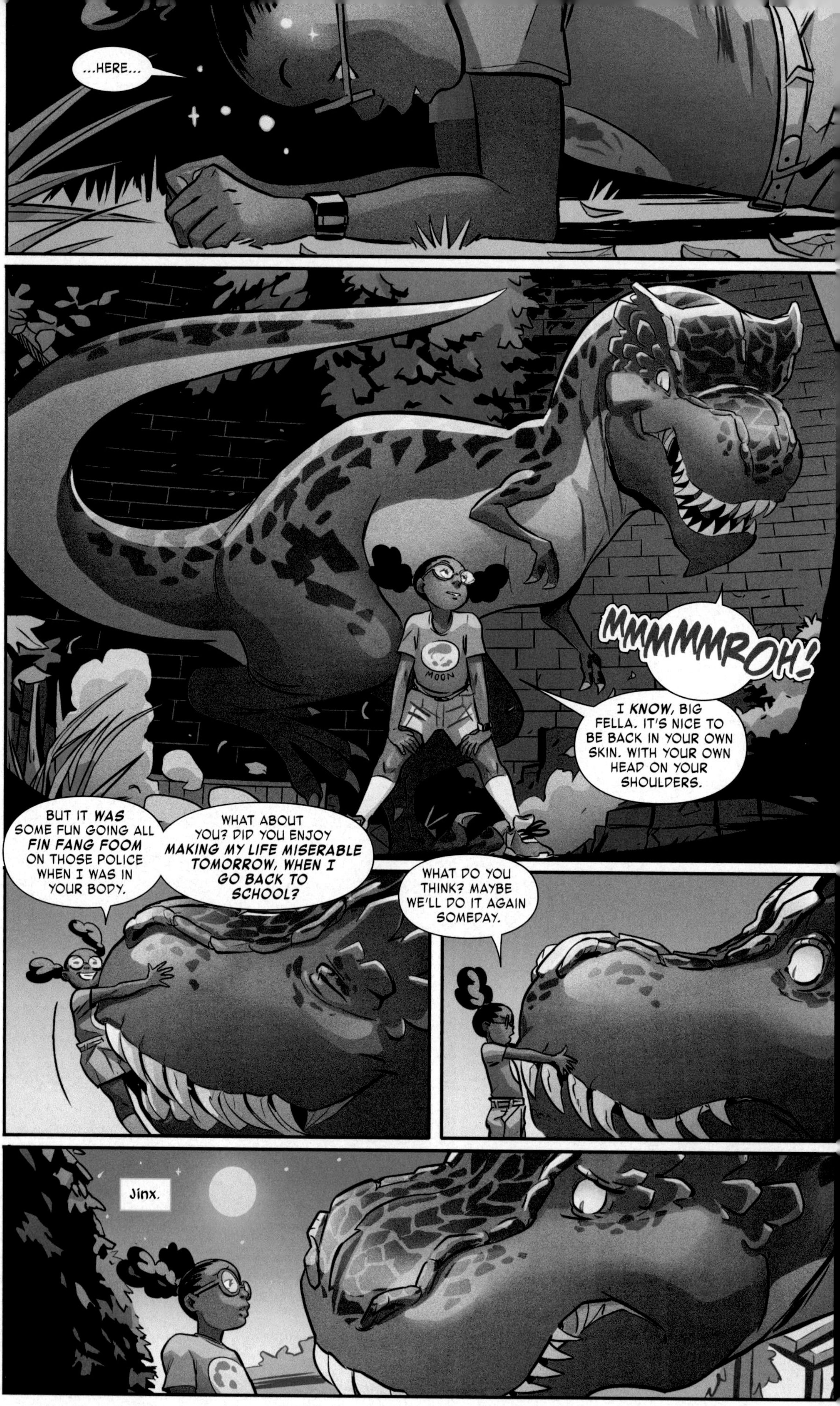
...HERE...
MMMMMROH!
I KNOW, BIG FELLA. IT'S NICE TO BE BACK IN YOUR OWN SKIN. WITH YOUR OWN HEAD ON YOUR SHOULDERS.
BUT IT WAS SOME FUN GOING ALL FIN FANG FOOM ON THOSE POLICE WHEN I WAS IN YOUR BODY.
WHAT ABOUT YOU? DID YOU ENJOY MAKING MY LIFE MISERABLE TOMORROW, WHEN I GO BACK TO SCHOOL?
WHAT DO YOU THINK? MAYBE WE'LL DO IT AGAIN SOMEDAY.
Jinx.

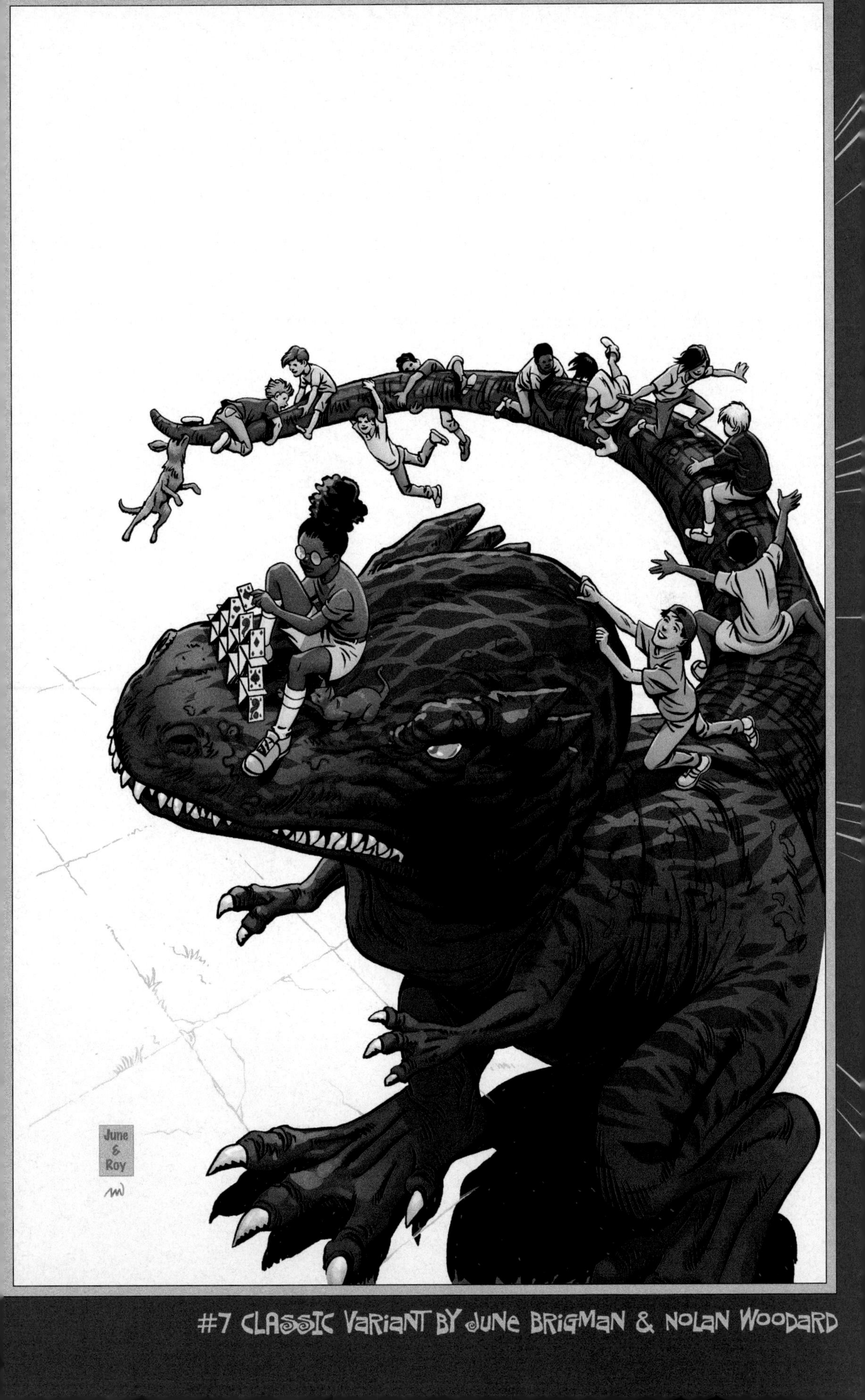
June & Roy

#7 CLASSIC VARIANT BY JUNE BRIGMAN & NOLAN WOODARD

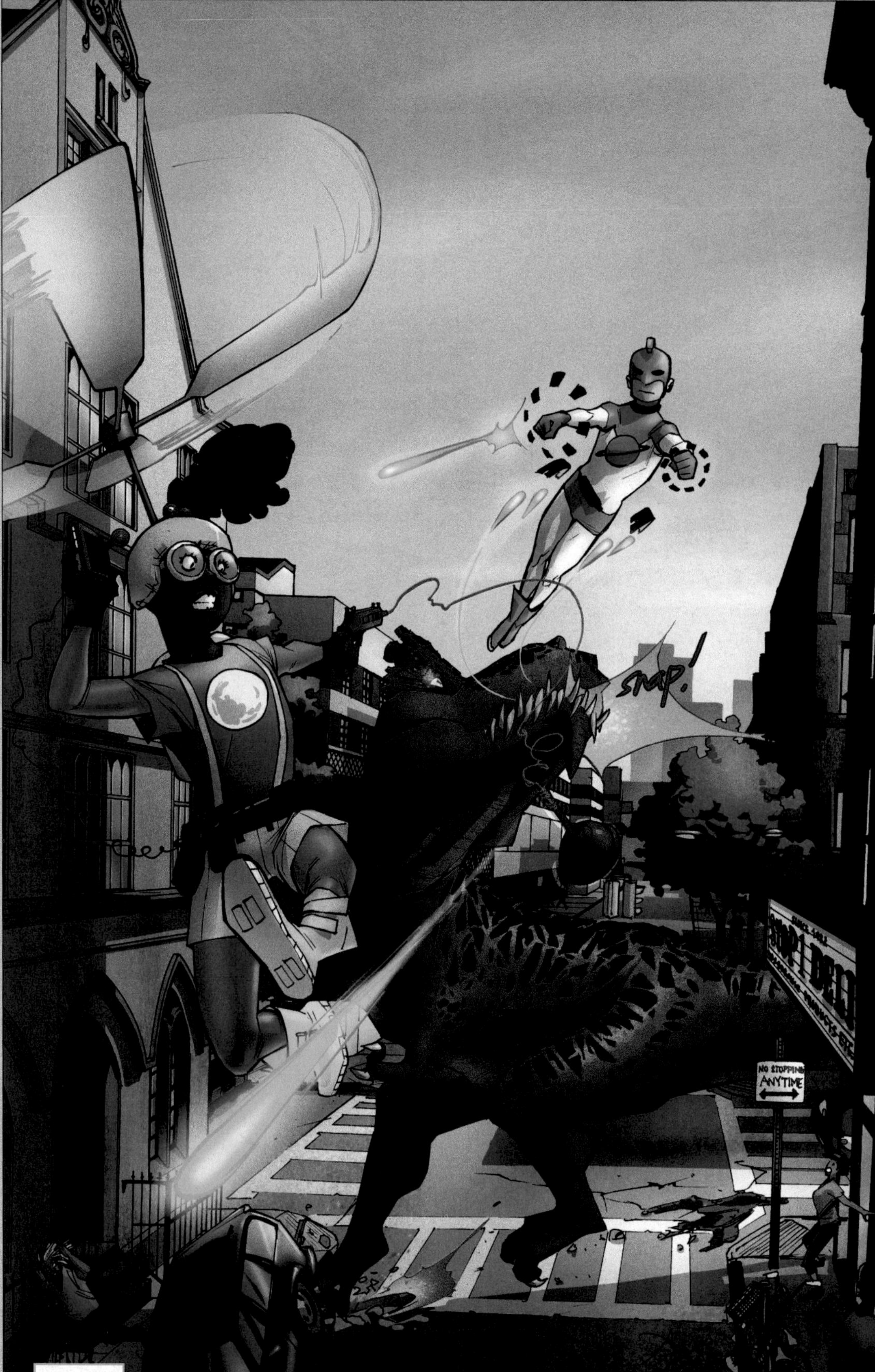
snap!
NO STOPPING
ANYTIME

CHAPTER 9

"MOON AND STARS"

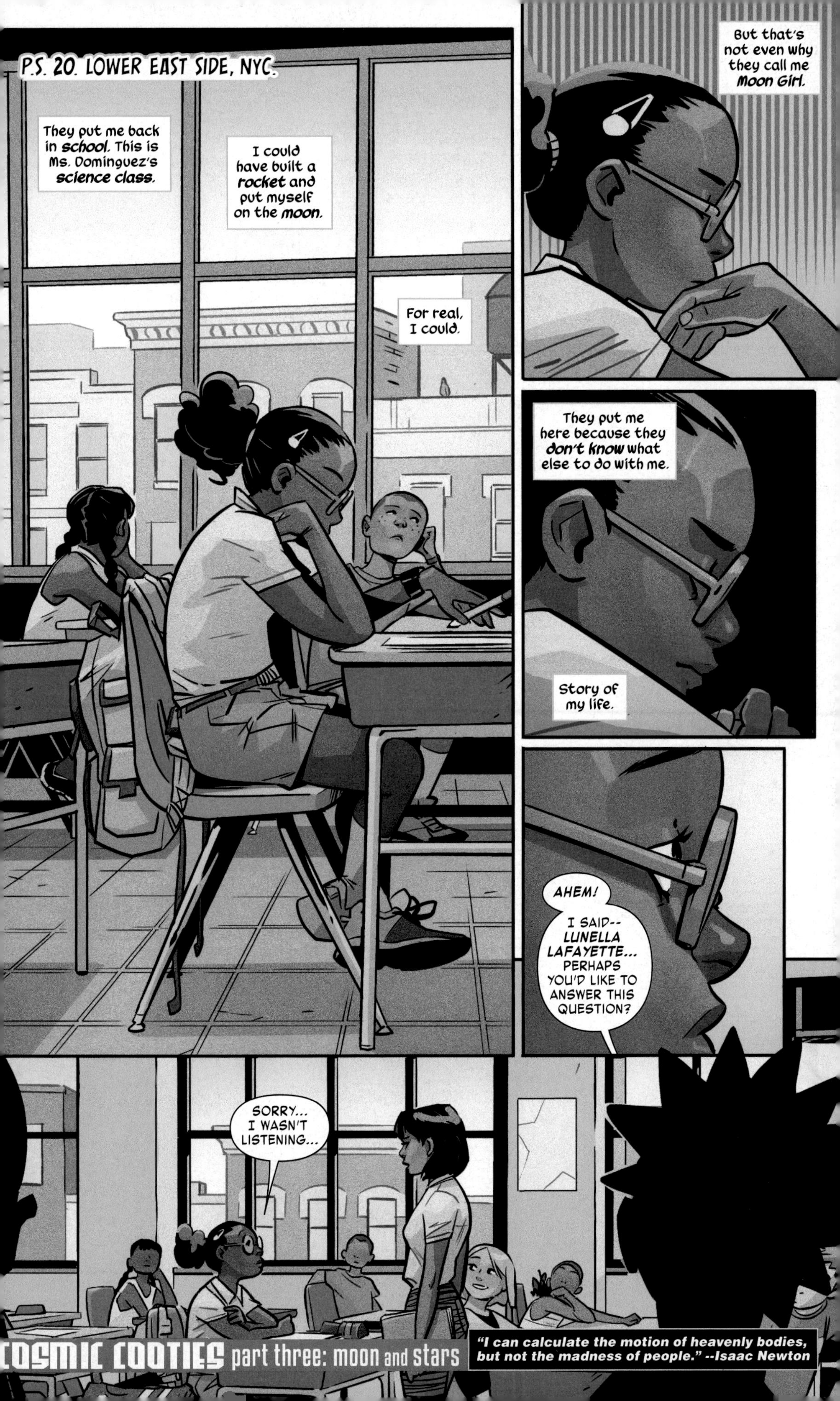

P.S. 20. LOWER EAST SIDE, NYC.
They put me back in school. This is Ms. Dominguez's science class.
I could have built a rocket and put myself on the moon.
For real, I could.
But that's not even why they call me Moon Girl.
They put me here because they don't know what else to do with me.
Story of my life.
AHEM!
I SAID-- LUNELLA LAFAYETTE... PERHAPS YOU'D LIKE TO ANSWER THIS QUESTION?
SORRY... I WASN'T LISTENING...
COSMIC COOTIES part three: moon and stars
"I can calculate the motion of heavenly bodies, but not the madness of people." --Isaac Newton

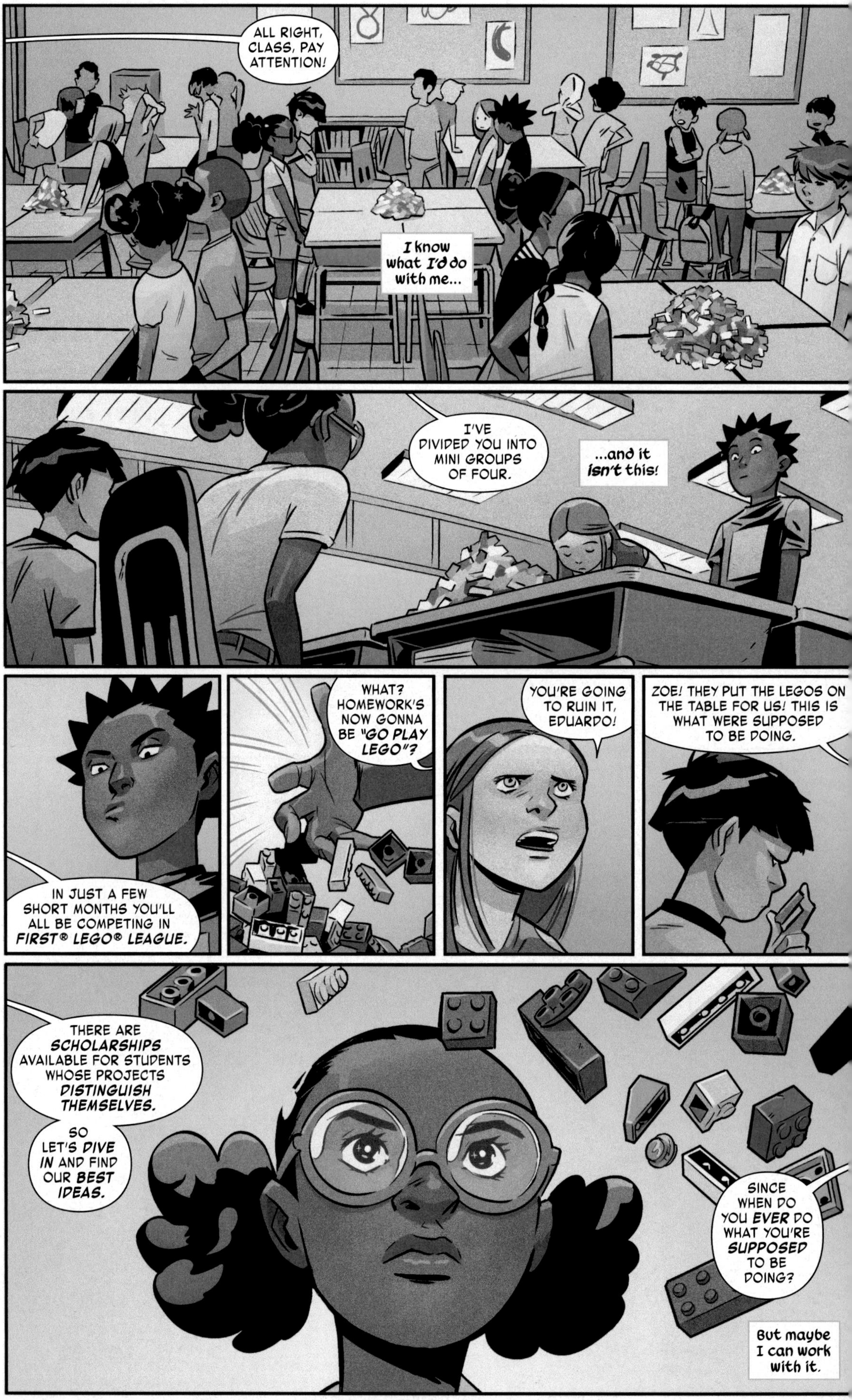

ALL RIGHT, CLASS, PAY ATTENTION!
I know what I'd do with me...
I'VE DIVIDED YOU INTO MINI GROUPS OF FOUR.
...and it isn't this!
IN JUST A FEW SHORT MONTHS YOU'LL ALL BE COMPETING IN FIRST® LEGO® LEAGUE.
WHAT? HOMEWORK'S NOW GONNA BE "GO PLAY LEGO"?
YOU'RE GOING TO RUIN IT, EDUARDO!
ZOE! THEY PUT THE LEGOS ON THE TABLE FOR US! THIS IS WHAT WERE SUPPOSED TO BE DOING.
THERE ARE SCHOLARSHIPS AVAILABLE FOR STUDENTS WHOSE PROJECTS DISTINGUISH THEMSELVES.
SO LET'S DIVE IN AND FIND OUR BEST IDEAS.
SINCE WHEN DO YOU EVER DO WHAT YOU'RE SUPPOSED TO BE DOING?
But maybe I can work with it.

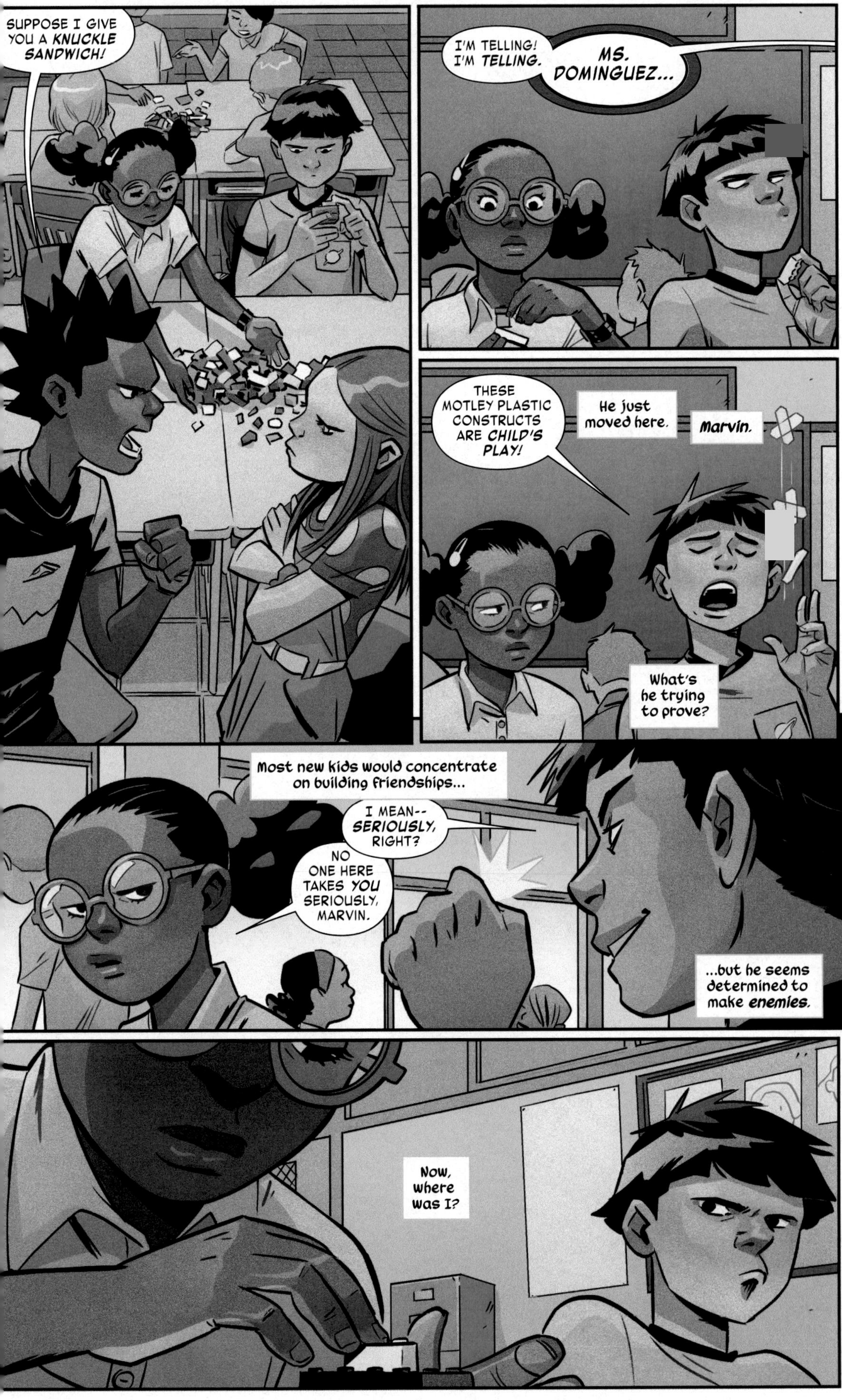
SUPPOSE I GIVE YOU A KNUCKLE SANDWICH!
I'M TELLING! I'M TELLING.
MS. DOMINGUEZ...
THESE MOTLEY PLASTIC CONSTRUCTS ARE CHILD'S PLAY!
He just moved here.
Marvin.
What's he trying to prove?
Most new kids would concentrate on building friendships...
I MEAN-- SERIOUSLY, RIGHT?
NO ONE HERE TAKES YOU SERIOUSLY, MARVIN.
...but he seems determined to make enemies.
Now, where was I?

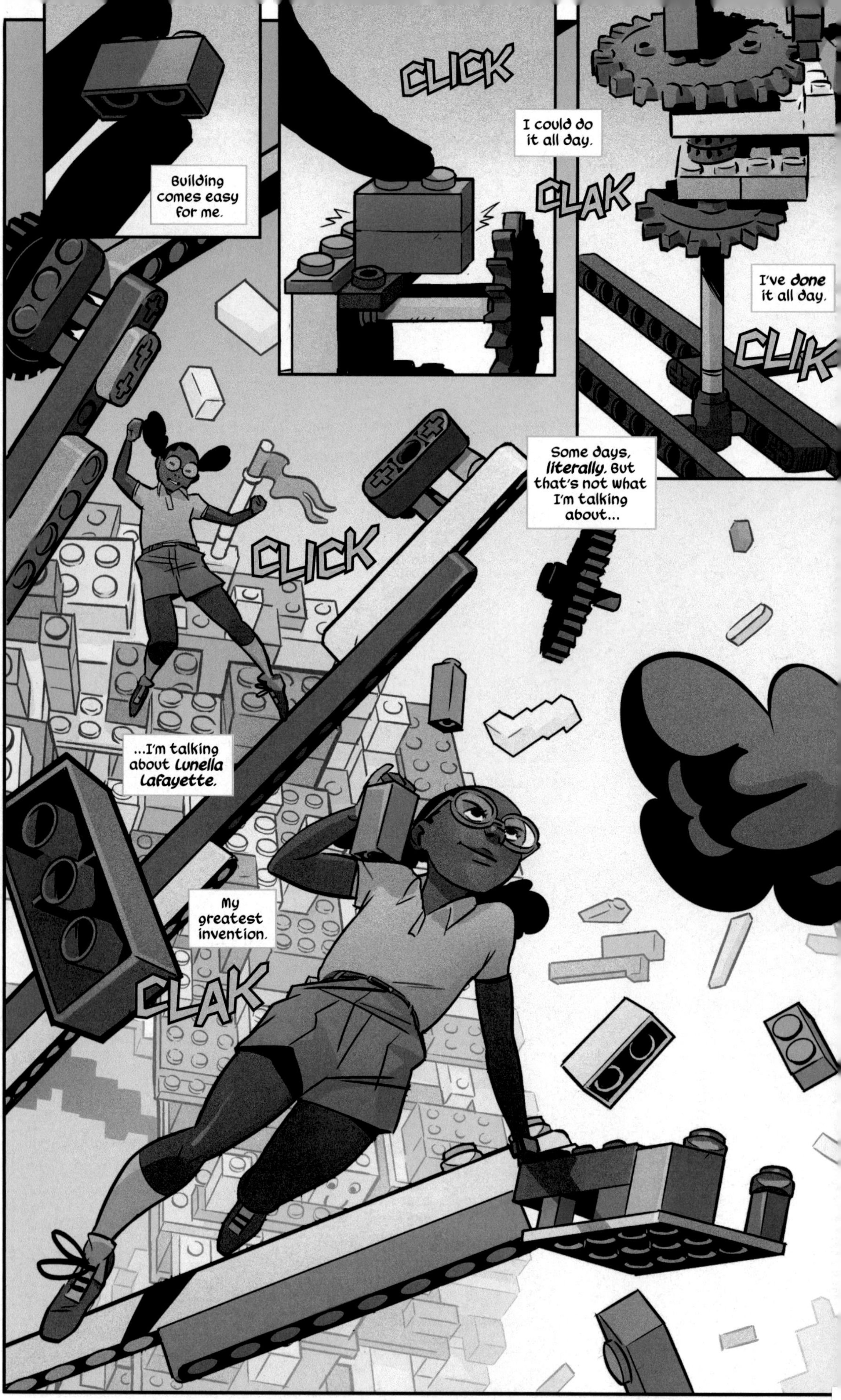
Building comes easy for me.
CLICK
I could do it all day.
CLAK
I've *done* it all day.
CLIK
Some days, *literally.* But that's not what I'm talking about...
CLICK
...I'm talking about *Lunella Lafayette.*
My greatest invention.
CLAK

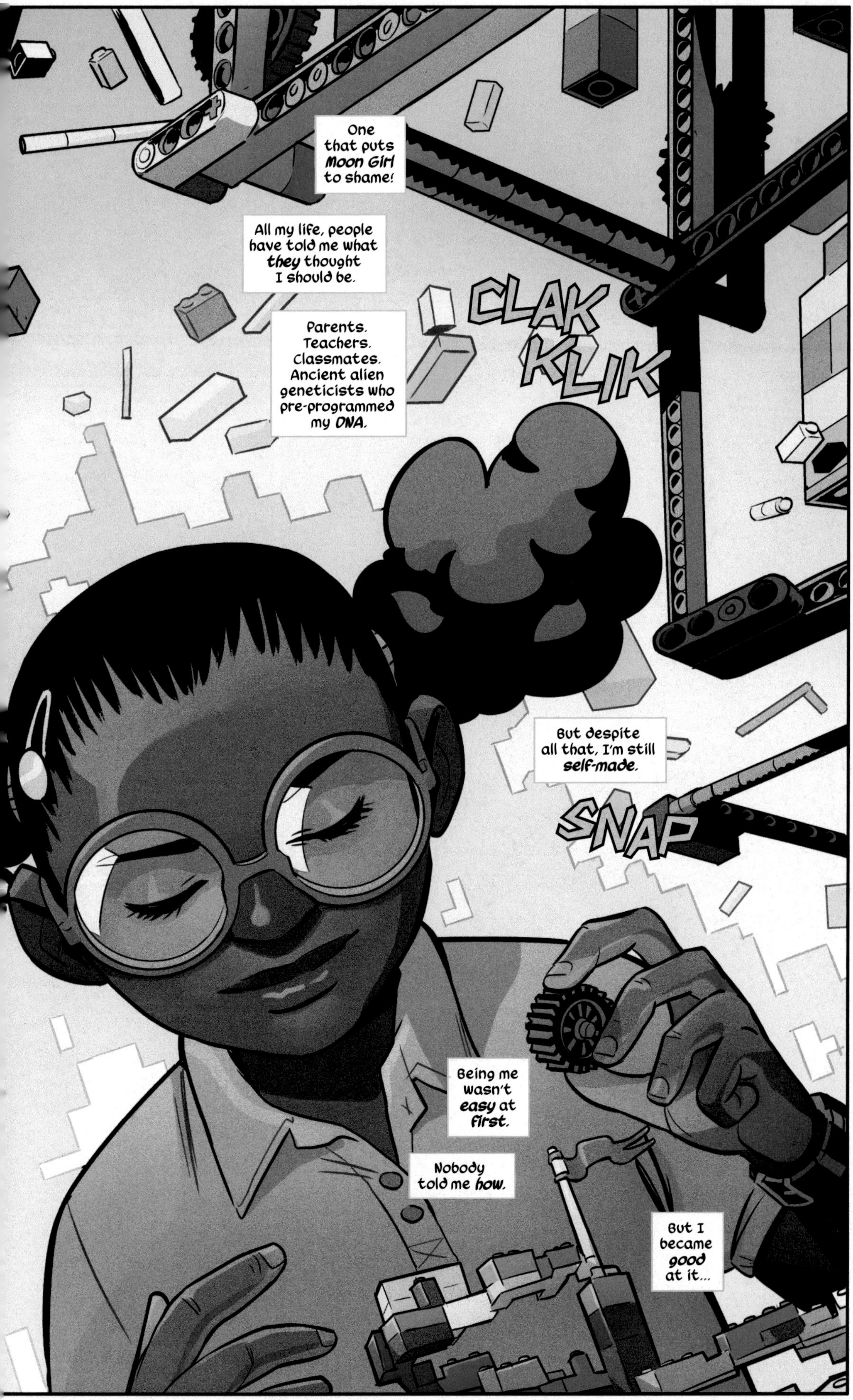

One that puts *Moon Girl* to shame!
All my life, people have told me what *they* thought I should be.
Parents. Teachers. Classmates. Ancient alien geneticists who pre-programmed my *DNA*.
CLAK
KLIK
But despite all that, I'm still *self-made*.
SNAP
Being me wasn't *easy* at *first*.
Nobody told me *how*.
But I became *good* at it...

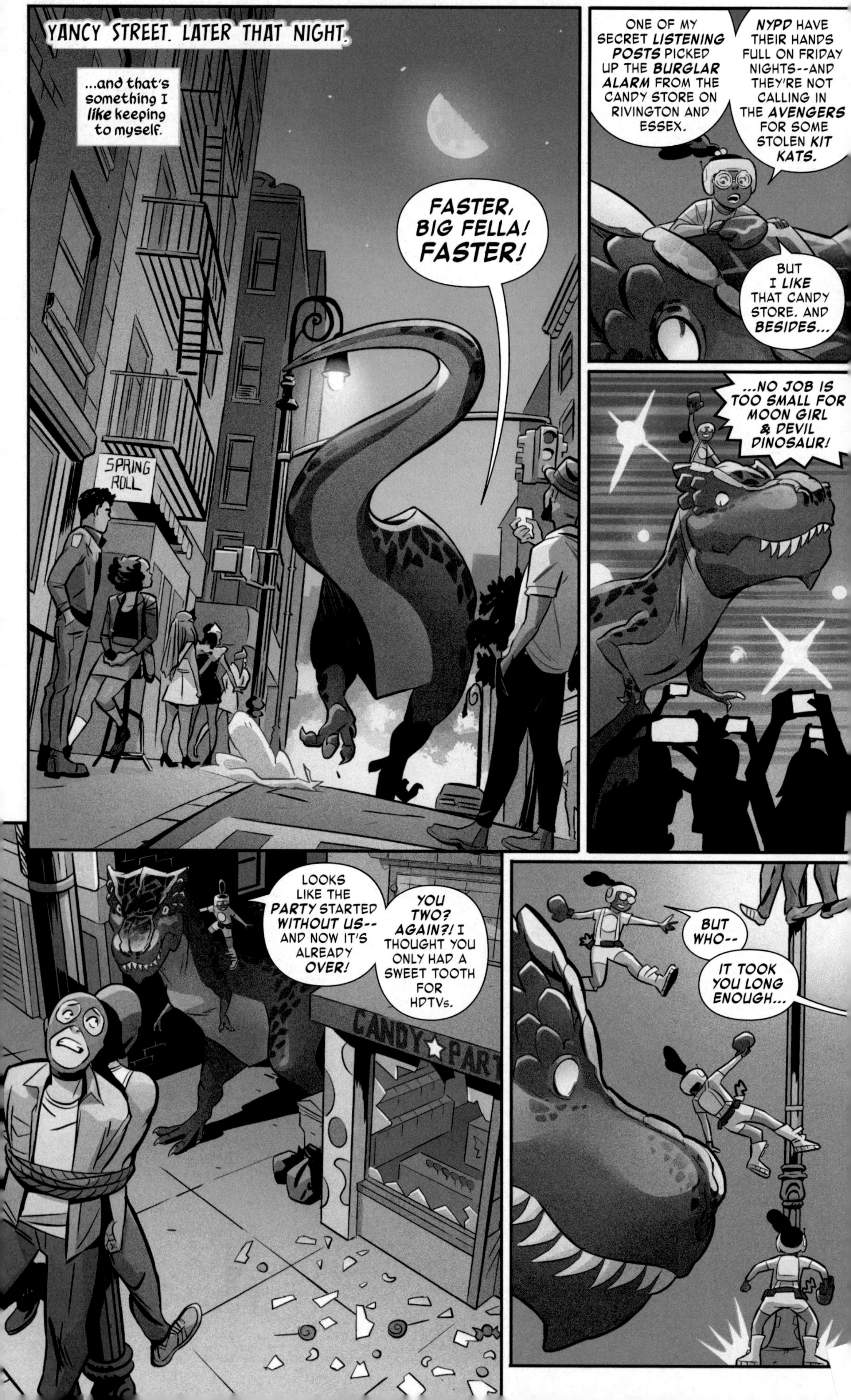

YANCY STREET. LATER THAT NIGHT.
...and that's something I like keeping to myself.
SPRING ROLL
FASTER, BIG FELLA! FASTER!
ONE OF MY SECRET LISTENING POSTS PICKED UP THE BURGLAR ALARM FROM THE CANDY STORE ON RIVINGTON AND ESSEX.
NYPD HAVE THEIR HANDS FULL ON FRIDAY NIGHTS--AND THEY'RE NOT CALLING IN THE AVENGERS FOR SOME STOLEN KIT KATS.
BUT I LIKE THAT CANDY STORE. AND BESIDES...
...NO JOB IS TOO SMALL FOR MOON GIRL & DEVIL DINOSAUR!
LOOKS LIKE THE PARTY STARTED WITHOUT US--AND NOW IT'S ALREADY OVER!
YOU TWO? AGAIN?! I THOUGHT YOU ONLY HAD A SWEET TOOTH FOR HDTVs.
CANDY PART
BUT WHO--
IT TOOK YOU LONG ENOUGH...

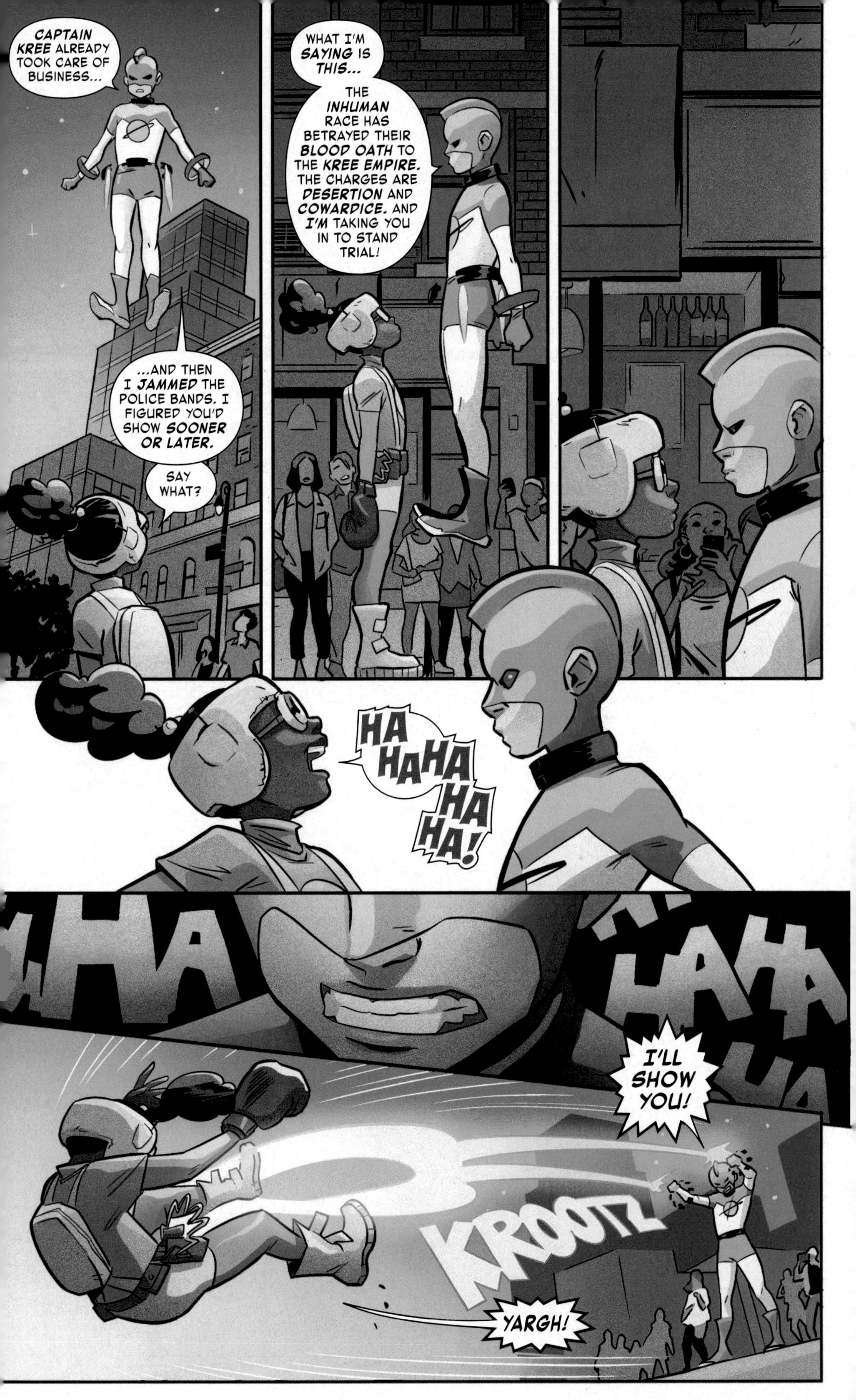
CAPTAIN KREE ALREADY TOOK CARE OF BUSINESS...
...AND THEN I JAMMED THE POLICE BANDS. I FIGURED YOU'D SHOW SOONER OR LATER.
SAY WHAT?
WHAT I'M SAYING IS THIS...
THE INHUMAN RACE HAS BETRAYED THEIR BLOOD OATH TO THE KREE EMPIRE. THE CHARGES ARE DESERTION AND COWARDICE. AND I'M TAKING YOU IN TO STAND TRIAL!
HA HAHA HA HA!
HA
HAHA HA
I'LL SHOW YOU!
KROOTZ
YARGH!

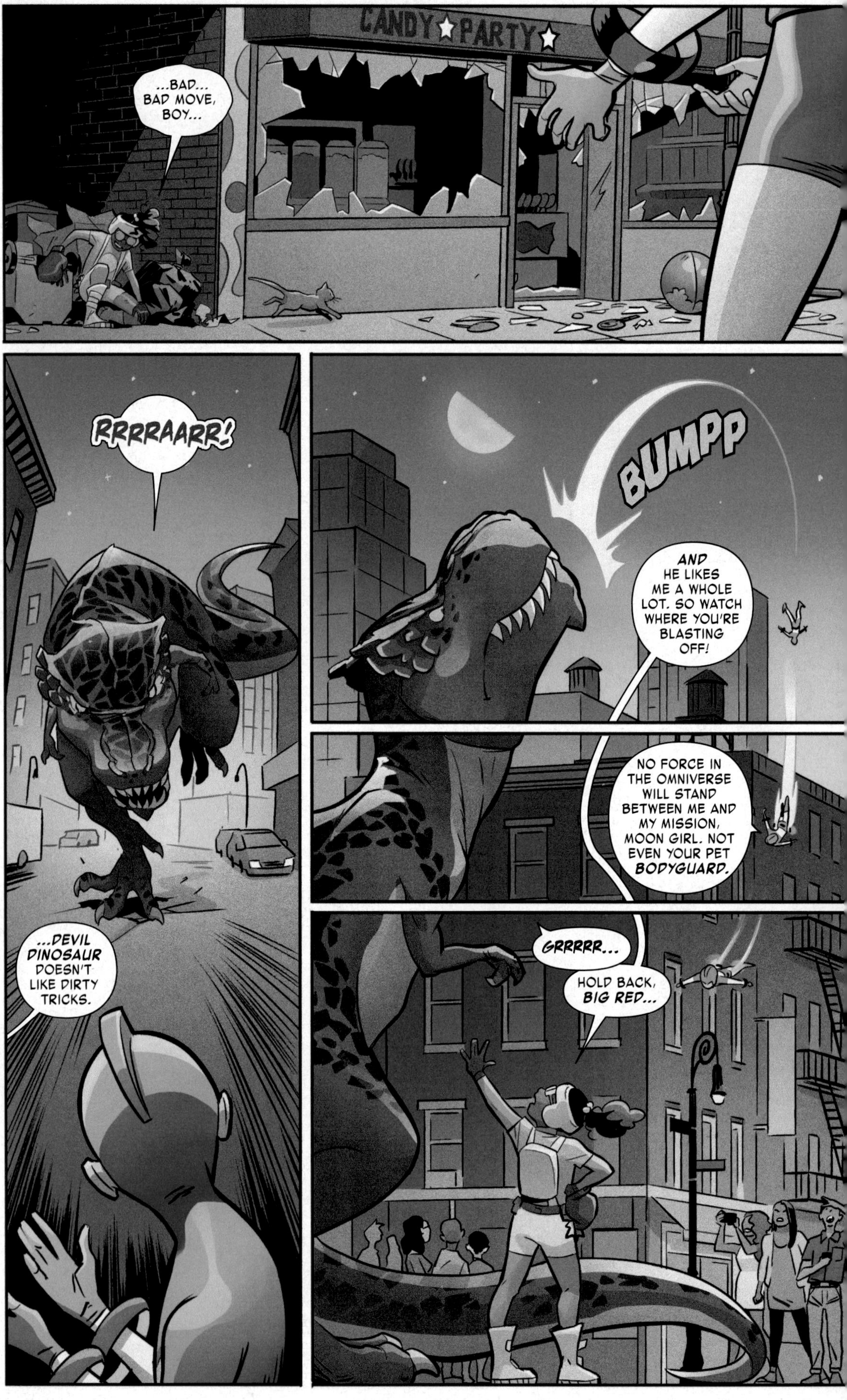
CANDY PARTY
...BAD... BAD MOVE, BOY...
RRRRAARR!
...DEVIL DINOSAUR DOESN'T LIKE DIRTY TRICKS.
BUMPP
AND HE LIKES ME A WHOLE LOT. SO WATCH WHERE YOU'RE BLASTING OFF!
NO FORCE IN THE OMNIVERSE WILL STAND BETWEEN ME AND MY MISSION, MOON GIRL. NOT EVEN YOUR PET BODYGUARD.
GRRRRR...
HOLD BACK, BIG RED...

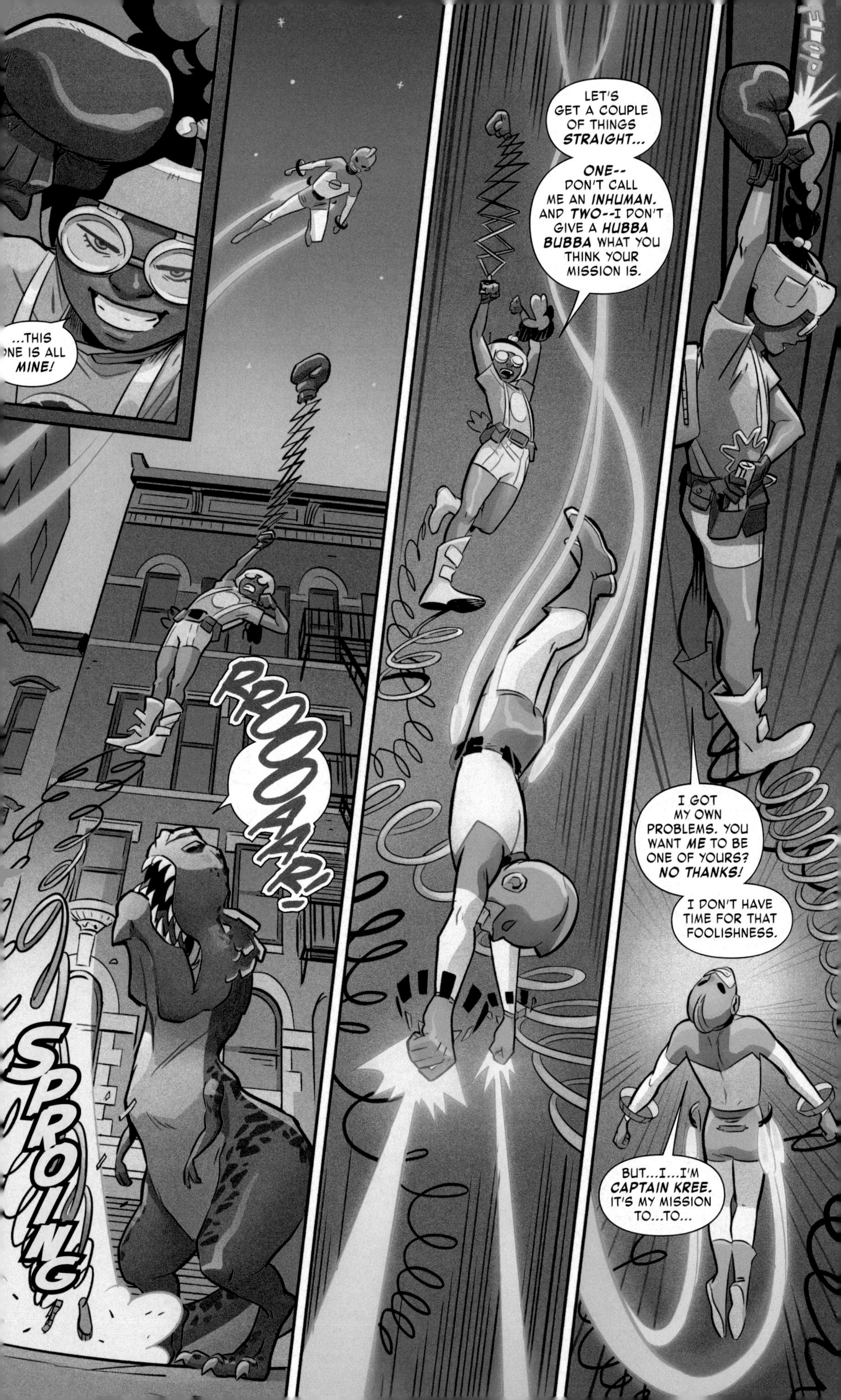

...THIS
ONE IS ALL
MINE!
RAOOOAAR!
SPROING
LET'S GET A COUPLE OF THINGS STRAIGHT...
ONE-- DON'T CALL ME AN INHUMAN. AND TWO--I DON'T GIVE A HUBBA BUBBA WHAT YOU THINK YOUR MISSION IS.
I GOT MY OWN PROBLEMS. YOU WANT ME TO BE ONE OF YOURS? NO THANKS!
I DON'T HAVE TIME FOR THAT FOOLISHNESS.
BUT...I...I'M CAPTAIN KREE. IT'S MY MISSION TO...TO...

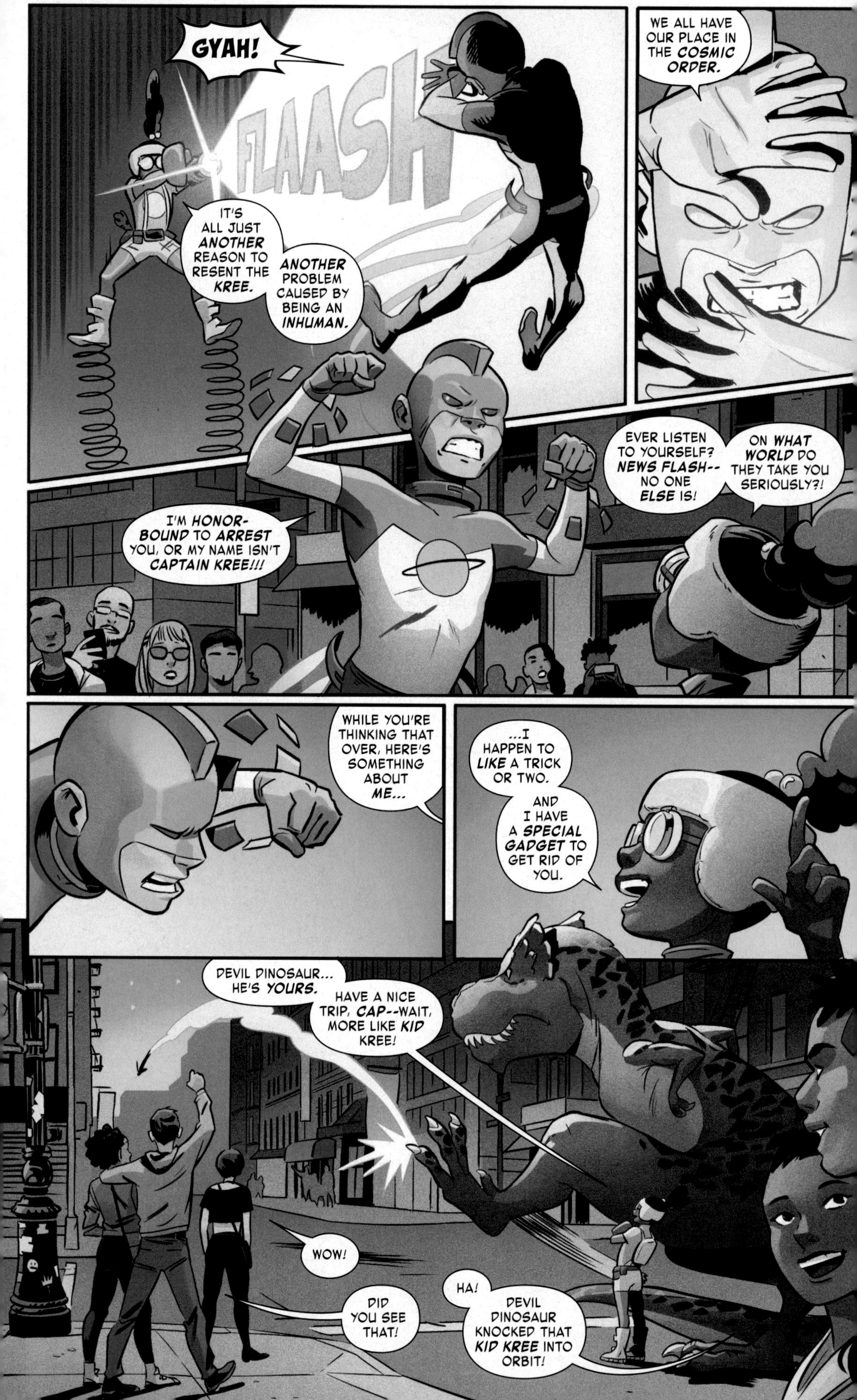
GYAH!
FLAASH
IT'S ALL JUST ANOTHER REASON TO RESENT THE KREE.
ANOTHER PROBLEM CAUSED BY BEING AN INHUMAN.
WE ALL HAVE OUR PLACE IN THE COSMIC ORDER.
I'M HONOR-BOUND TO ARREST YOU, OR MY NAME ISN'T CAPTAIN KREE!!!
EVER LISTEN TO YOURSELF? NEWS FLASH-- NO ONE ELSE IS!
ON WHAT WORLD DO THEY TAKE YOU SERIOUSLY?!
WHILE YOU'RE THINKING THAT OVER, HERE'S SOMETHING ABOUT ME...
...I HAPPEN TO LIKE A TRICK OR TWO.
AND I HAVE A SPECIAL GADGET TO GET RID OF YOU.
DEVIL DINOSAUR... HE'S YOURS.
HAVE A NICE TRIP, CAP--WAIT, MORE LIKE KID KREE!
WOW!
DID YOU SEE THAT!
HA!
DEVIL DINOSAUR KNOCKED THAT KID KREE INTO ORBIT!

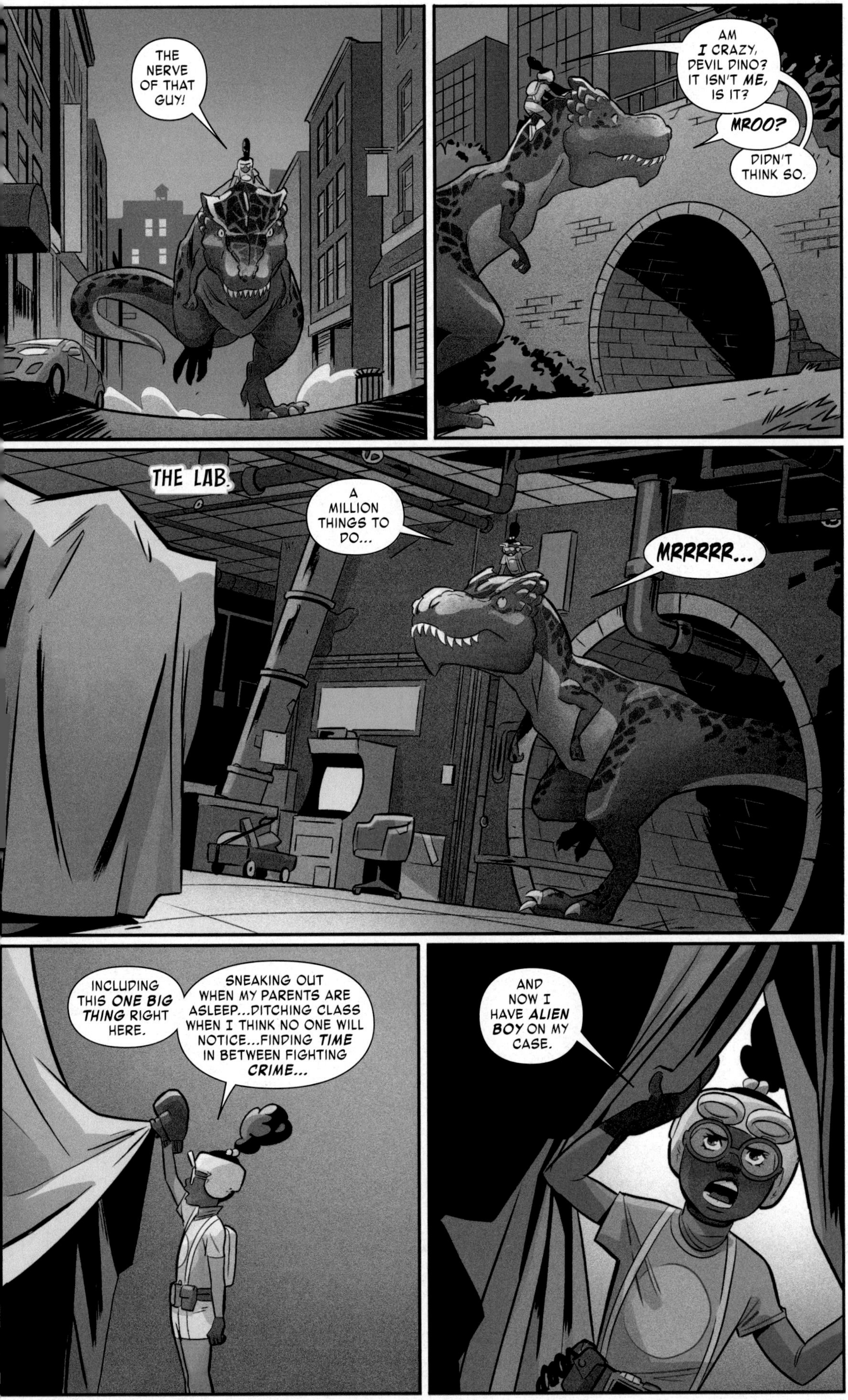
THE NERVE OF THAT GUY!
AM I CRAZY, DEVIL DINO? IT ISN'T ME, IS IT?
MROO?
DIDN'T THINK SO.
THE LAB.
A MILLION THINGS TO DO...
MRRRRR...
INCLUDING THIS ONE BIG THING RIGHT HERE.
SNEAKING OUT WHEN MY PARENTS ARE ASLEEP...DITCHING CLASS WHEN I THINK NO ONE WILL NOTICE...FINDING TIME IN BETWEEN FIGHTING CRIME...
AND NOW I HAVE ALIEN BOY ON MY CASE.

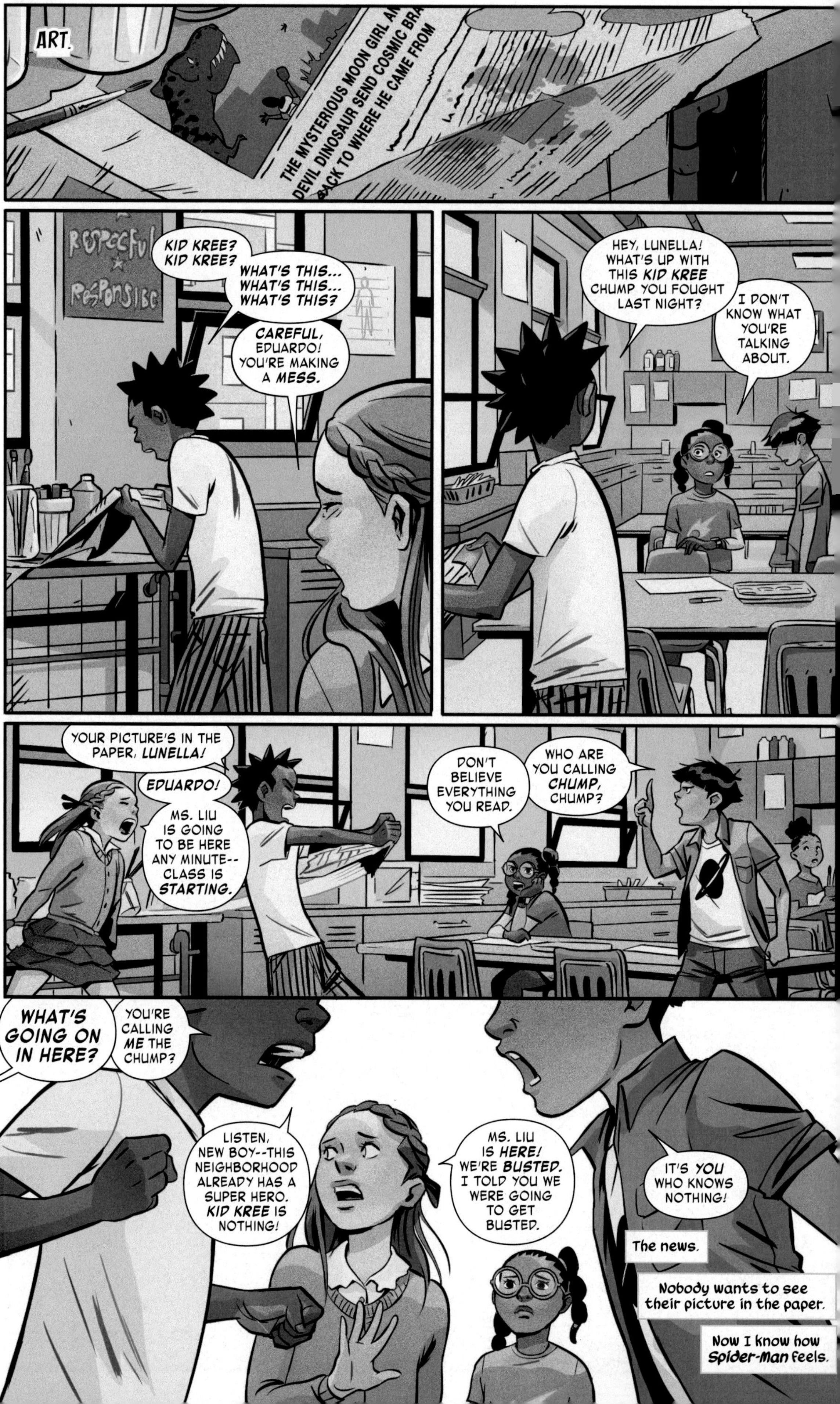
ART.
THE MYSTERIOUS MOON GIRL AND DEVIL DINOSAUR SEND COSMIC BRA... BACK TO WHERE HE CAME FROM
RESPECTFUL RESPONSIBLE
KID KREE? KID KREE?
WHAT'S THIS... WHAT'S THIS... WHAT'S THIS?
CAREFUL, EDUARDO! YOU'RE MAKING A MESS.
HEY, LUNELLA! WHAT'S UP WITH THIS KID KREE CHUMP YOU FOUGHT LAST NIGHT?
I DON'T KNOW WHAT YOU'RE TALKING ABOUT.
YOUR PICTURE'S IN THE PAPER, LUNELLA!
EDUARDO!
MS. LIU IS GOING TO BE HERE ANY MINUTE-- CLASS IS STARTING.
DON'T BELIEVE EVERYTHING YOU READ.
WHO ARE YOU CALLING CHUMP, CHUMP?
WHAT'S GOING ON IN HERE?
YOU'RE CALLING ME THE CHUMP?
LISTEN, NEW BOY--THIS NEIGHBORHOOD ALREADY HAS A SUPER HERO. KID KREE IS NOTHING!
MS. LIU IS HERE! WE'RE BUSTED. I TOLD YOU WE WERE GOING TO GET BUSTED.
IT'S YOU WHO KNOWS NOTHING!
The news.
Nobody wants to see their picture in the paper.
Now I know how Spider-Man feels.

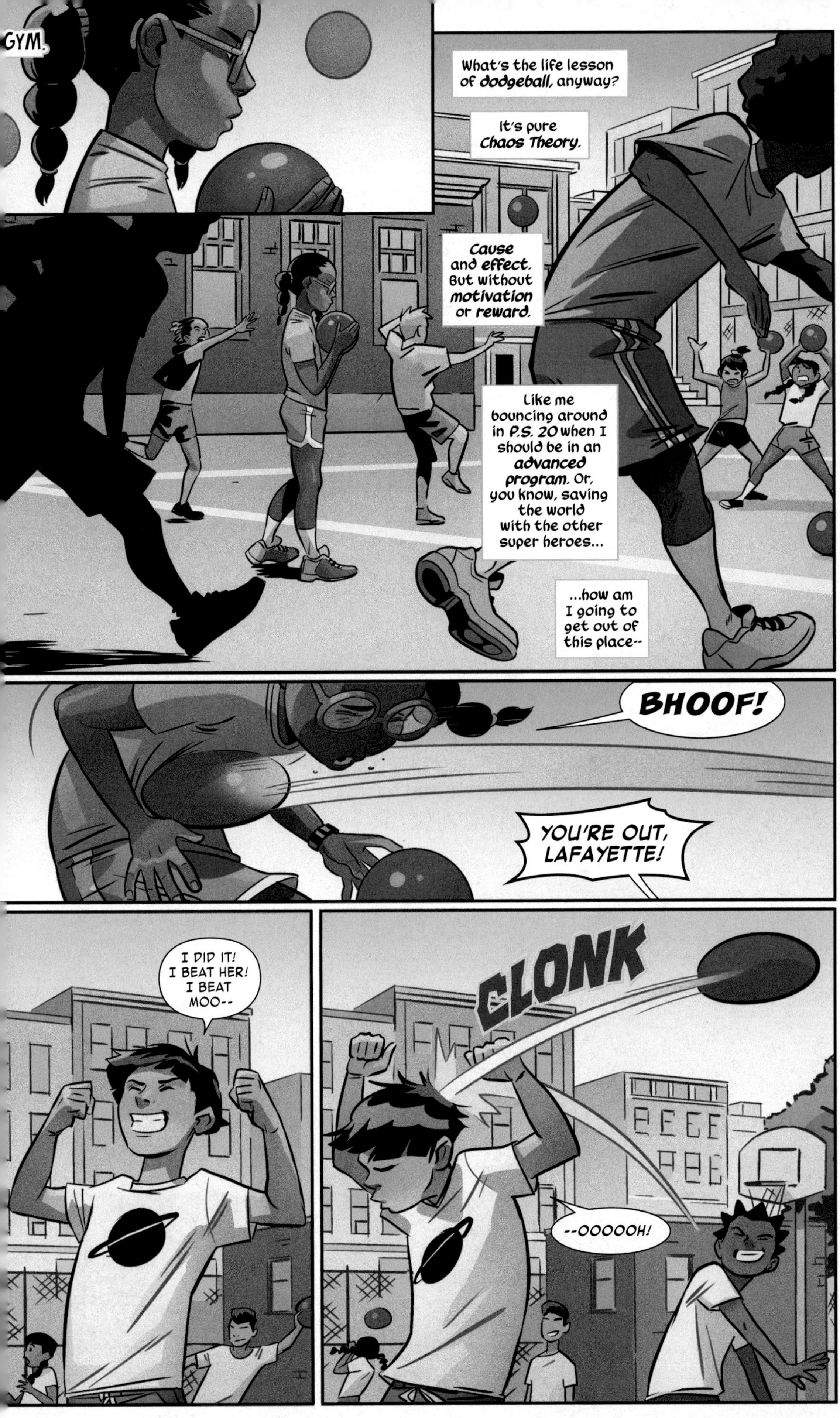
GYM.
What's the life lesson of dodgeball, anyway?
It's pure Chaos Theory.
Cause and effect. But without motivation or reward.
Like me bouncing around in P.S. 20 when I should be in an advanced program. Or, you know, saving the world with the other super heroes...
...how am I going to get out of this place--
BHOOF!
YOU'RE OUT, LAFAYETTE!
I DID IT! I BEAT HER! I BEAT MOO--
CLONK
--OOOOOH!

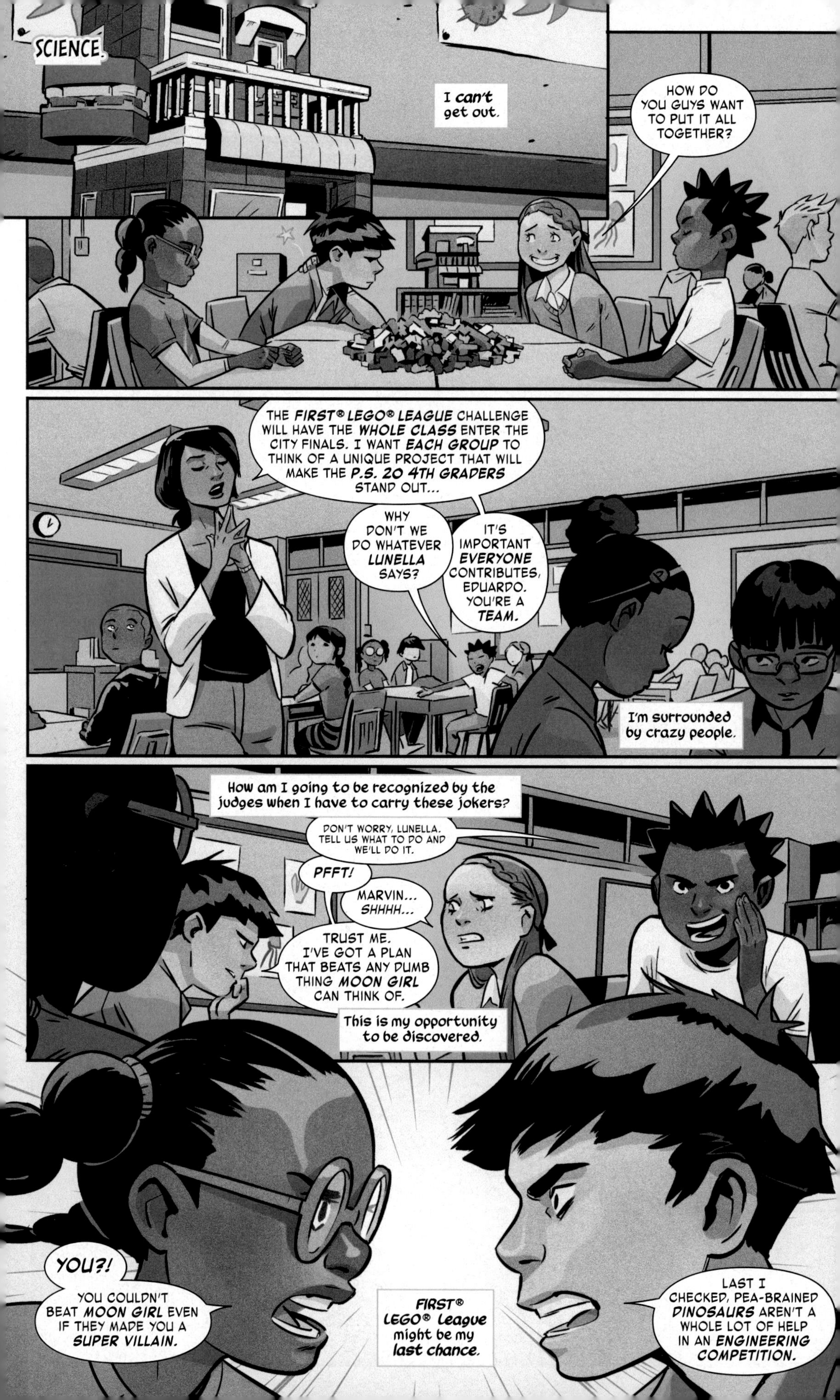
SCIENCE.
I can't get out.
HOW DO YOU GUYS WANT TO PUT IT ALL TOGETHER?
THE FIRST® LEGO® LEAGUE CHALLENGE WILL HAVE THE WHOLE CLASS ENTER THE CITY FINALS. I WANT EACH GROUP TO THINK OF A UNIQUE PROJECT THAT WILL MAKE THE P.S. 20 4TH GRADERS STAND OUT...
WHY DON'T WE DO WHATEVER LUNELLA SAYS?
IT'S IMPORTANT EVERYONE CONTRIBUTES, EDUARDO. YOU'RE A TEAM.
I'm surrounded by crazy people.
How am I going to be recognized by the judges when I have to carry these jokers?
DON'T WORRY, LUNELLA. TELL US WHAT TO DO AND WE'LL DO IT.
PFFT!
MARVIN... SHHHH...
TRUST ME. I'VE GOT A PLAN THAT BEATS ANY DUMB THING MOON GIRL CAN THINK OF.
This is my opportunity to be discovered.
YOU?!
YOU COULDN'T BEAT MOON GIRL EVEN IF THEY MADE YOU A SUPER VILLAIN.
FIRST® LEGO® League might be my last chance.
LAST I CHECKED, PEA-BRAINED DINOSAURS AREN'T A WHOLE LOT OF HELP IN AN ENGINEERING COMPETITION.

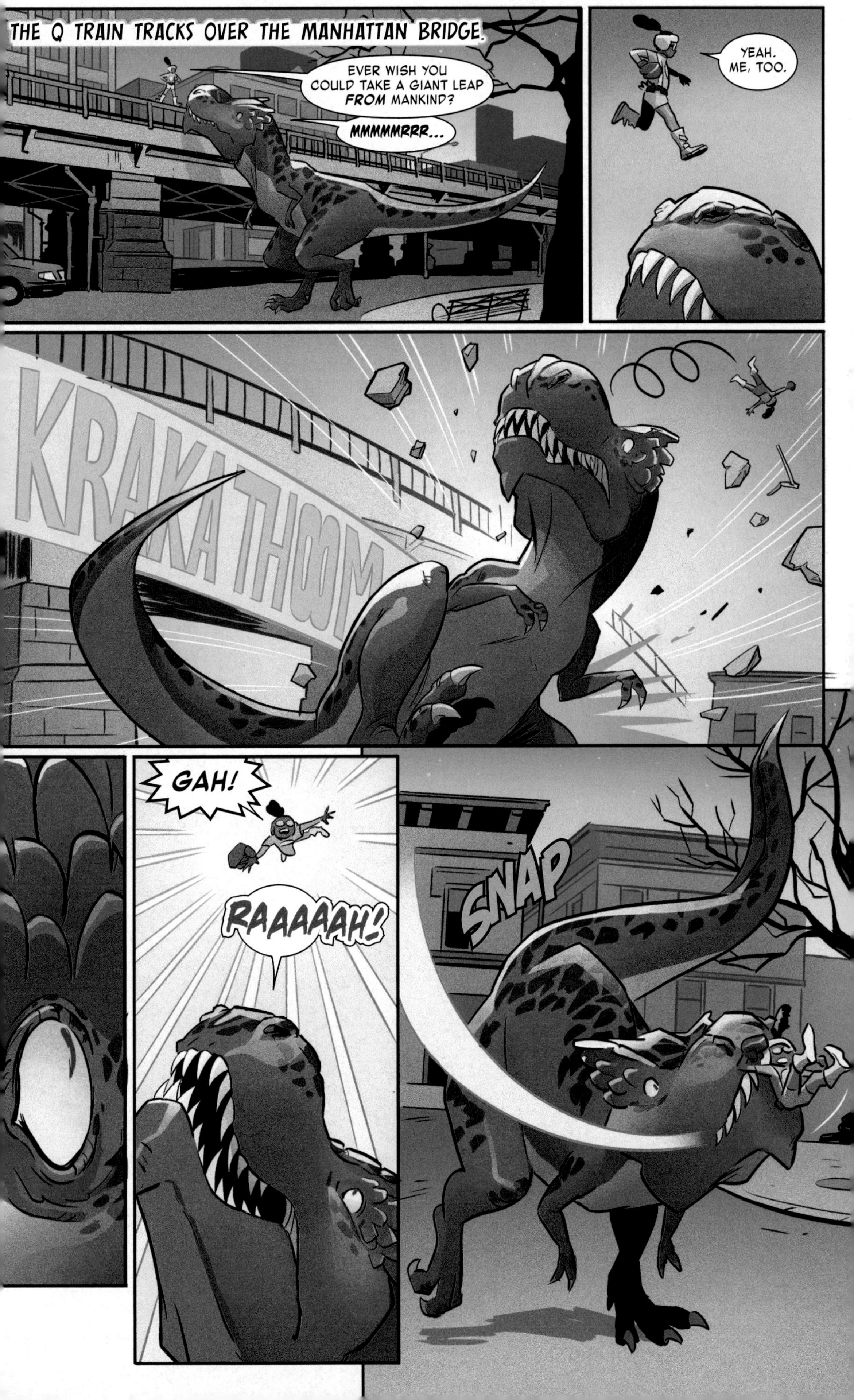
THE Q TRAIN TRACKS OVER THE MANHATTAN BRIDGE.
EVER WISH YOU COULD TAKE A GIANT LEAP FROM MANKIND?
MMMMMRRR...
YEAH. ME, TOO.
KRAKATHOOM
GAH!
RAAAAAH!
SNAP

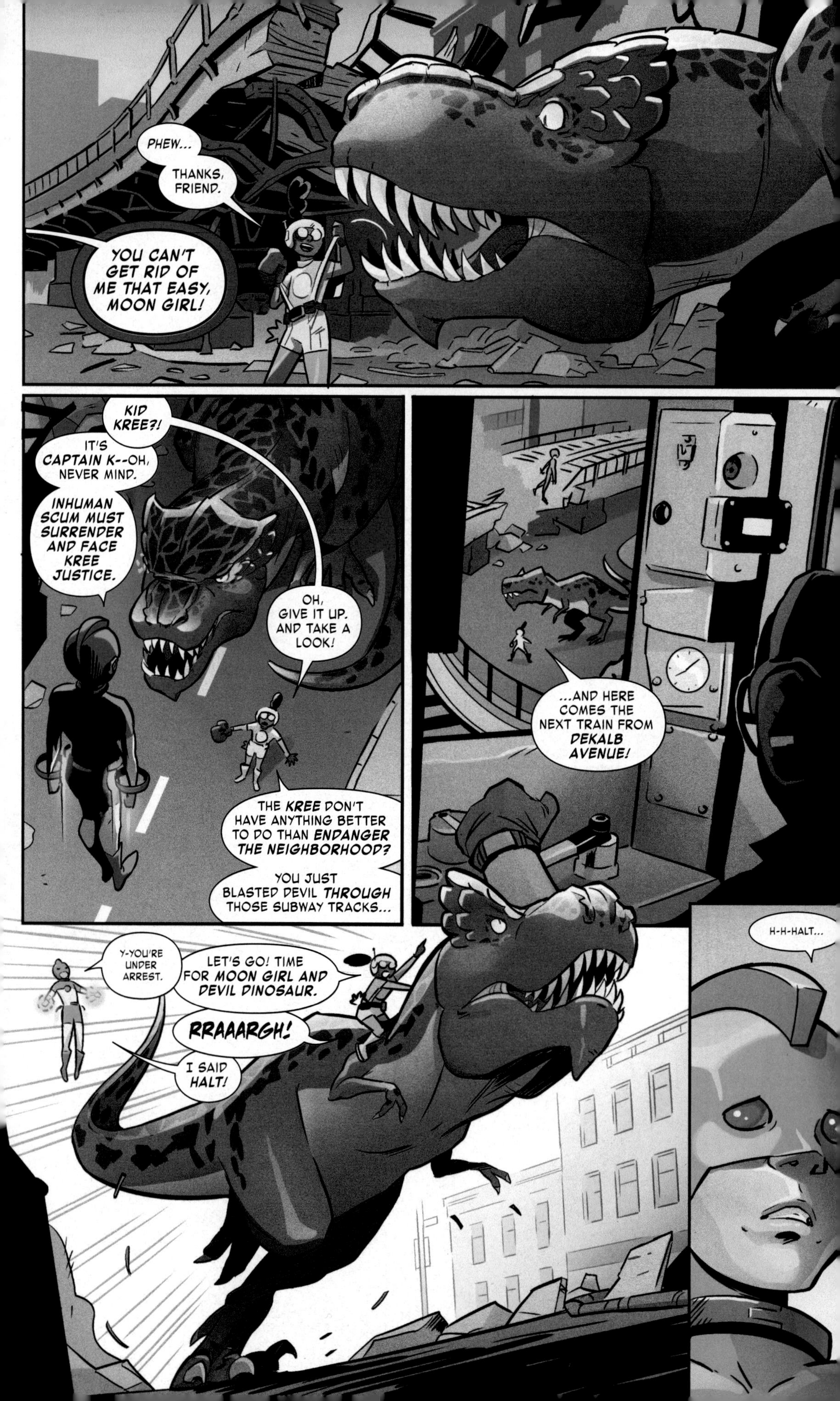

PHEW...
THANKS, FRIEND.
YOU CAN'T GET RID OF ME THAT EASY, MOON GIRL!
KID KREE?!
IT'S CAPTAIN K--OH, NEVER MIND.
INHUMAN SCUM MUST SURRENDER AND FACE KREE JUSTICE.
OH, GIVE IT UP. AND TAKE A LOOK!
THE KREE DON'T HAVE ANYTHING BETTER TO DO THAN ENDANGER THE NEIGHBORHOOD?
YOU JUST BLASTED DEVIL THROUGH THOSE SUBWAY TRACKS...
...AND HERE COMES THE NEXT TRAIN FROM DEKALB AVENUE!
Y-YOU'RE UNDER ARREST.
LET'S GO! TIME FOR MOON GIRL AND DEVIL DINOSAUR.
RRAAARGH!
I SAID HALT!
H-H-HALT...

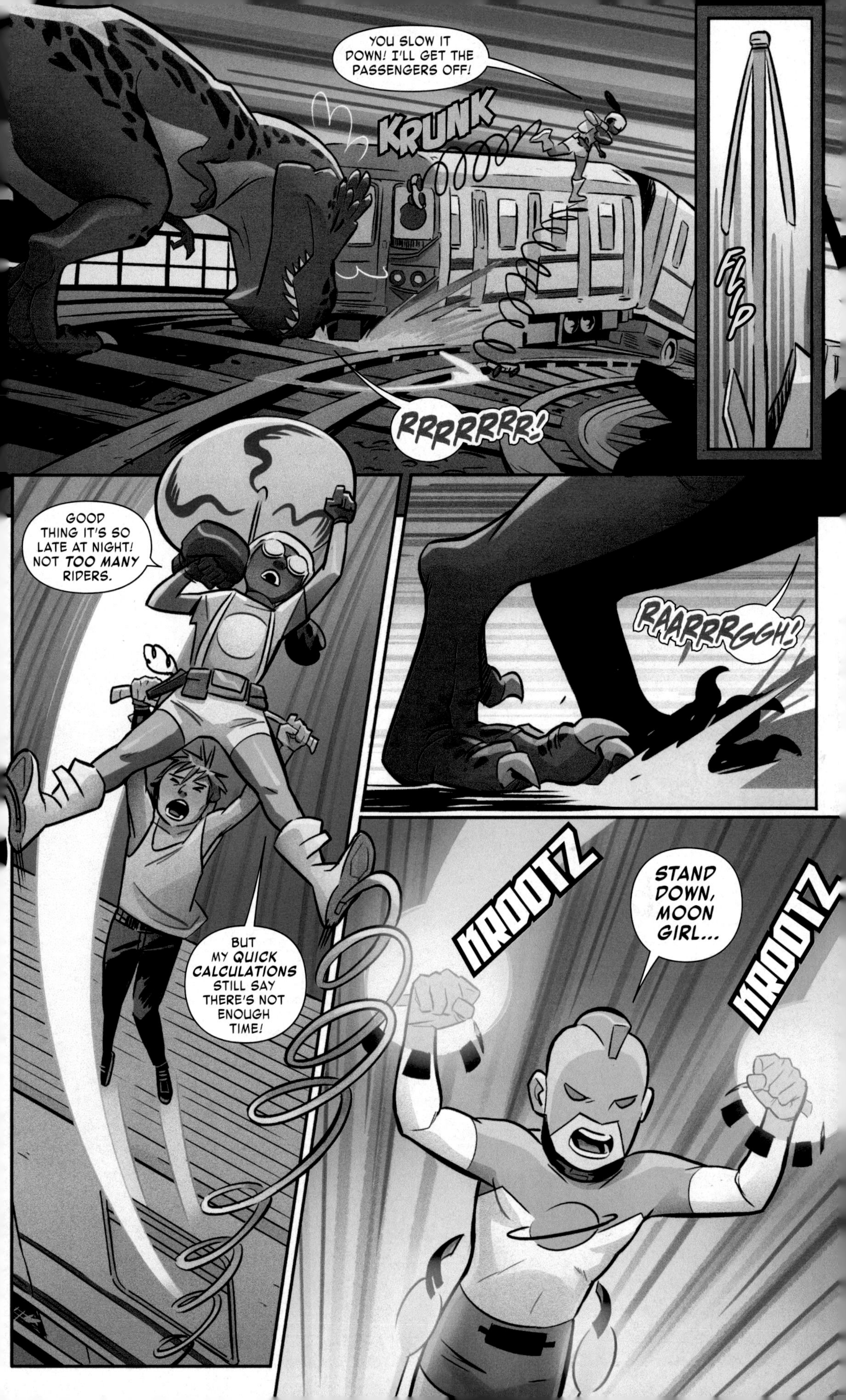
YOU SLOW IT DOWN! I'LL GET THE PASSENGERS OFF!
KRUNK
RRRRRRR!
FLIP
GOOD THING IT'S SO LATE AT NIGHT! NOT TOO MANY RIDERS.
RAARRRGGH!
BUT MY QUICK CALCULATIONS STILL SAY THERE'S NOT ENOUGH TIME!
KROOTZ
STAND DOWN, MOON GIRL...
KROOTZ

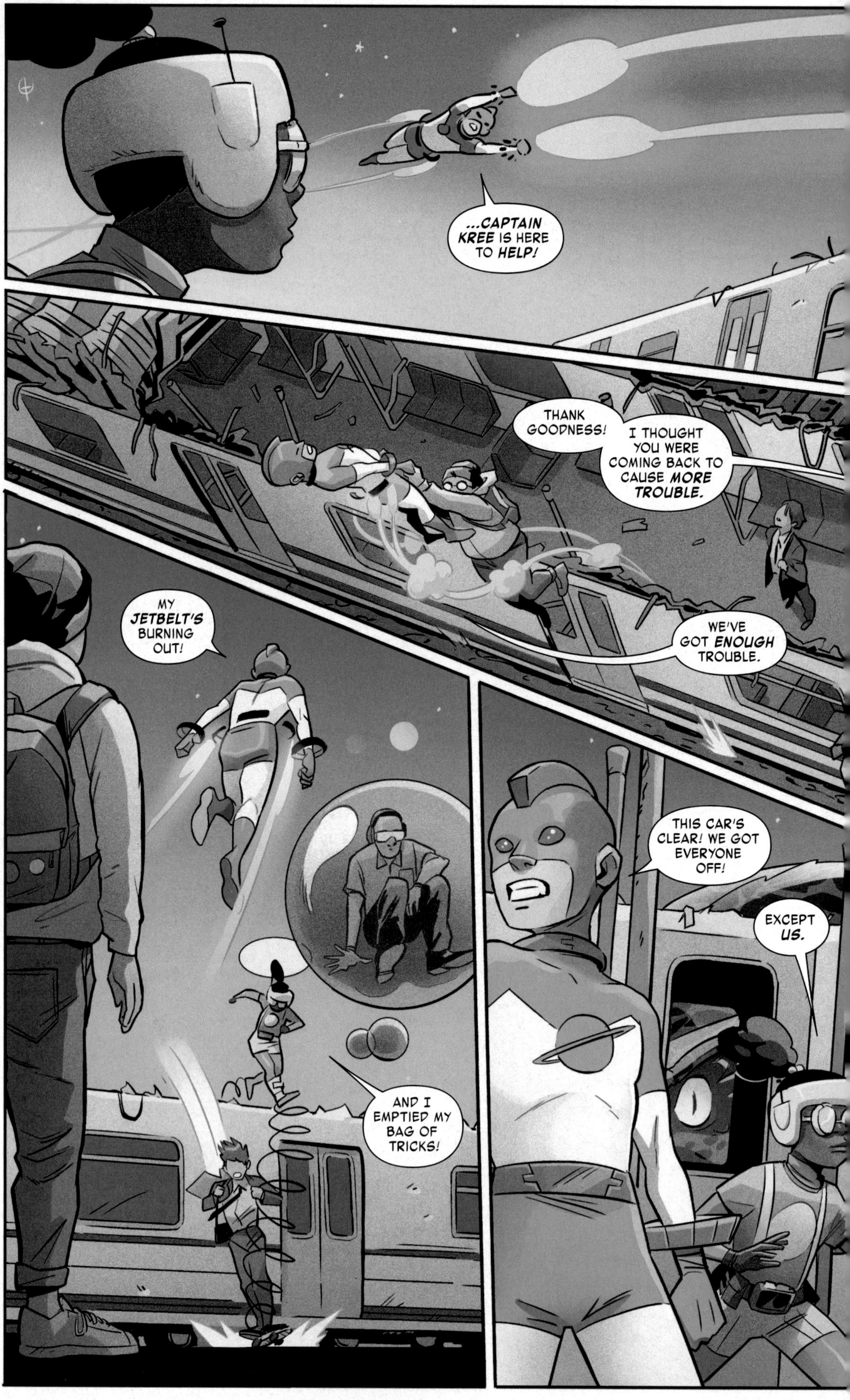
...CAPTAIN KREE IS HERE TO HELP!
THANK GOODNESS!
I THOUGHT YOU WERE COMING BACK TO CAUSE MORE TROUBLE.
WE'VE GOT ENOUGH TROUBLE.
MY JETBELT'S BURNING OUT!
AND I EMPTIED MY BAG OF TRICKS!
THIS CAR'S CLEAR! WE GOT EVERYONE OFF!
EXCEPT US.

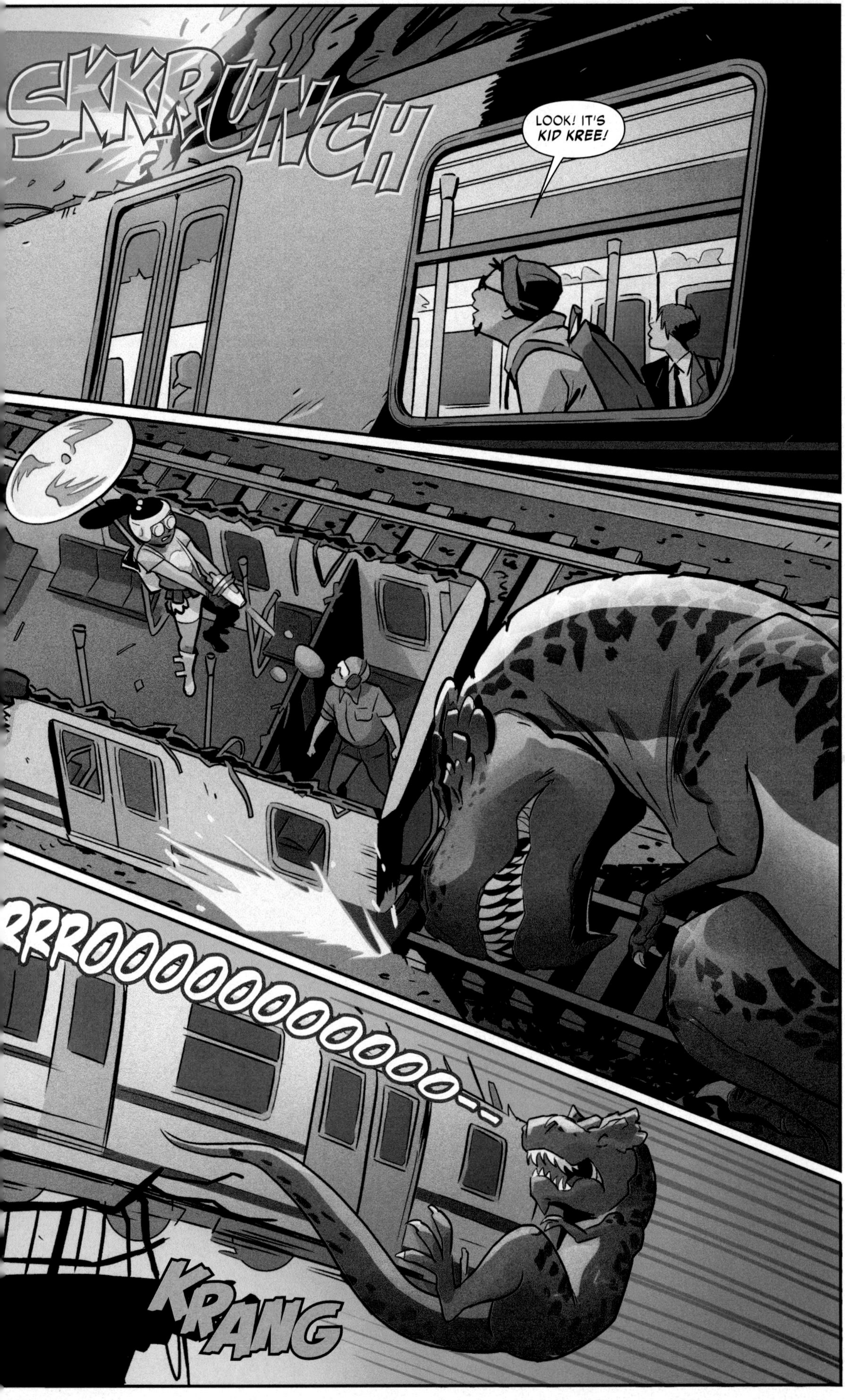
SKKRUNCH
LOOK! IT'S KID KREE!
RRROOOOOOOOOOOOO--
KRANG

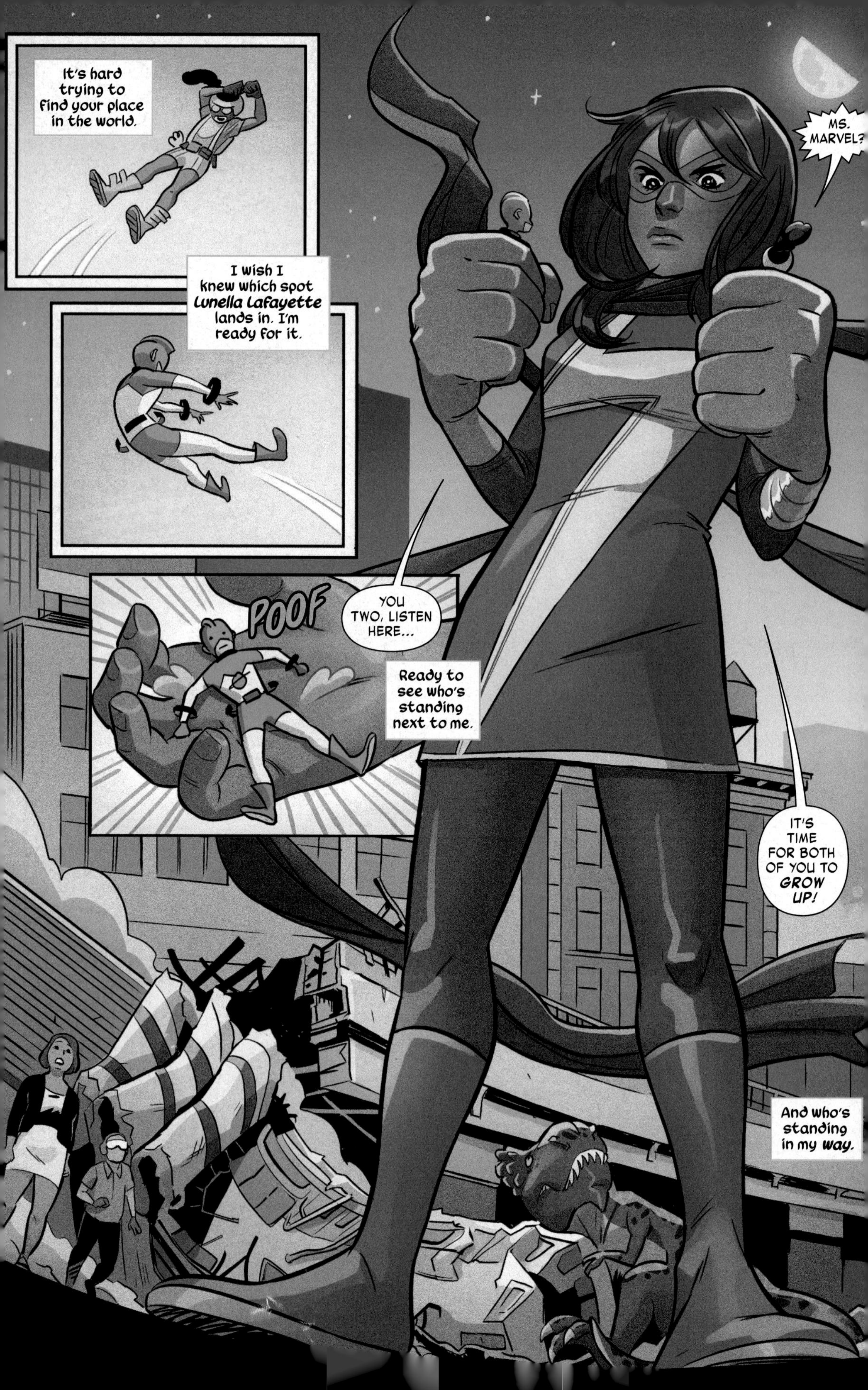

It's hard trying to find your place in the world.
I wish I knew which spot Lunella Lafayette lands in. I'm ready for it.
MS. MARVEL?
POOF
YOU TWO, LISTEN HERE...
Ready to see who's standing next to me.
IT'S TIME FOR BOTH OF YOU TO GROW UP!
And who's standing in my way.

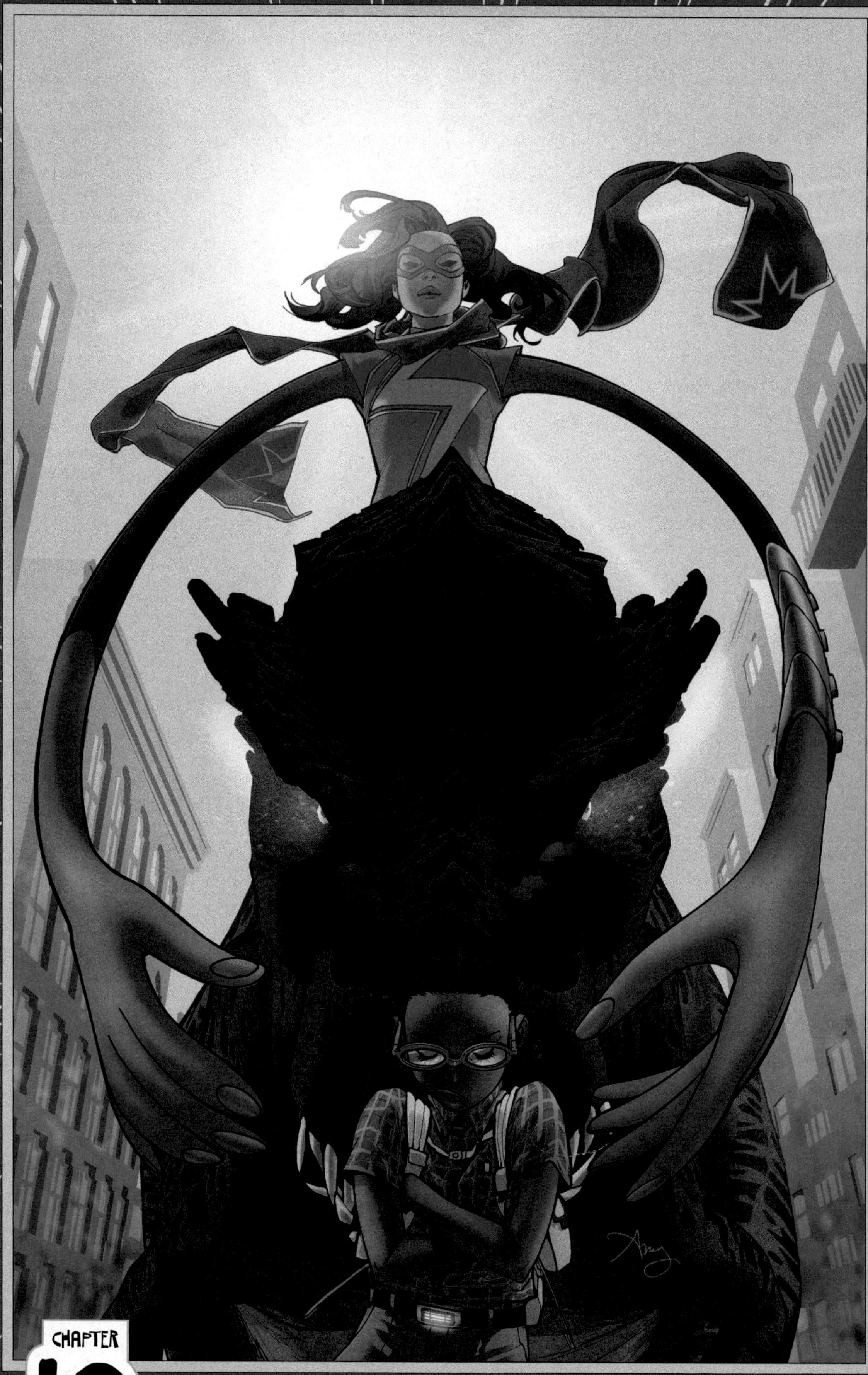

CHAPTER 10 "The IN-CROWD"

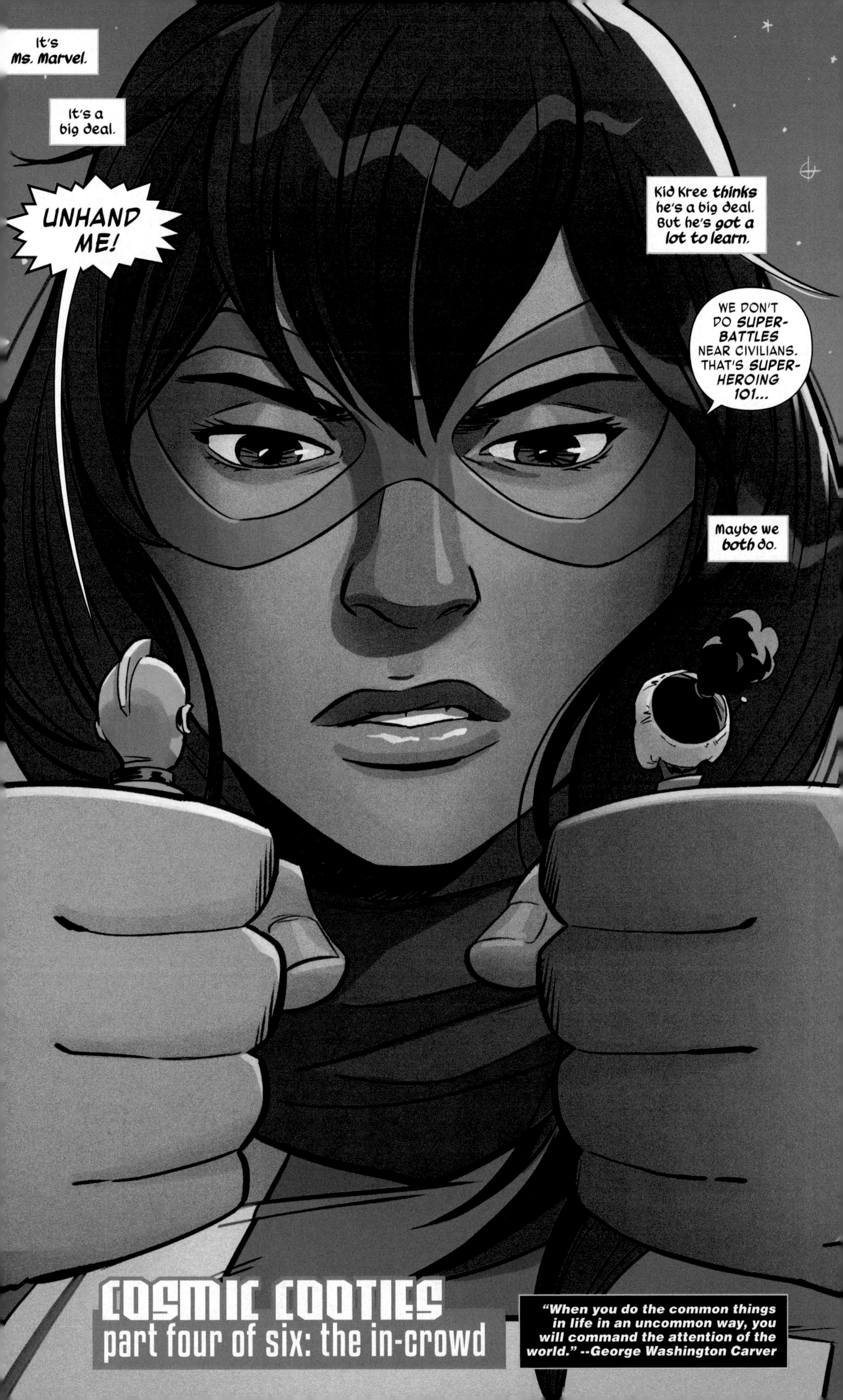
It's Ms. Marvel.
It's a big deal.
UNHAND ME!
Kid Kree thinks he's a big deal. But he's got a lot to learn.
WE DON'T DO SUPER-BATTLES NEAR CIVILIANS. THAT'S SUPER-HEROING 101...
Maybe we both do.
COSMIC COOTIES
part four of six: the in-crowd
"When you do the common things in life in an uncommon way, you will command the attention of the world." --George Washington Carver

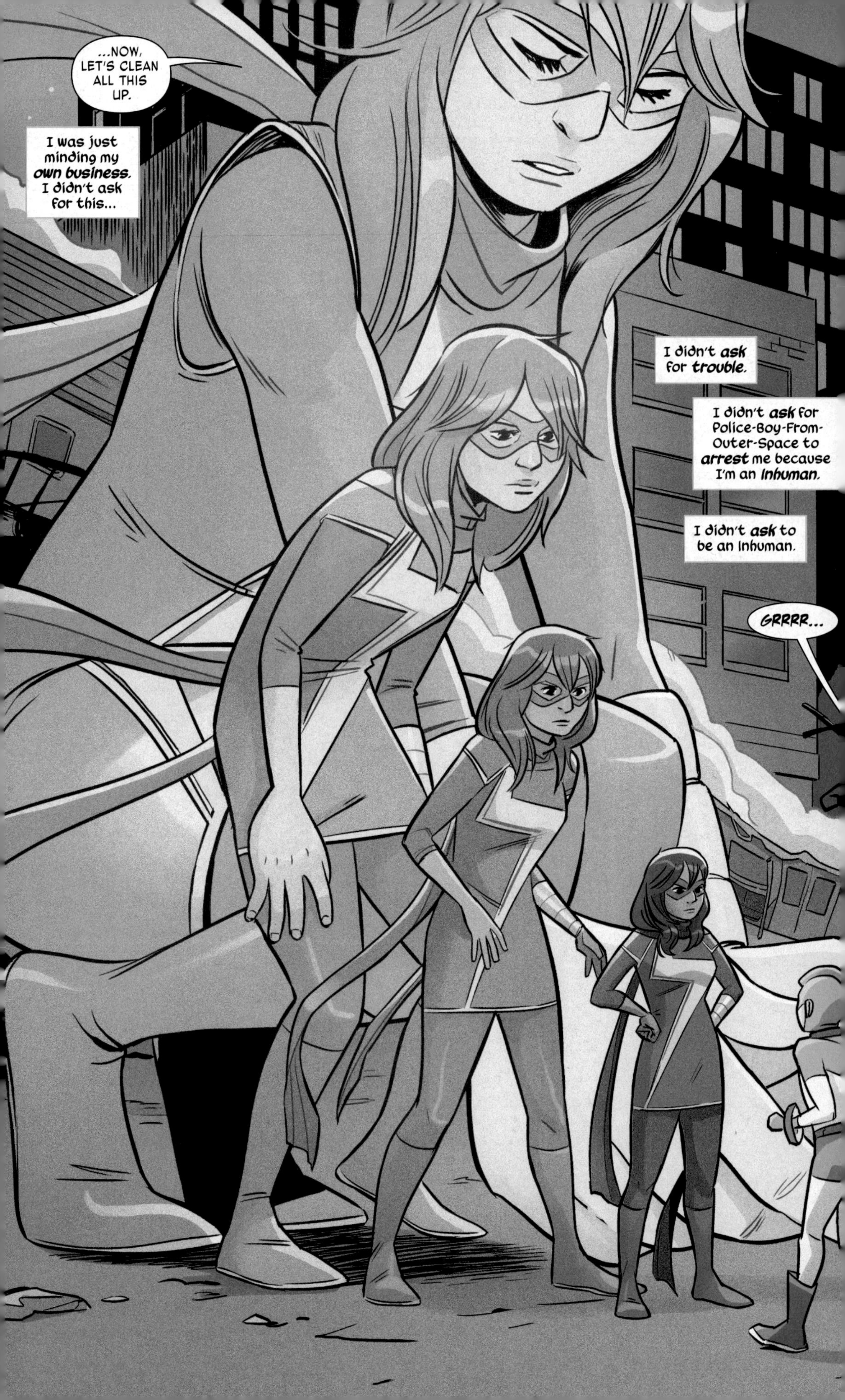
...NOW, LET'S CLEAN ALL THIS UP.
I was just minding my own business. I didn't ask for this...
I didn't ask for trouble.
I didn't ask for Police-Boy-From-Outer-Space to arrest me because I'm an Inhuman.
I didn't ask to be an Inhuman.
GRRRR...

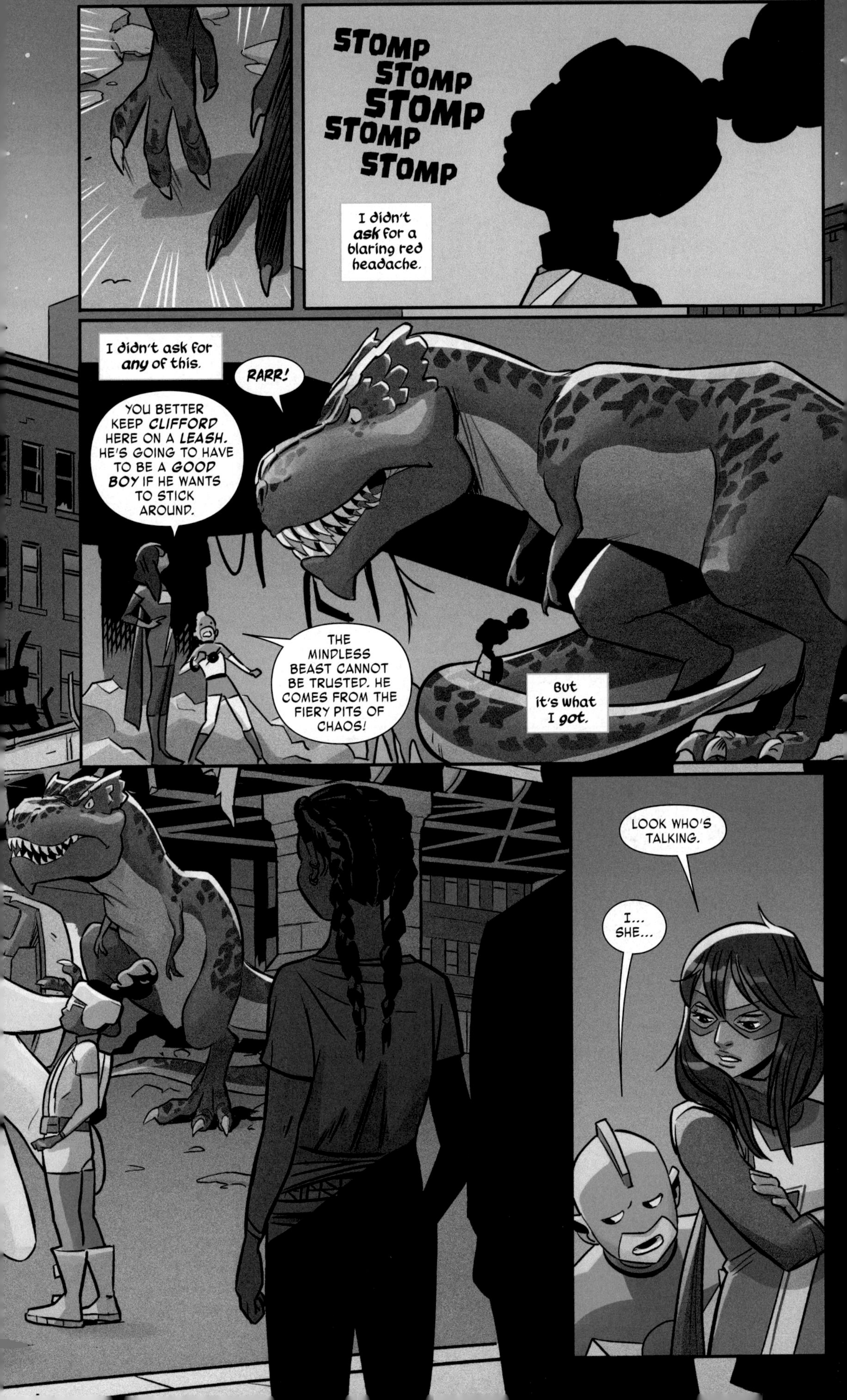

STOMP STOMP STOMP STOMP STOMP
I didn't ask for a blaring red headache.
I didn't ask for any of this.
RARR!
YOU BETTER KEEP CLIFFORD HERE ON A LEASH. HE'S GOING TO HAVE TO BE A GOOD BOY IF HE WANTS TO STICK AROUND.
THE MINDLESS BEAST CANNOT BE TRUSTED. HE COMES FROM THE FIERY PITS OF CHAOS!
But it's what I got.
LOOK WHO'S TALKING.
I... SHE...

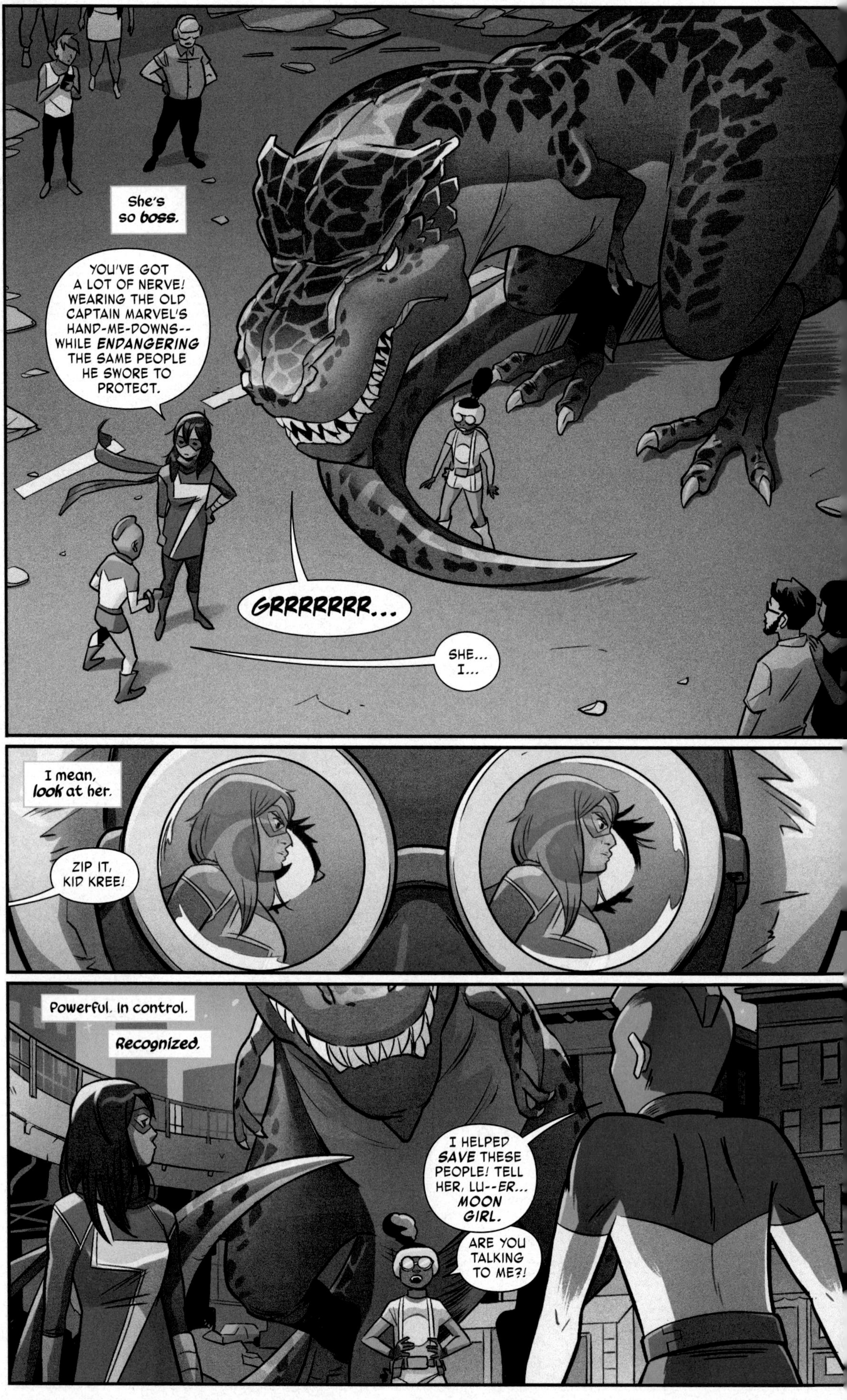
She's so boss.
YOU'VE GOT A LOT OF NERVE! WEARING THE OLD CAPTAIN MARVEL'S HAND-ME-DOWNS-- WHILE ENDANGERING THE SAME PEOPLE HE SWORE TO PROTECT.
GRRRRRRR...
SHE... I...
I mean, look at her.
ZIP IT, KID KREE!
Powerful. In control.
Recognized.
I HELPED SAVE THESE PEOPLE! TELL HER, LU--ER... MOON GIRL.
ARE YOU TALKING TO ME?!

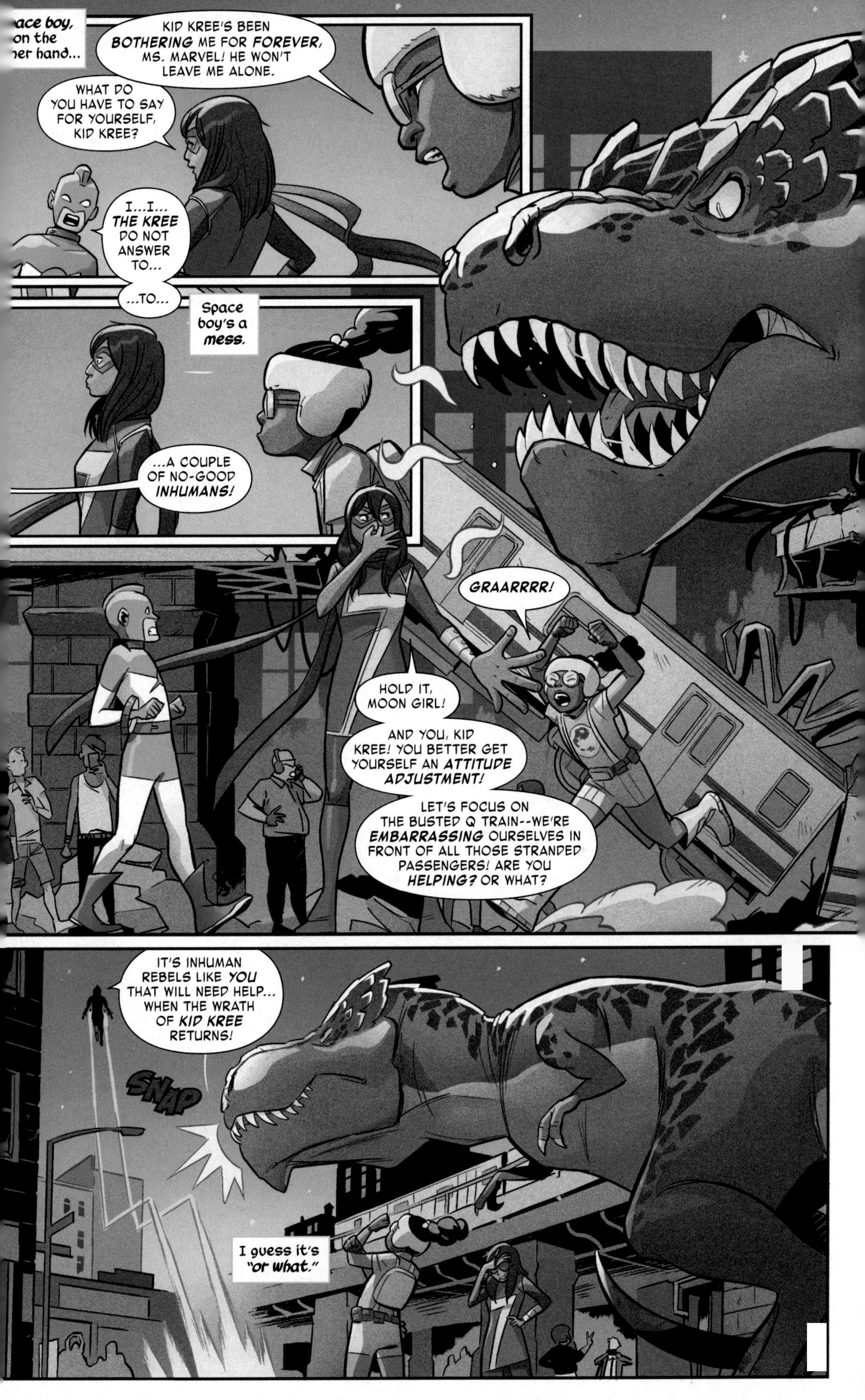
ace boy, on the her hand...
KID KREE'S BEEN BOTHERING ME FOR FOREVER, MS. MARVEL! HE WON'T LEAVE ME ALONE.
WHAT DO YOU HAVE TO SAY FOR YOURSELF, KID KREE?
I...I... THE KREE DO NOT ANSWER TO...
...TO...
Space boy's a mess.
...A COUPLE OF NO-GOOD INHUMANS!
GRAARRRR!
HOLD IT, MOON GIRL!
AND YOU, KID KREE! YOU BETTER GET YOURSELF AN ATTITUDE ADJUSTMENT!
LET'S FOCUS ON THE BUSTED Q TRAIN--WE'RE EMBARRASSING OURSELVES IN FRONT OF ALL THOSE STRANDED PASSENGERS! ARE YOU HELPING? OR WHAT?
IT'S INHUMAN REBELS LIKE YOU THAT WILL NEED HELP... WHEN THE WRATH OF KID KREE RETURNS!
SNAP
I guess it's "or what."

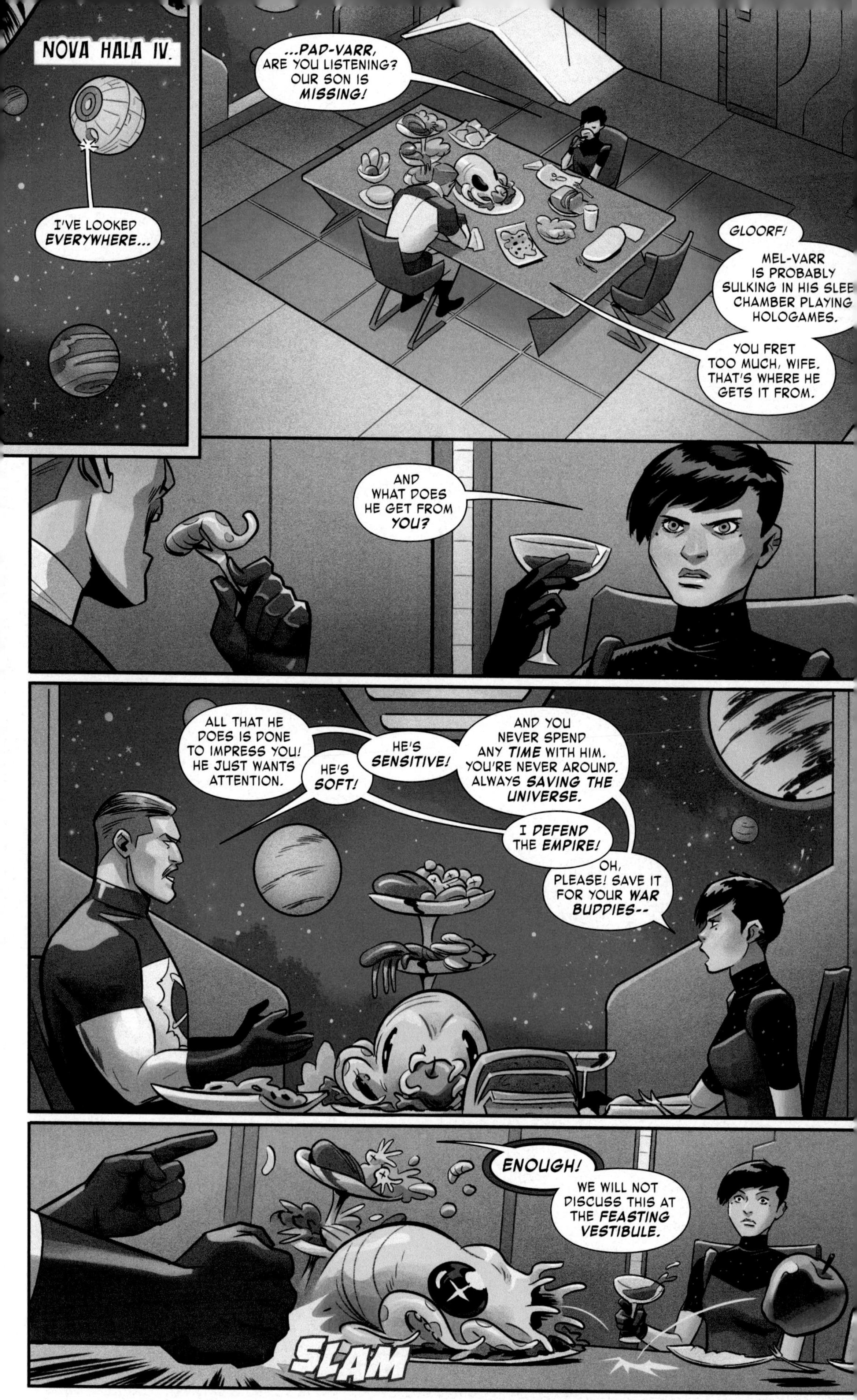
NOVA HALA IV.
I'VE LOOKED EVERYWHERE...
...PAD-VARR, ARE YOU LISTENING? OUR SON IS MISSING!
GLOORF!
MEL-VARR IS PROBABLY SULKING IN HIS SLEE CHAMBER PLAYING HOLOGAMES.
YOU FRET TOO MUCH, WIFE. THAT'S WHERE HE GETS IT FROM.
AND WHAT DOES HE GET FROM YOU?
ALL THAT HE DOES IS DONE TO IMPRESS YOU! HE JUST WANTS ATTENTION.
HE'S SOFT!
HE'S SENSITIVE!
AND YOU NEVER SPEND ANY TIME WITH HIM. YOU'RE NEVER AROUND. ALWAYS SAVING THE UNIVERSE.
I DEFEND THE EMPIRE!
OH, PLEASE! SAVE IT FOR YOUR WAR BUDDIES--
ENOUGH!
WE WILL NOT DISCUSS THIS AT THE FEASTING VESTIBULE.
SLAM

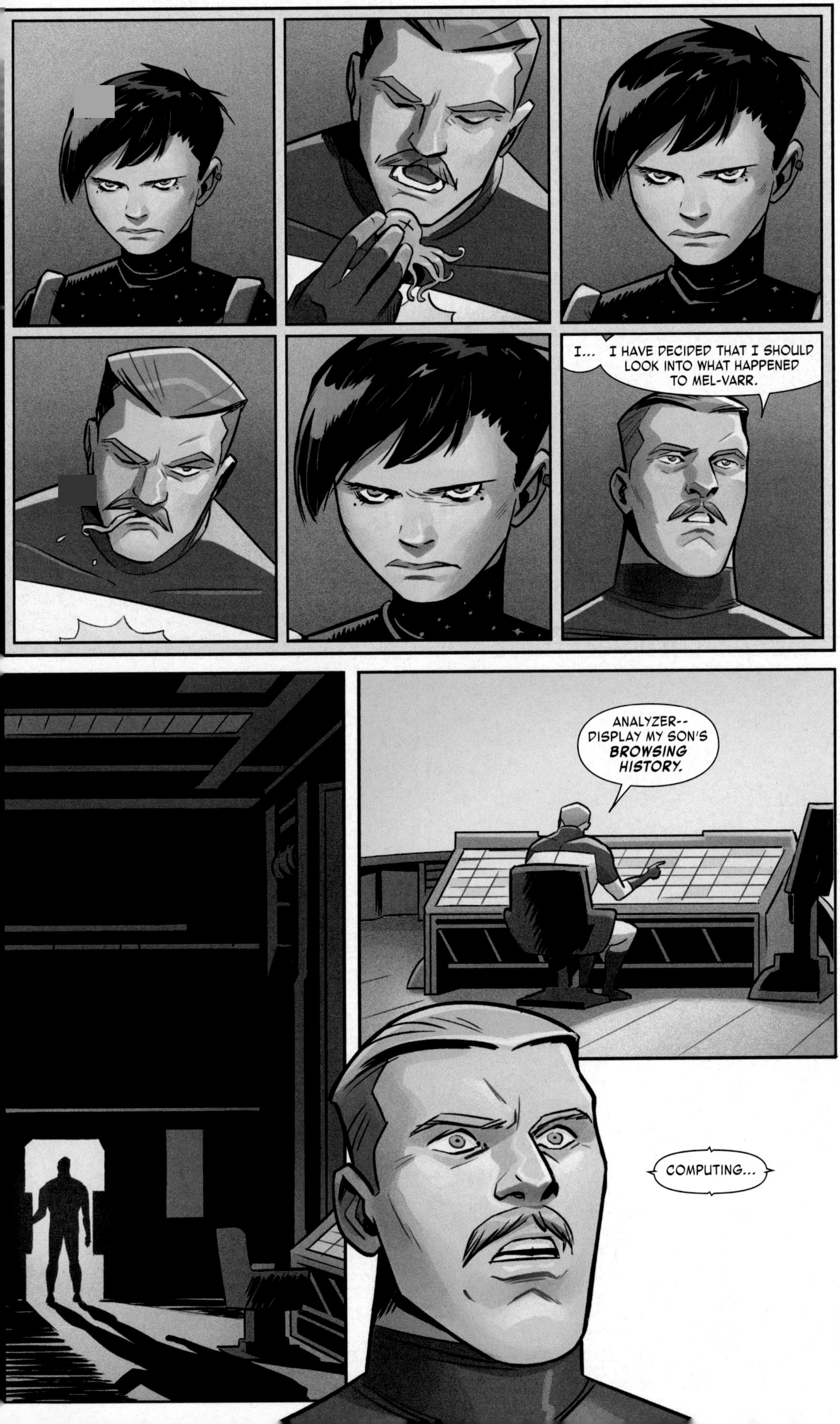
I... I HAVE DECIDED THAT I SHOULD LOOK INTO WHAT HAPPENED TO MEL-VARR.
ANALYZER-- DISPLAY MY SON'S **BROWSING HISTORY.**
COMPUTING...

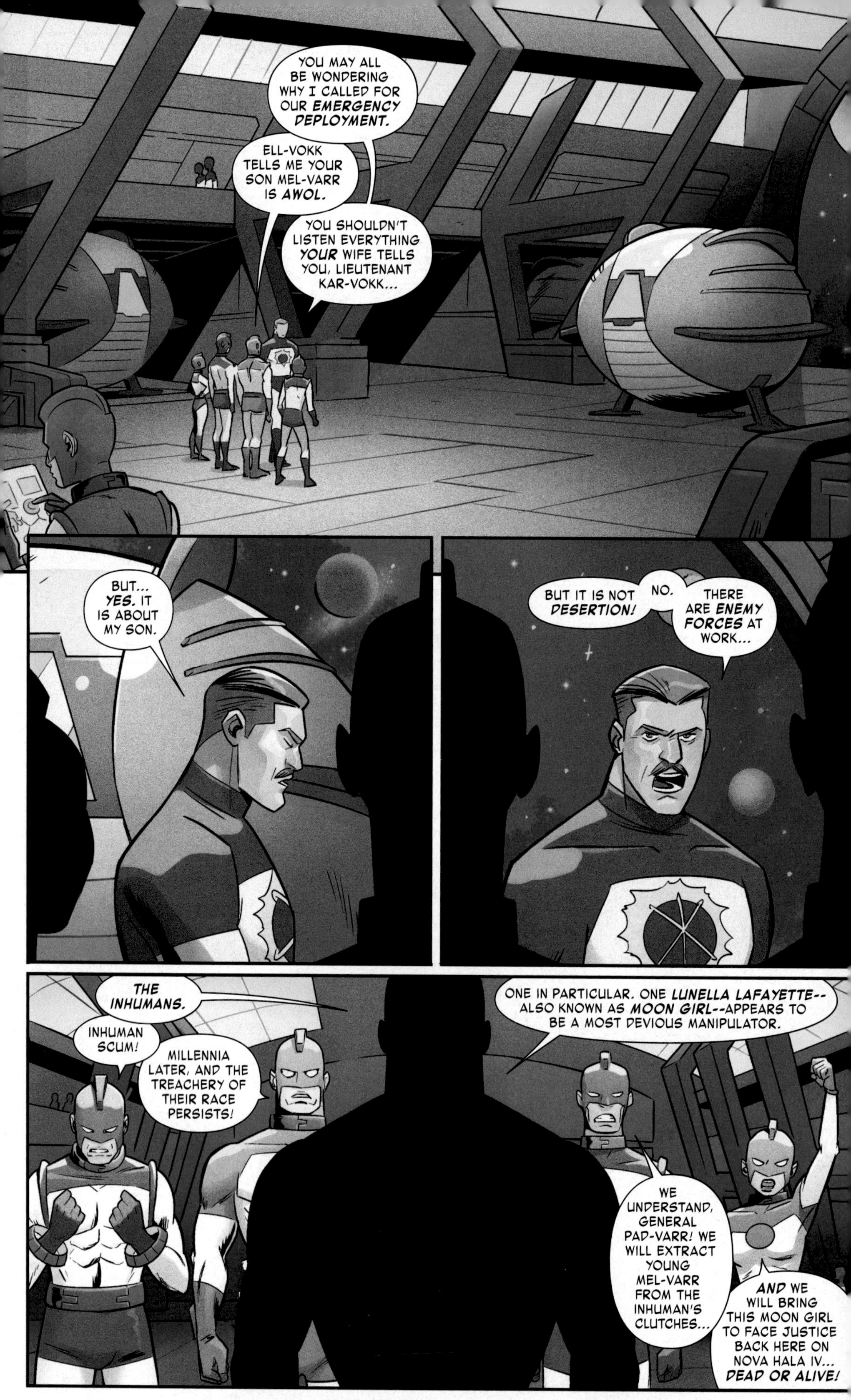
YOU MAY ALL BE WONDERING WHY I CALLED FOR OUR EMERGENCY DEPLOYMENT.
ELL-VOKK TELLS ME YOUR SON MEL-VARR IS AWOL.
YOU SHOULDN'T LISTEN EVERYTHING YOUR WIFE TELLS YOU, LIEUTENANT KAR-VOKK...
BUT... YES. IT IS ABOUT MY SON.
BUT IT IS NOT DESERTION!
NO.
THERE ARE ENEMY FORCES AT WORK...
THE INHUMANS.
INHUMAN SCUM!
MILLENNIA LATER, AND THE TREACHERY OF THEIR RACE PERSISTS!
ONE IN PARTICULAR. ONE LUNELLA LAFAYETTE--ALSO KNOWN AS MOON GIRL--APPEARS TO BE A MOST DEVIOUS MANIPULATOR.
WE UNDERSTAND, GENERAL PAD-VARR! WE WILL EXTRACT YOUNG MEL-VARR FROM THE INHUMAN'S CLUTCHES...
AND WE WILL BRING THIS MOON GIRL TO FACE JUSTICE BACK HERE ON NOVA HALA IV... DEAD OR ALIVE!

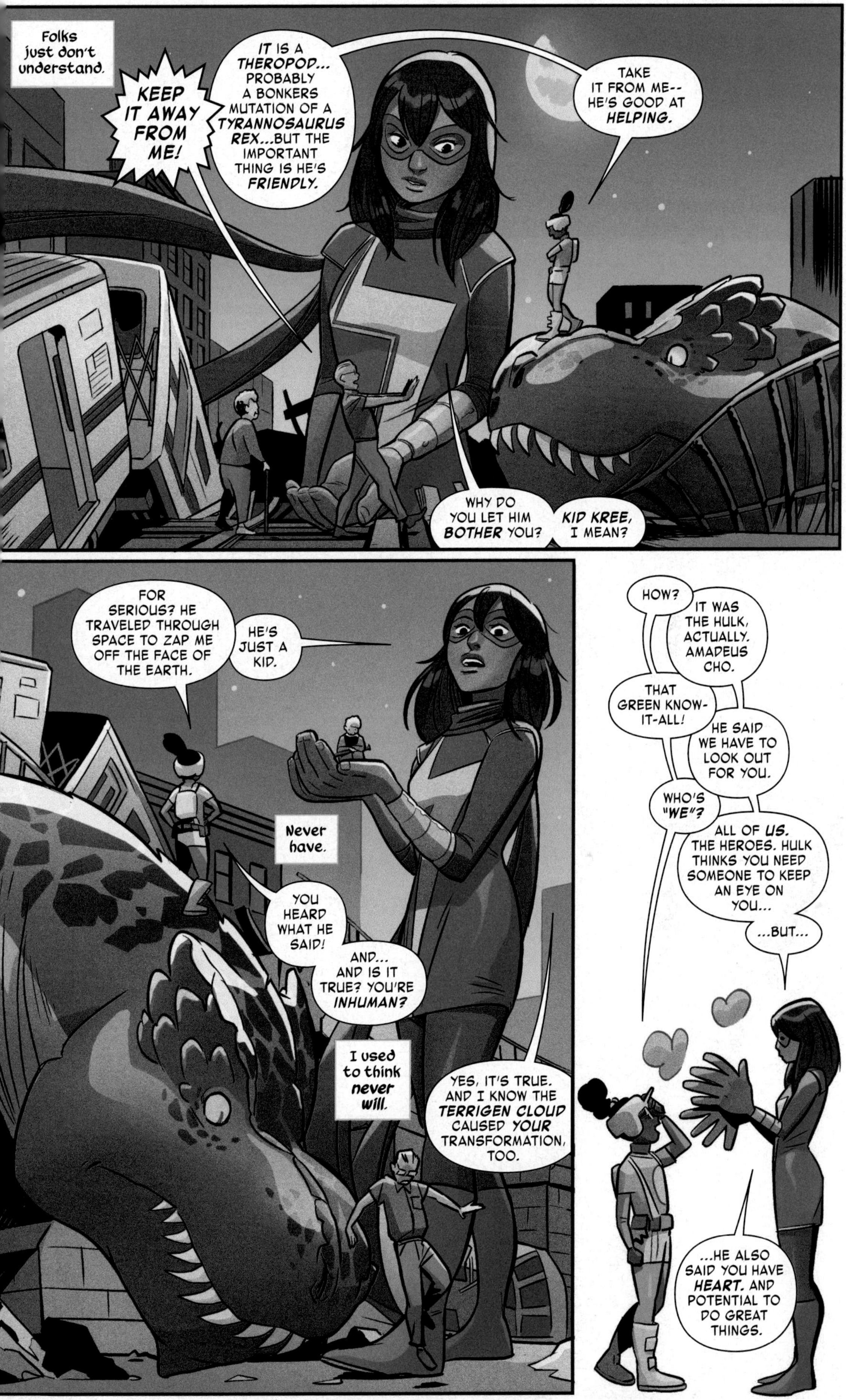
Folks just don't understand.
KEEP IT AWAY FROM ME!
IT IS A THEROPOD... PROBABLY A BONKERS MUTATION OF A TYRANNOSAURUS REX...BUT THE IMPORTANT THING IS HE'S FRIENDLY.
TAKE IT FROM ME-- HE'S GOOD AT HELPING.
WHY DO YOU LET HIM BOTHER YOU?
KID KREE, I MEAN?
FOR SERIOUS? HE TRAVELED THROUGH SPACE TO ZAP ME OFF THE FACE OF THE EARTH.
HE'S JUST A KID.
Never have.
YOU HEARD WHAT HE SAID!
AND... AND IS IT TRUE? YOU'RE INHUMAN?
I used to think never will.
YES, IT'S TRUE. AND I KNOW THE TERRIGEN CLOUD CAUSED YOUR TRANSFORMATION, TOO.
HOW?
IT WAS THE HULK, ACTUALLY. AMADEUS CHO.
THAT GREEN KNOW-IT-ALL!
HE SAID WE HAVE TO LOOK OUT FOR YOU.
WHO'S "WE"?
ALL OF US. THE HEROES. HULK THINKS YOU NEED SOMEONE TO KEEP AN EYE ON YOU...
...BUT...
...HE ALSO SAID YOU HAVE HEART. AND POTENTIAL TO DO GREAT THINGS.

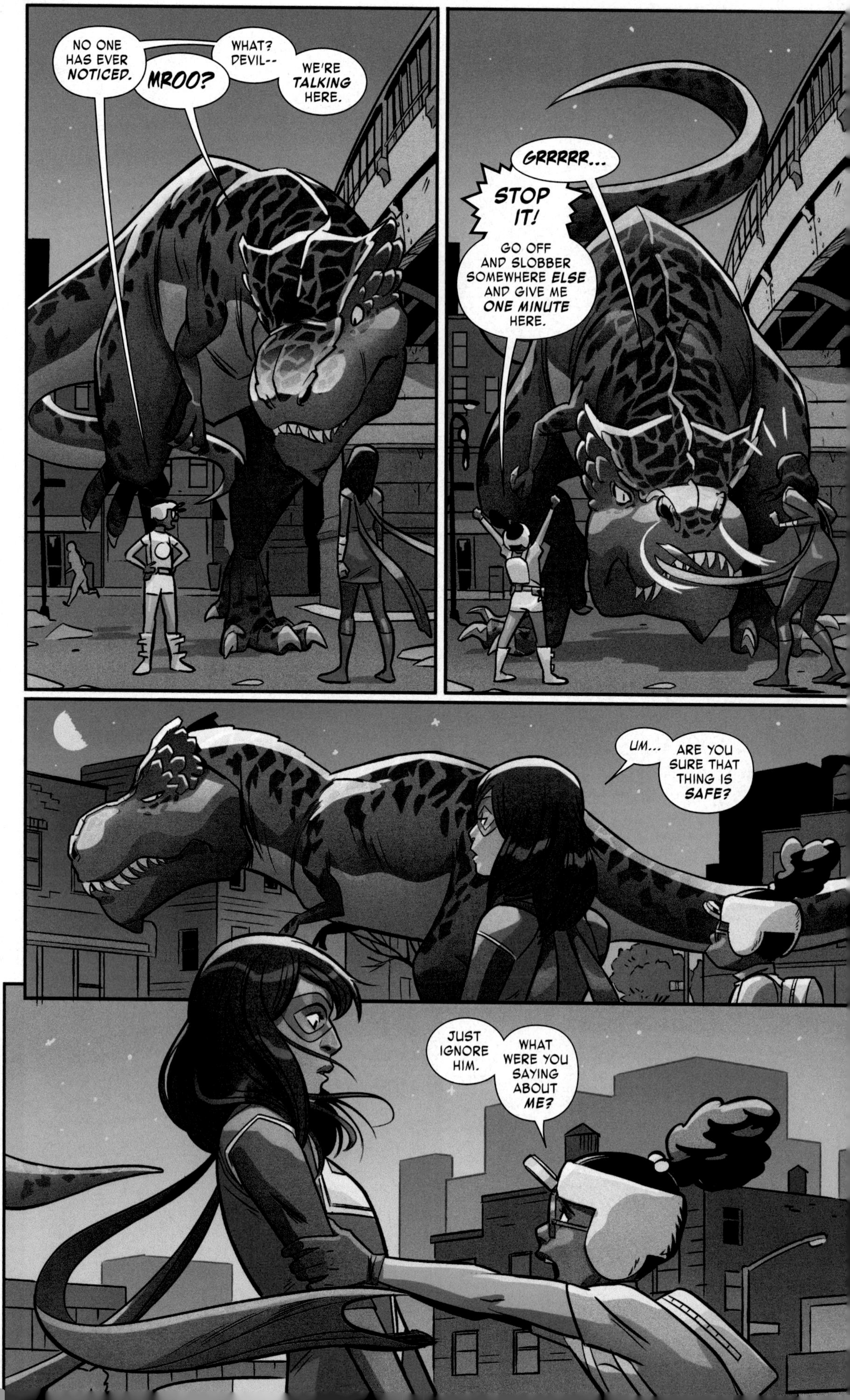
NO ONE HAS EVER NOTICED.
WHAT? DEVIL--
MROO?
WE'RE TALKING HERE.
GRRRRR...
STOP IT!
GO OFF AND SLOBBER SOMEWHERE ELSE AND GIVE ME ONE MINUTE HERE.
UM...
ARE YOU SURE THAT THING IS SAFE?
JUST IGNORE HIM.
WHAT WERE YOU SAYING ABOUT ME?

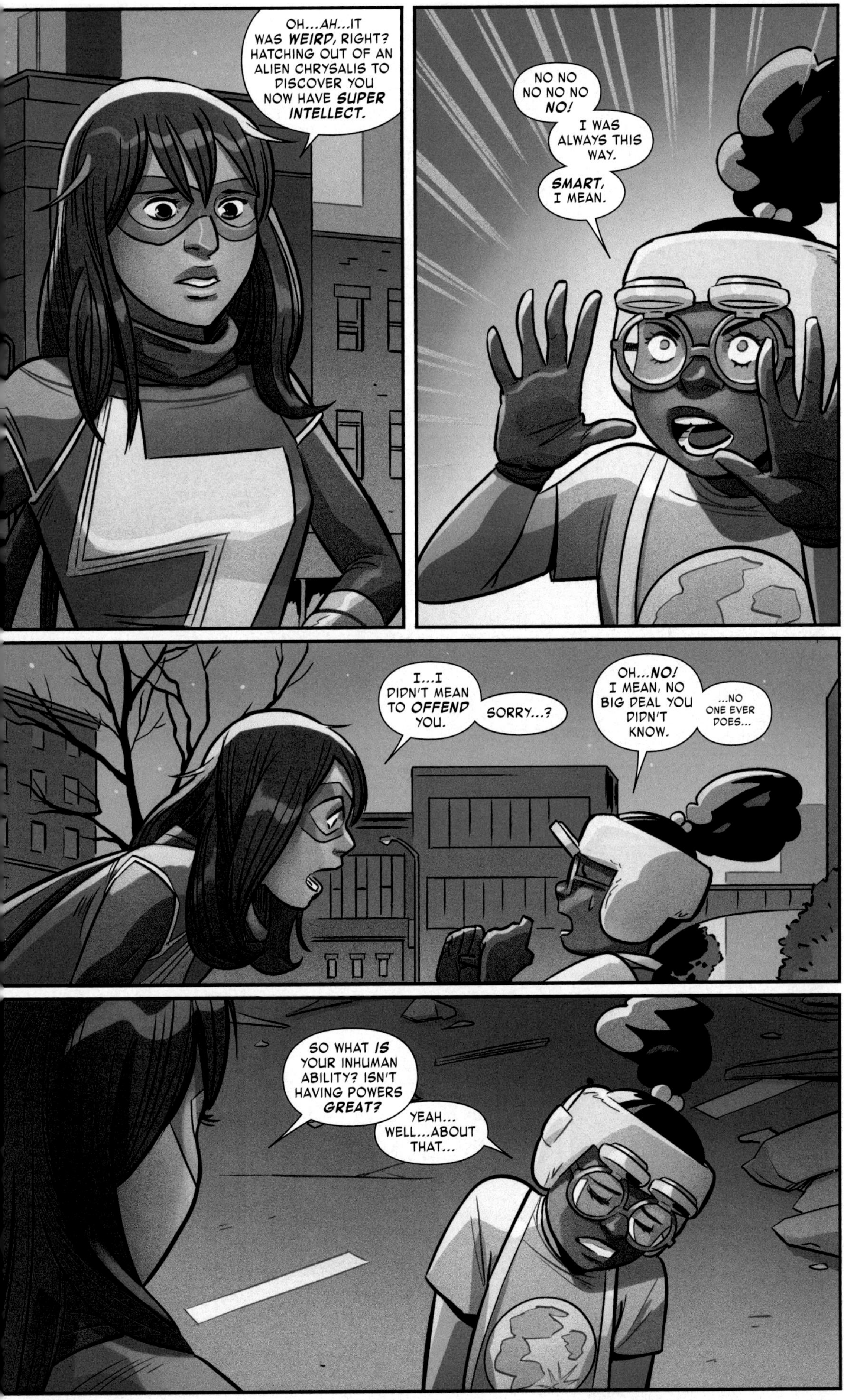
OH...AH...IT WAS WEIRD, RIGHT? HATCHING OUT OF AN ALIEN CHRYSALIS TO DISCOVER YOU NOW HAVE SUPER INTELLECT.
NO NO NO NO NO NO!
I WAS ALWAYS THIS WAY.
SMART, I MEAN.
I...I DIDN'T MEAN TO OFFEND YOU.
SORRY...?
OH...NO! I MEAN, NO BIG DEAL YOU DIDN'T KNOW.
...NO ONE EVER DOES...
SO WHAT IS YOUR INHUMAN ABILITY? ISN'T HAVING POWERS GREAT?
YEAH... WELL...ABOUT THAT...

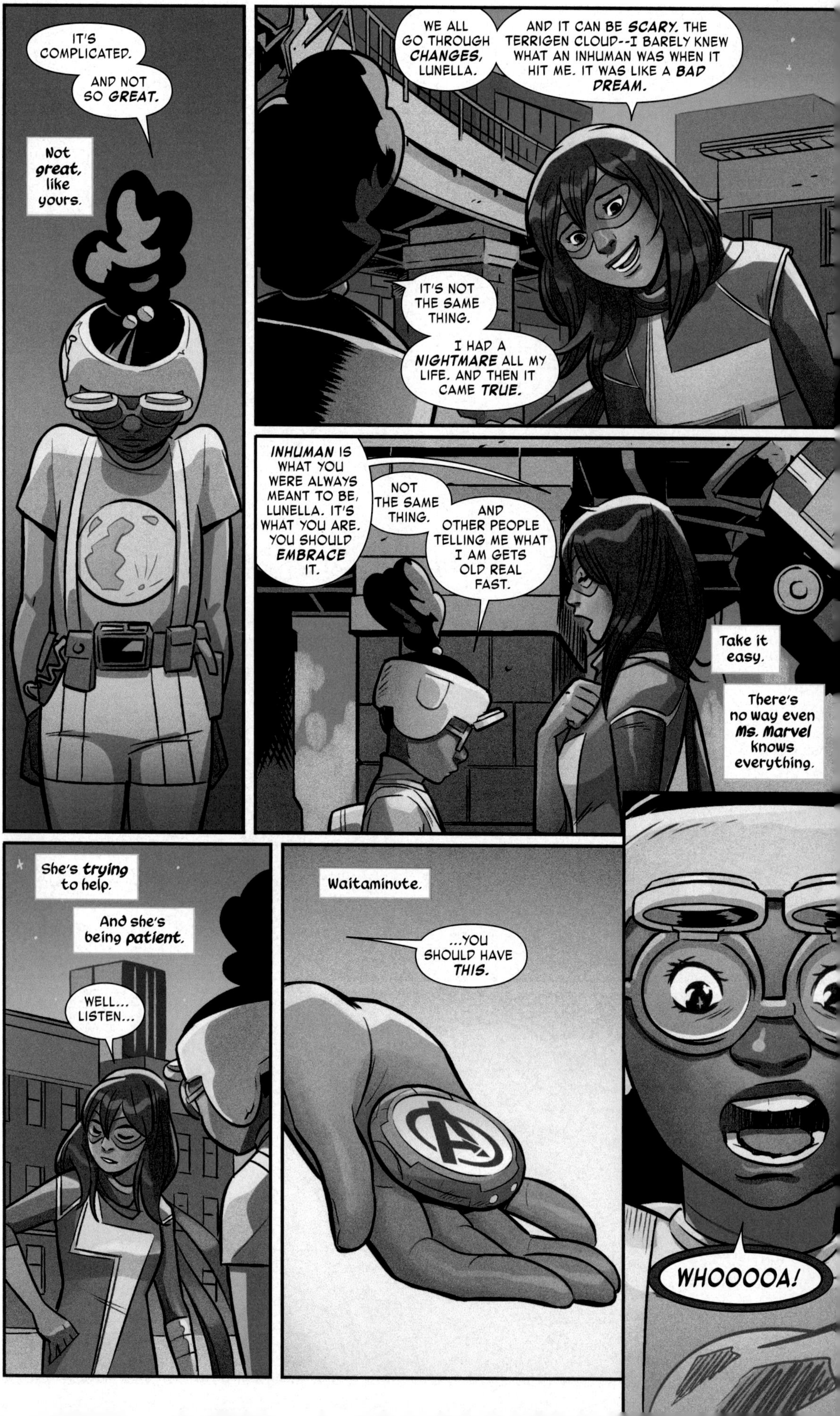
IT'S COMPLICATED.
AND NOT SO GREAT.
Not great, like yours.
WE ALL GO THROUGH CHANGES, LUNELLA.
AND IT CAN BE SCARY. THE TERRIGEN CLOUD--I BARELY KNEW WHAT AN INHUMAN WAS WHEN IT HIT ME. IT WAS LIKE A BAD DREAM.
IT'S NOT THE SAME THING.
I HAD A NIGHTMARE ALL MY LIFE. AND THEN IT CAME TRUE.
INHUMAN IS WHAT YOU WERE ALWAYS MEANT TO BE, LUNELLA. IT'S WHAT YOU ARE. YOU SHOULD EMBRACE IT.
NOT THE SAME THING.
AND OTHER PEOPLE TELLING ME WHAT I AM GETS OLD REAL FAST.
Take it easy.
There's no way even Ms. Marvel knows everything.
She's trying to help.
And she's being patient.
WELL... LISTEN...
Waitaminute.
...YOU SHOULD HAVE THIS.
WHOOOOA!

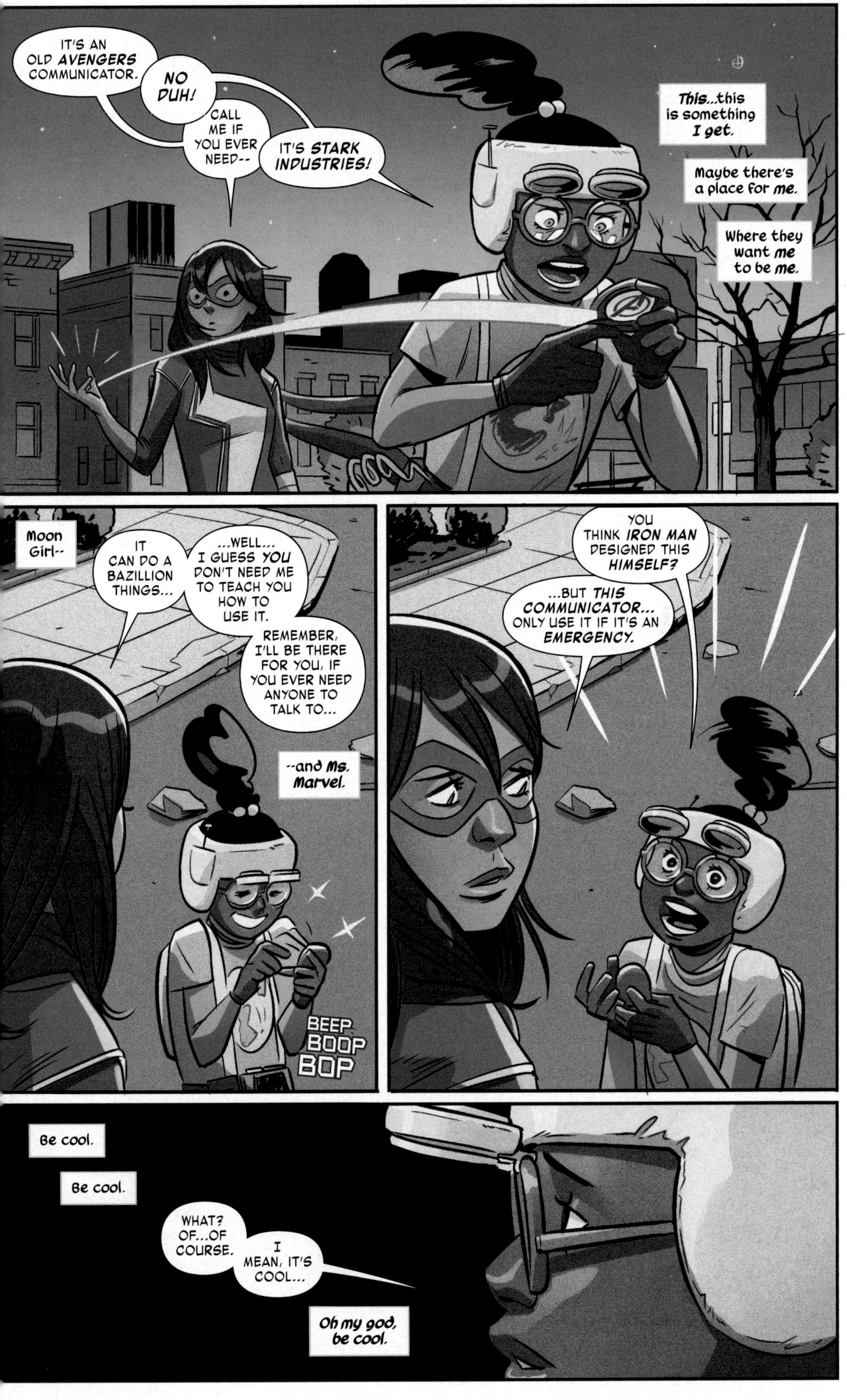

IT'S AN OLD AVENGERS COMMUNICATOR.
NO DUH!
CALL ME IF YOU EVER NEED--
IT'S STARK INDUSTRIES!
This...this is something I get.
Maybe there's a place for me.
Where they want me to be me.
Moon Girl--
IT CAN DO A BAZILLION THINGS...
...WELL... I GUESS YOU DON'T NEED ME TO TEACH YOU HOW TO USE IT.
REMEMBER, I'LL BE THERE FOR YOU, IF YOU EVER NEED ANYONE TO TALK TO...
--and Ms. Marvel.
BEEP BOOP BOP
YOU THINK IRON MAN DESIGNED THIS HIMSELF?
...BUT THIS COMMUNICATOR... ONLY USE IT IF IT'S AN EMERGENCY.
Be cool.
Be cool.
WHAT? OF...OF COURSE.
I MEAN, IT'S COOL...
Oh my god, be cool.

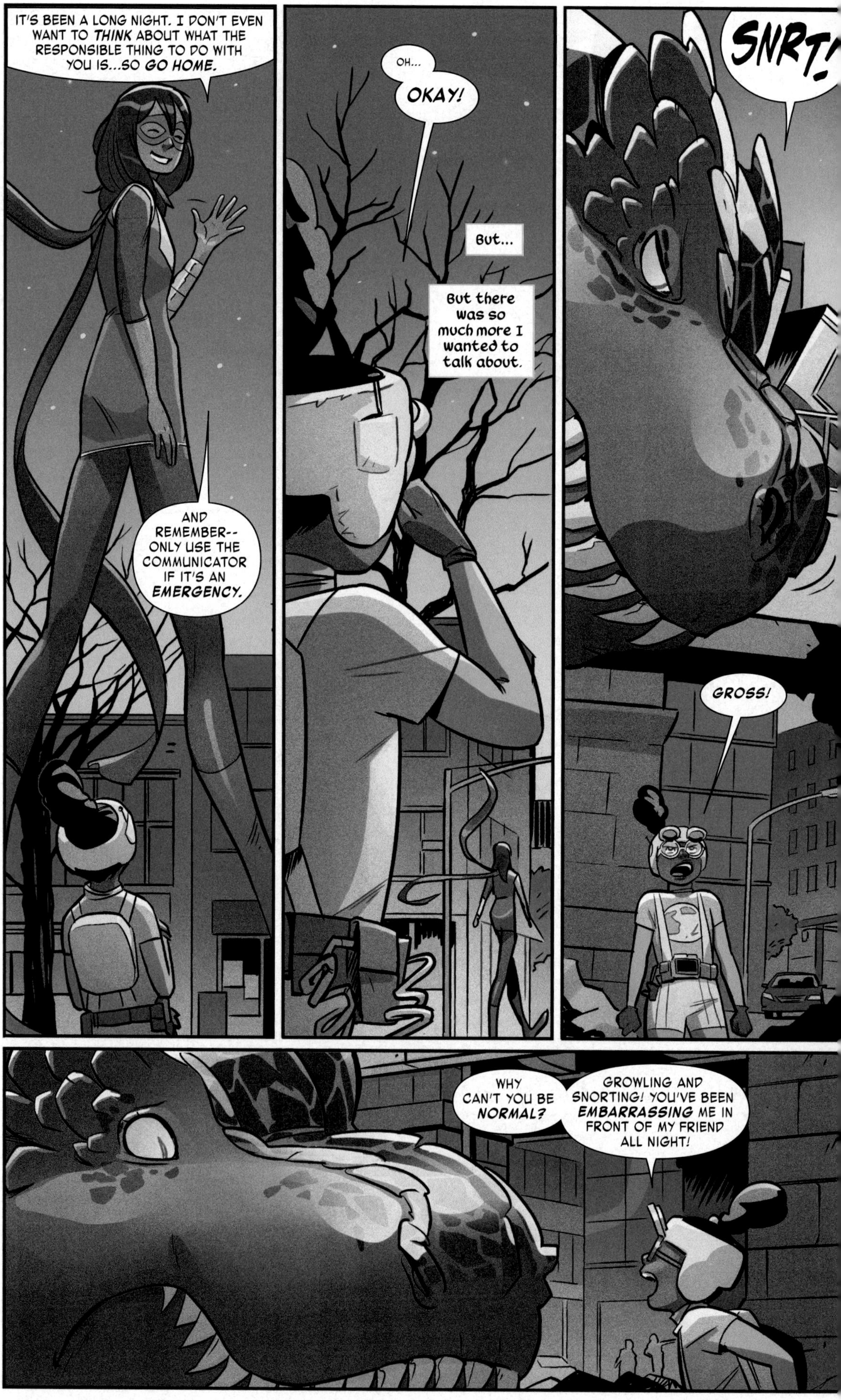
IT'S BEEN A LONG NIGHT. I DON'T EVEN WANT TO THINK ABOUT WHAT THE RESPONSIBLE THING TO DO WITH YOU IS...SO GO HOME.
AND REMEMBER-- ONLY USE THE COMMUNICATOR IF IT'S AN EMERGENCY.
OH...
OKAY!
But...
But there was so much more I wanted to talk about.
SNRT!
GROSS!
WHY CAN'T YOU BE NORMAL?
GROWLING AND SNORTING! YOU'VE BEEN EMBARRASSING ME IN FRONT OF MY FRIEND ALL NIGHT!

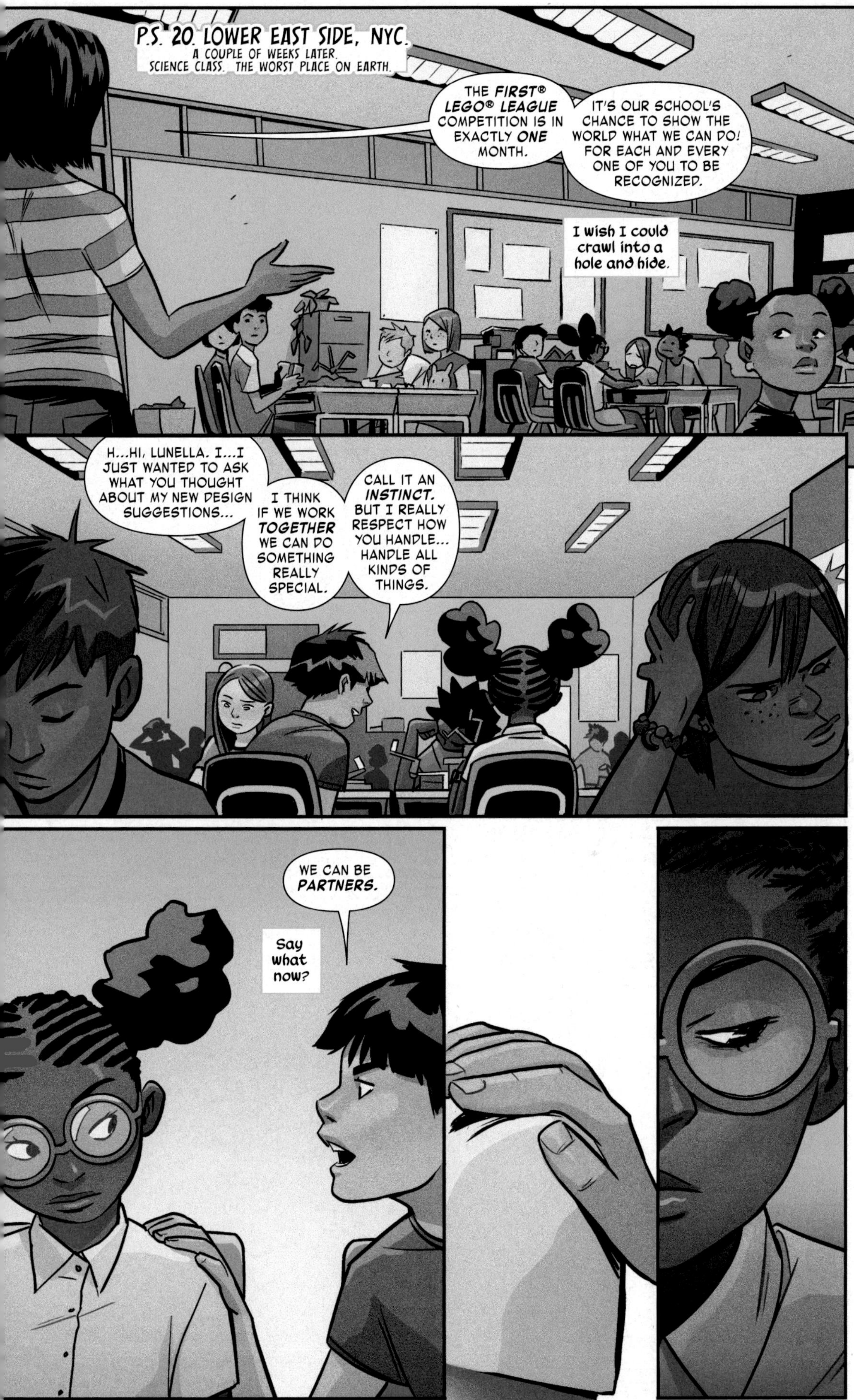

P.S. 20. LOWER EAST SIDE, NYC.
A COUPLE OF WEEKS LATER. SCIENCE CLASS. THE WORST PLACE ON EARTH.
THE FIRST® LEGO® LEAGUE COMPETITION IS IN EXACTLY ONE MONTH.
IT'S OUR SCHOOL'S CHANCE TO SHOW THE WORLD WHAT WE CAN DO! FOR EACH AND EVERY ONE OF YOU TO BE RECOGNIZED.
I wish I could crawl into a hole and hide.
H...HI, LUNELLA. I...I JUST WANTED TO ASK WHAT YOU THOUGHT ABOUT MY NEW DESIGN SUGGESTIONS...
I THINK IF WE WORK TOGETHER WE CAN DO SOMETHING REALLY SPECIAL.
CALL IT AN INSTINCT. BUT I REALLY RESPECT HOW YOU HANDLE... HANDLE ALL KINDS OF THINGS.
WE CAN BE PARTNERS.
Say what now?

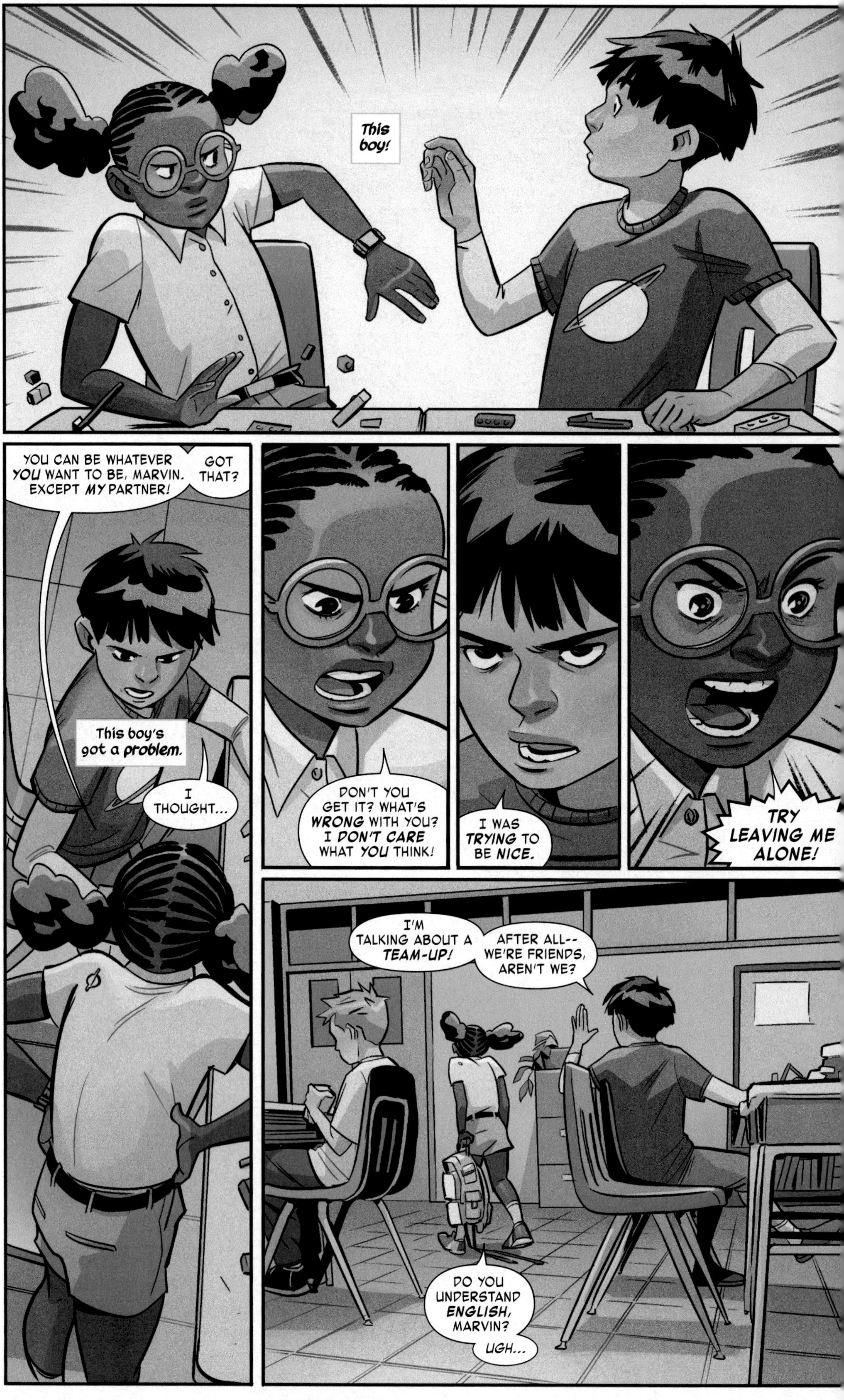

This boy!
YOU CAN BE WHATEVER YOU WANT TO BE, MARVIN. EXCEPT MY PARTNER!
GOT THAT?
This boy's got a problem.
I THOUGHT...
DON'T YOU GET IT? WHAT'S WRONG WITH YOU? I DON'T CARE WHAT YOU THINK!
I WAS TRYING TO BE NICE.
TRY LEAVING ME ALONE!
I'M TALKING ABOUT A TEAM-UP!
AFTER ALL-- WE'RE FRIENDS, AREN'T WE?
DO YOU UNDERSTAND ENGLISH, MARVIN?
UGH...

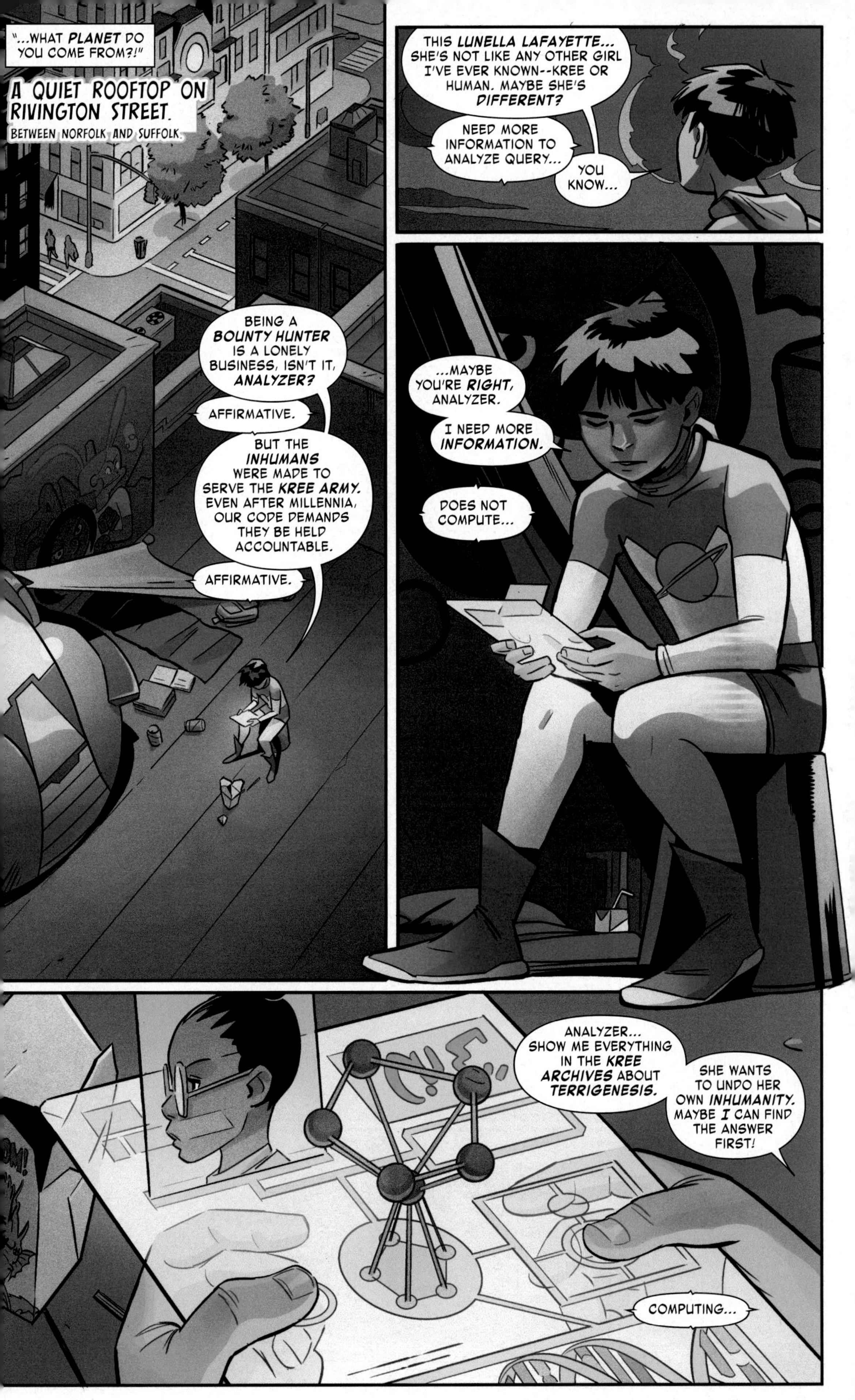
"...WHAT PLANET DO YOU COME FROM?!"
A QUIET ROOFTOP ON RIVINGTON STREET.
BETWEEN NORFOLK AND SUFFOLK.
BEING A BOUNTY HUNTER IS A LONELY BUSINESS, ISN'T IT, ANALYZER?
AFFIRMATIVE.
BUT THE INHUMANS WERE MADE TO SERVE THE KREE ARMY. EVEN AFTER MILLENNIA, OUR CODE DEMANDS THEY BE HELD ACCOUNTABLE.
AFFIRMATIVE.
THIS LUNELLA LAFAYETTE... SHE'S NOT LIKE ANY OTHER GIRL I'VE EVER KNOWN--KREE OR HUMAN. MAYBE SHE'S DIFFERENT?
NEED MORE INFORMATION TO ANALYZE QUERY...
YOU KNOW...
...MAYBE YOU'RE RIGHT, ANALYZER.
I NEED MORE INFORMATION.
DOES NOT COMPUTE...
ANALYZER... SHOW ME EVERYTHING IN THE KREE ARCHIVES ABOUT TERRIGENESIS.
SHE WANTS TO UNDO HER OWN INHUMANITY. MAYBE I CAN FIND THE ANSWER FIRST!
COMPUTING...

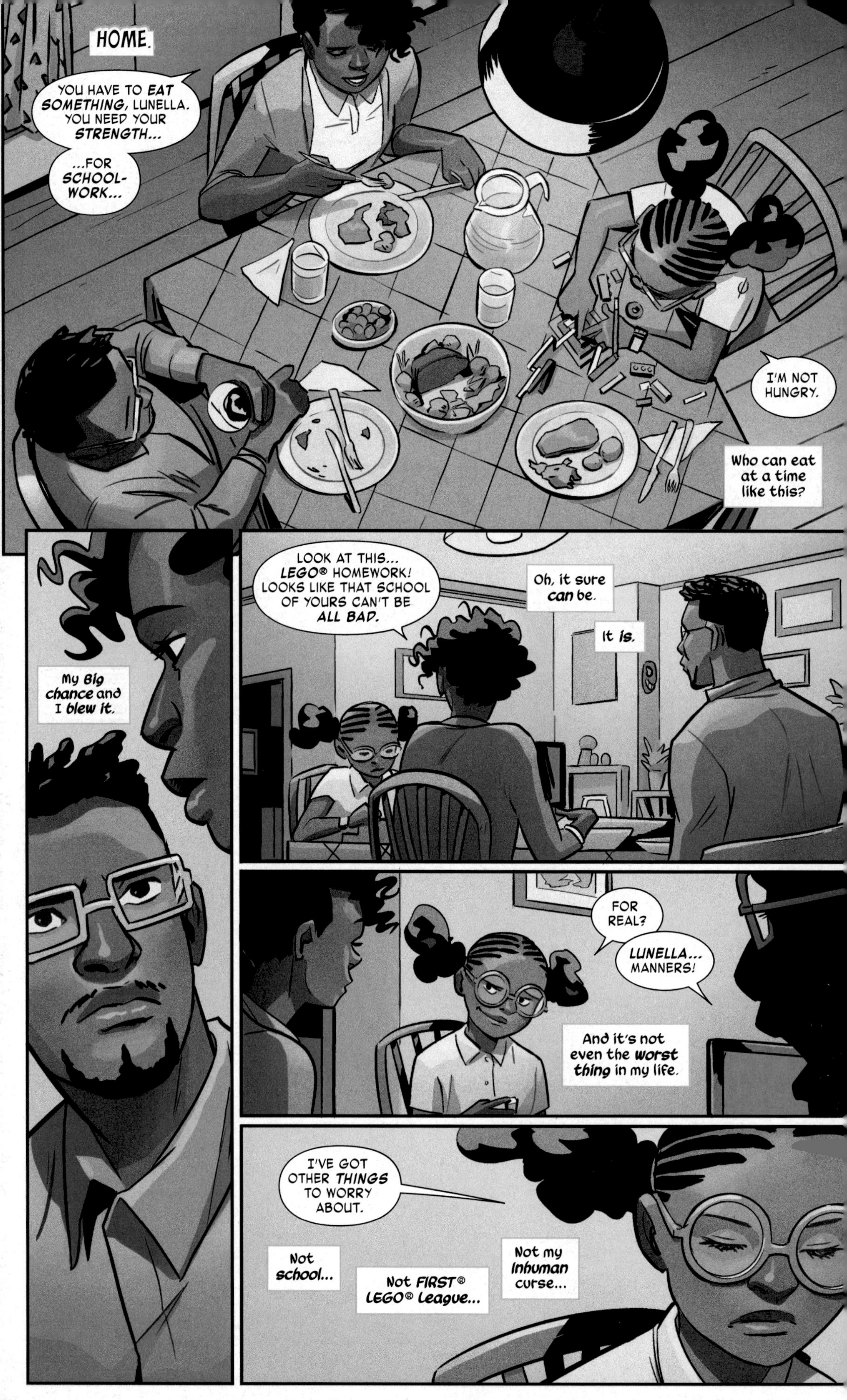
HOME.
YOU HAVE TO EAT SOMETHING, LUNELLA. YOU NEED YOUR STRENGTH...
...FOR SCHOOL-WORK...
I'M NOT HUNGRY.
Who can eat at a time like this?
My Big chance and I blew it.
LOOK AT THIS... LEGO® HOMEWORK! LOOKS LIKE THAT SCHOOL OF YOURS CAN'T BE ALL BAD.
Oh, it sure can be.
It is.
FOR REAL?
LUNELLA... MANNERS!
And it's not even the worst thing in my life.
I'VE GOT OTHER THINGS TO WORRY ABOUT.
Not school...
Not FIRST® LEGO® League...
Not my Inhuman curse...

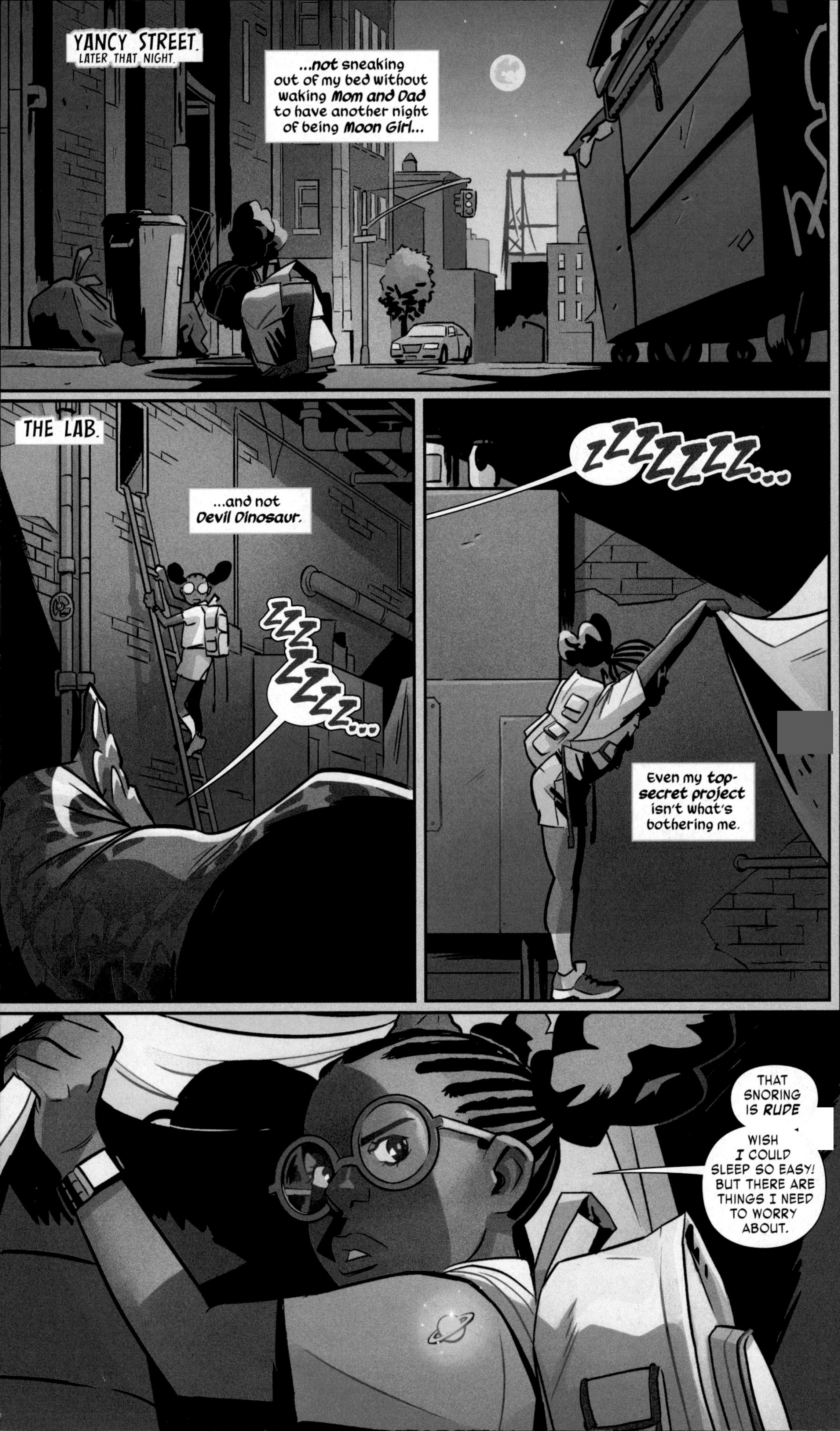
YANCY STREET. LATER THAT NIGHT.
...not sneaking out of my bed without waking Mom and Dad to have another night of being Moon Girl...
THE LAB.
...and not Devil Dinosaur.
ZZZZZZZ...
ZZZZZZZ...
Even my top-secret project isn't what's bothering me.
THAT SNORING IS RUDE
WISH I COULD SLEEP SO EASY! BUT THERE ARE THINGS I NEED TO WORRY ABOUT.

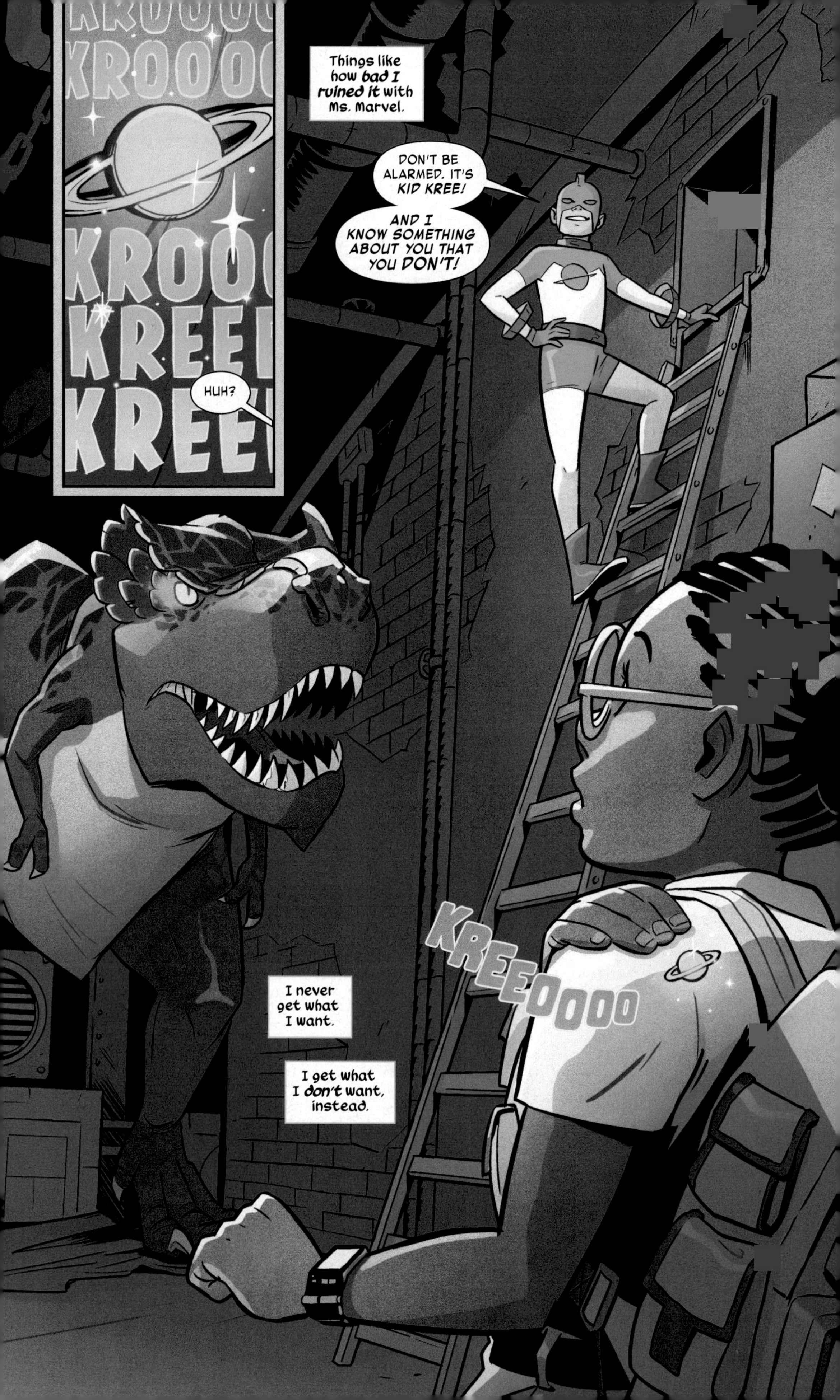
Things like how *bad I ruined it* with Ms. Marvel.
HUH?
DON'T BE ALARMED. IT'S *KID KREE!*
*AND I KNOW SOMETHING ABOUT YOU THAT YOU **DON'T!***
KREEOOOO
I never get what I want.
I get what I *don't* want, instead.

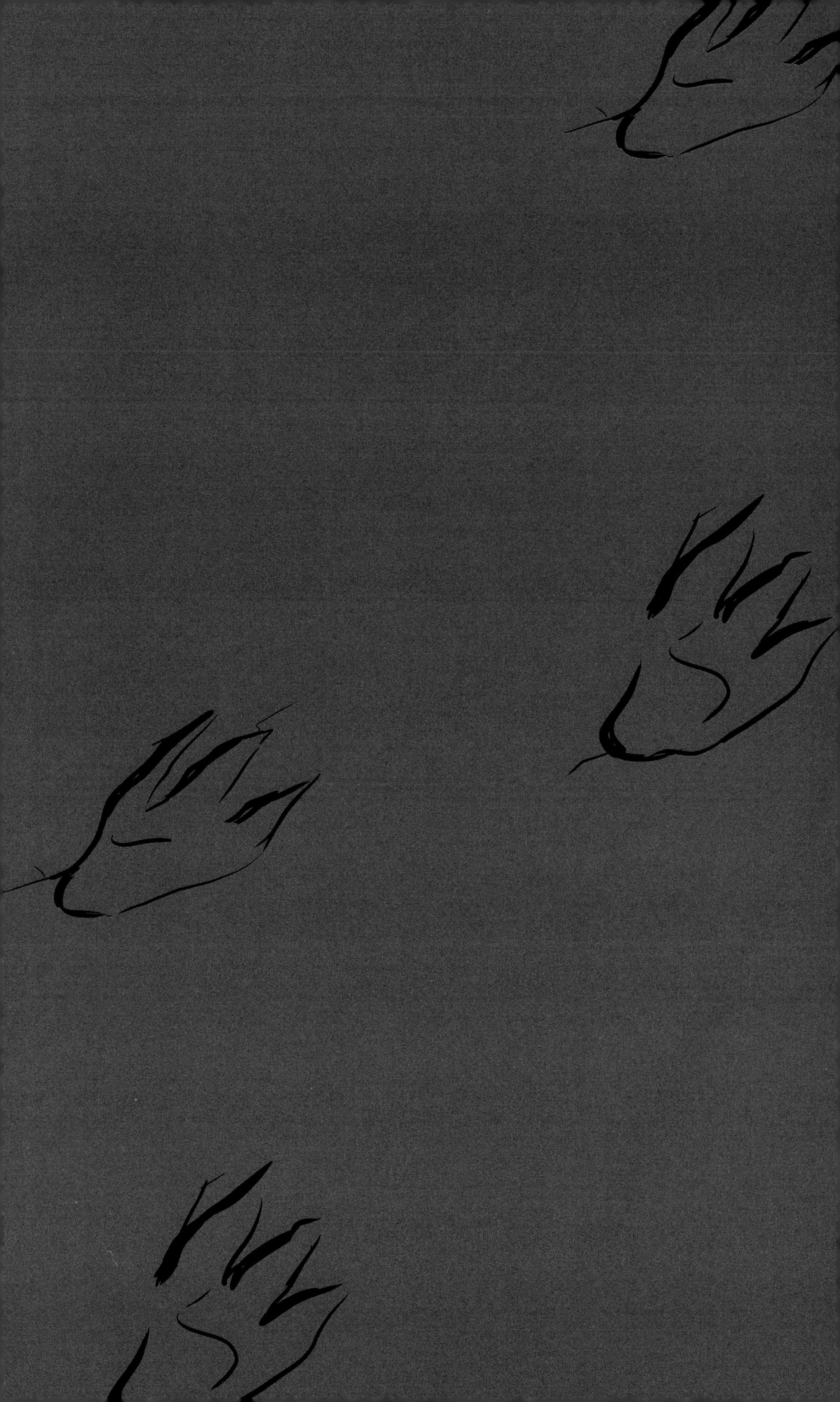

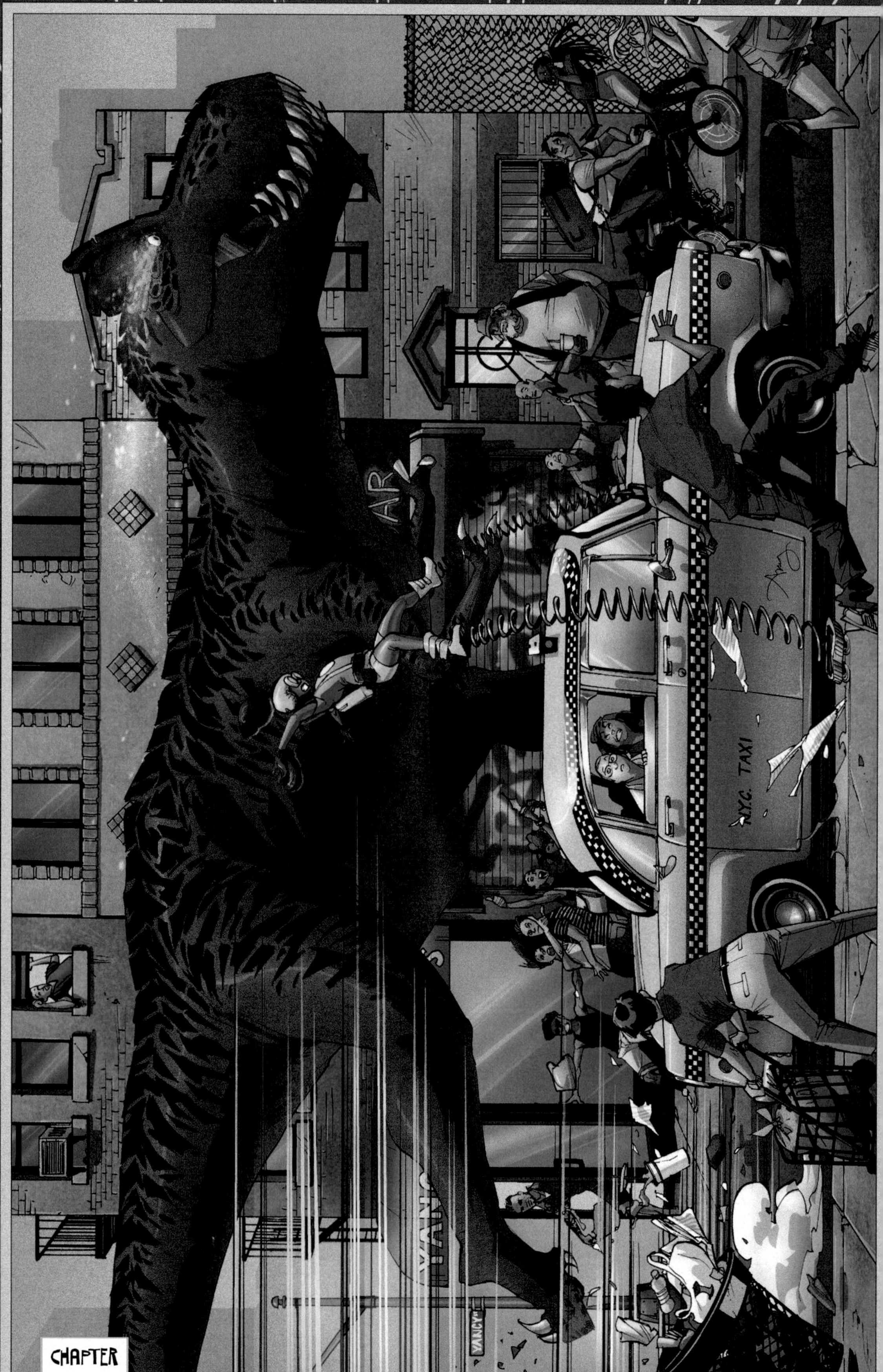
N.Y.C. TAXI

CHAPTER 11

"The Inhuman Thing To Do"

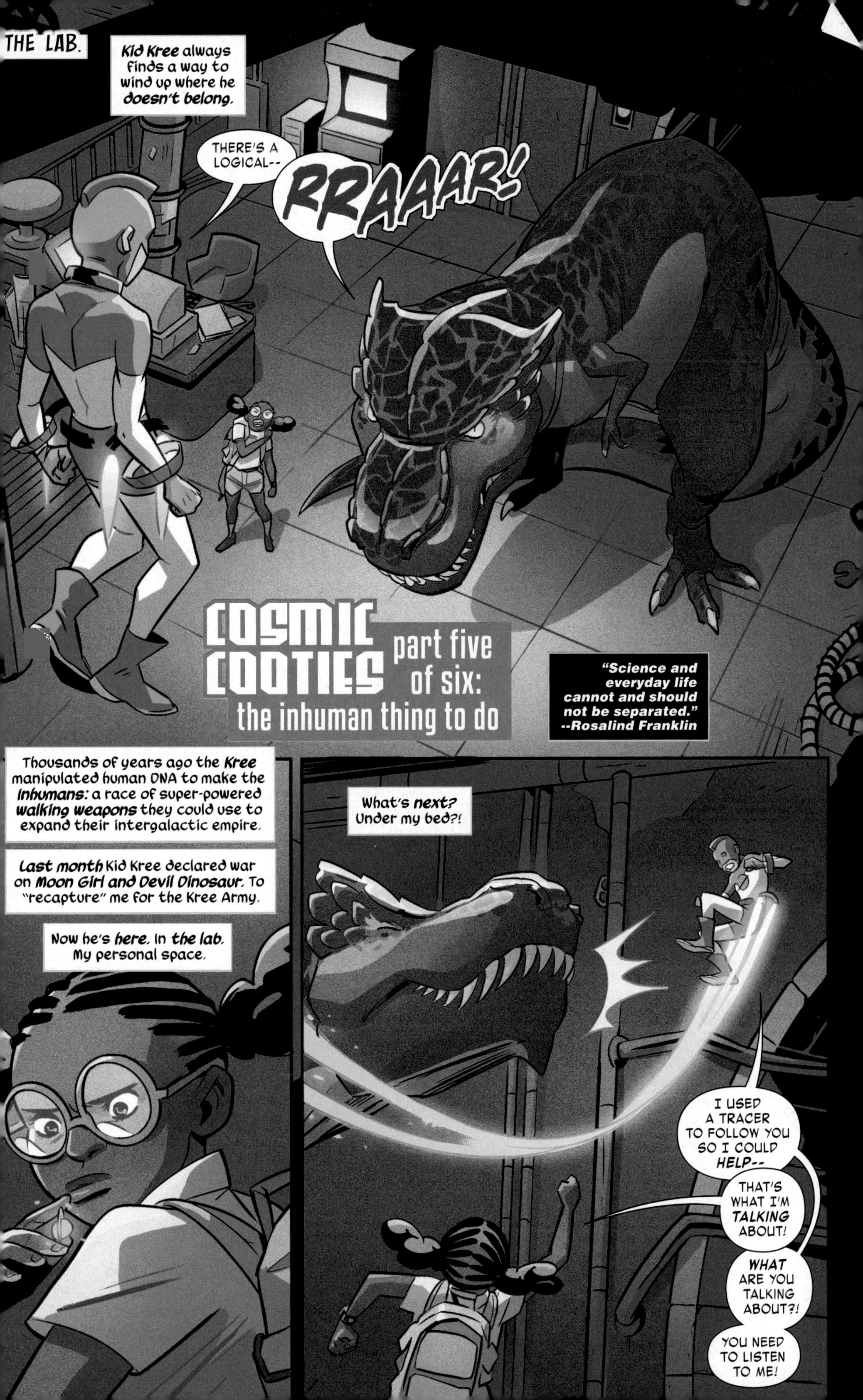
THE LAB.
Kid Kree always finds a way to wind up where he doesn't belong.
THERE'S A LOGICAL--
RRAAAR!
COSMIC COOTIES part five of six: the inhuman thing to do
"Science and everyday life cannot and should not be separated." --Rosalind Franklin
Thousands of years ago the Kree manipulated human DNA to make the Inhumans: a race of super-powered walking weapons they could use to expand their intergalactic empire.
Last month Kid Kree declared war on Moon Girl and Devil Dinosaur. To "recapture" me for the Kree Army.
Now he's here. In the lab. My personal space.
What's next? Under my bed?!
I USED A TRACER TO FOLLOW YOU SO I COULD HELP--
THAT'S WHAT I'M TALKING ABOUT!
WHAT ARE YOU TALKING ABOUT?!
YOU NEED TO LISTEN TO ME!

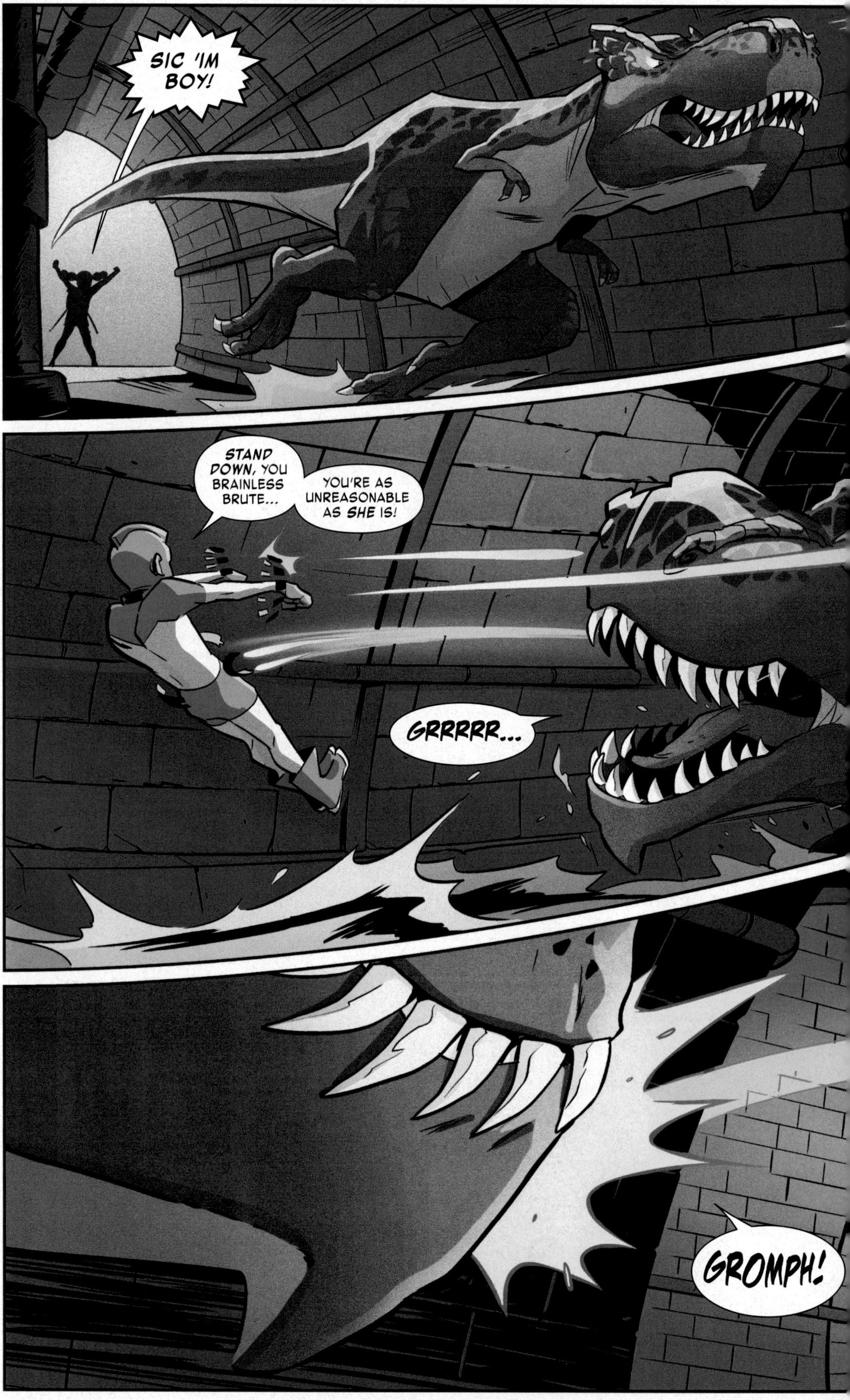
SIC 'IM BOY!
STAND DOWN, YOU BRAINLESS BRUTE...
YOU'RE AS UNREASONABLE AS SHE IS!
GRRRRR...
GROMPH!

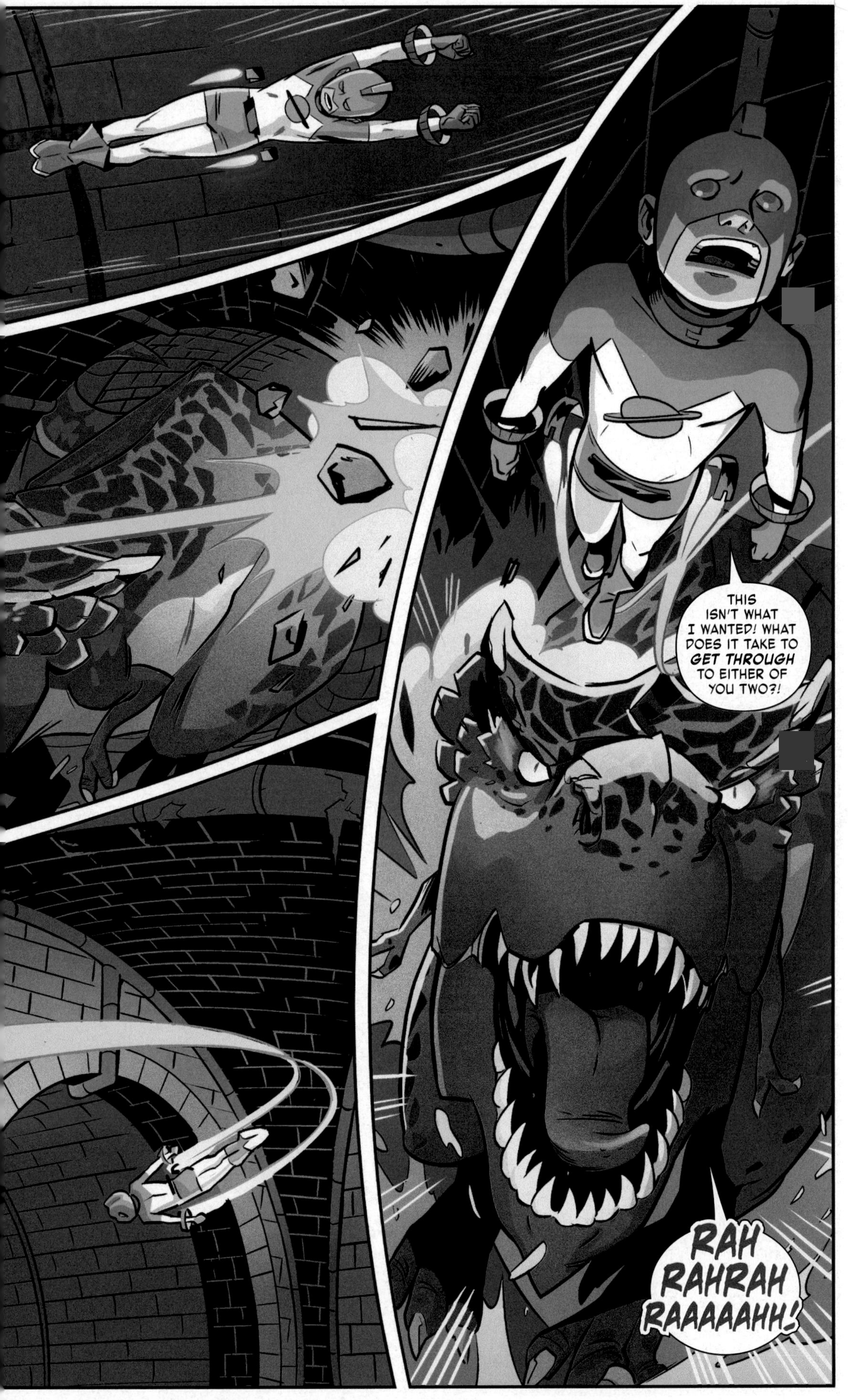
THIS ISN'T WHAT I WANTED! WHAT DOES IT TAKE TO ***GET THROUGH*** TO EITHER OF YOU TWO?!
RAH RAHRAH RAAAAAHH!

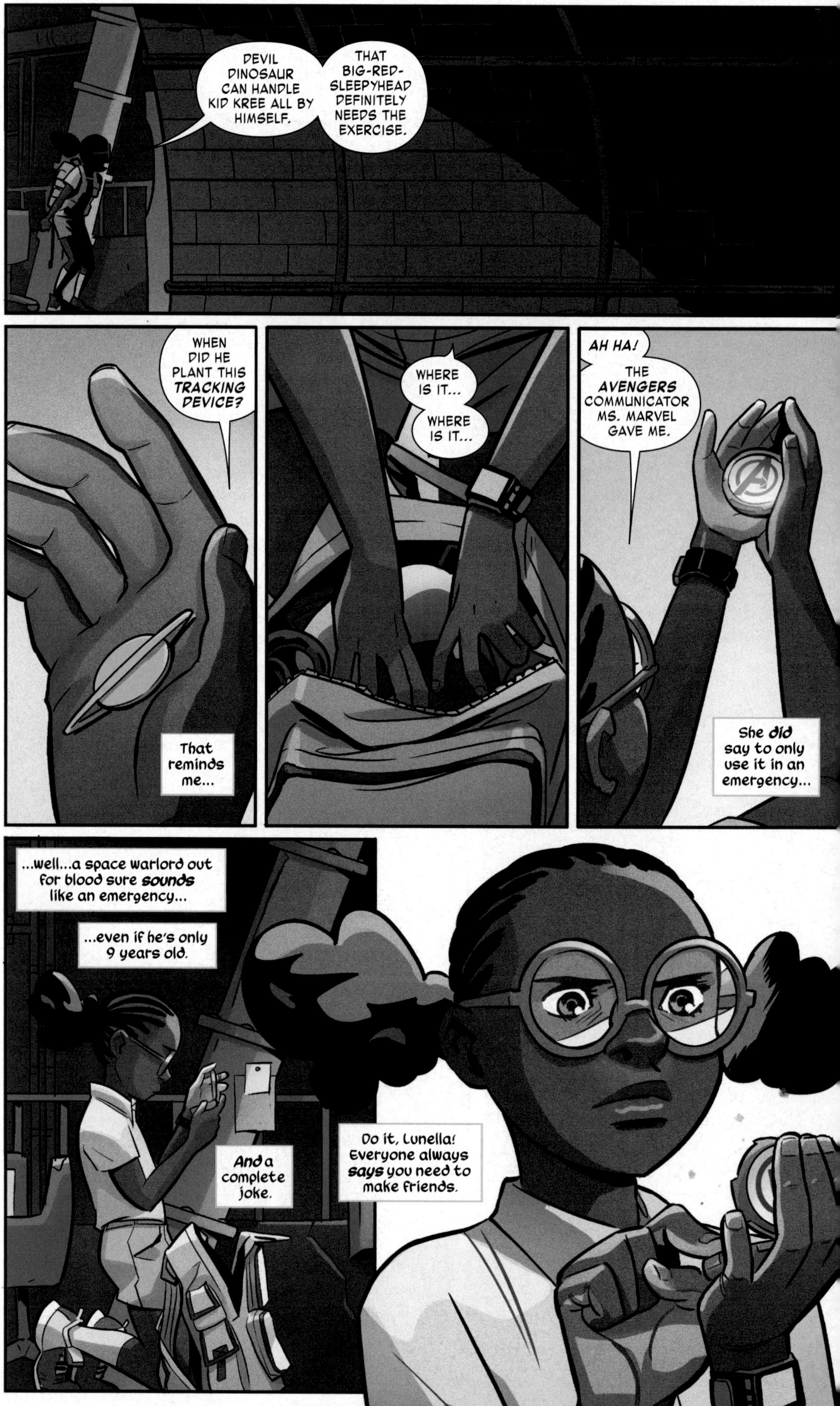
DEVIL DINOSAUR CAN HANDLE KID KREE ALL BY HIMSELF.
THAT BIG-RED-SLEEPYHEAD DEFINITELY NEEDS THE EXERCISE.
WHEN DID HE PLANT THIS TRACKING DEVICE?
That reminds me...
WHERE IS IT...
WHERE IS IT...
AH HA!
THE AVENGERS COMMUNICATOR MS. MARVEL GAVE ME.
She did say to only use it in an emergency...
...well...a space warlord out for blood sure sounds like an emergency...
...even if he's only 9 years old.
And a complete joke.
Do it, Lunella! Everyone always says you need to make friends.

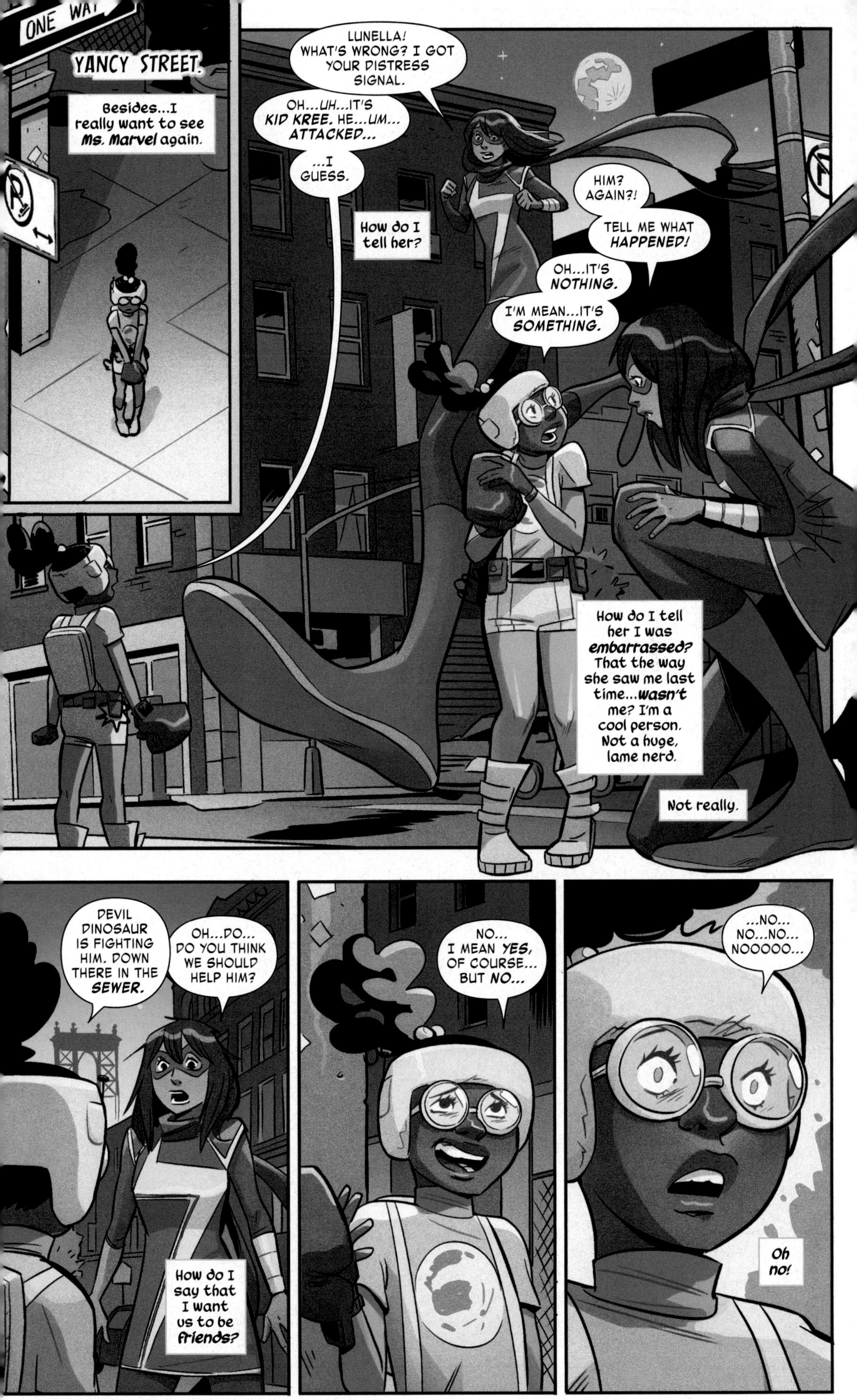

ONE WAY
YANCY STREET.
Besides...I really want to see Ms. Marvel again.
LUNELLA! WHAT'S WRONG? I GOT YOUR DISTRESS SIGNAL.
OH...UH...IT'S KID KREE. HE...UM... ATTACKED...
...I GUESS.
How do I tell her?
HIM? AGAIN?!
TELL ME WHAT HAPPENED!
OH...IT'S NOTHING.
I'M MEAN...IT'S SOMETHING.
How do I tell her I was embarrassed? That the way she saw me last time...wasn't me? I'm a cool person. Not a huge, lame nerd.
Not really.
DEVIL DINOSAUR IS FIGHTING HIM. DOWN THERE IN THE SEWER.
OH...DO... DO YOU THINK WE SHOULD HELP HIM?
How do I say that I want us to be friends?
NO... I MEAN YES, OF COURSE... BUT NO...
...NO... NO...NO... NOOOOO...
Oh no!

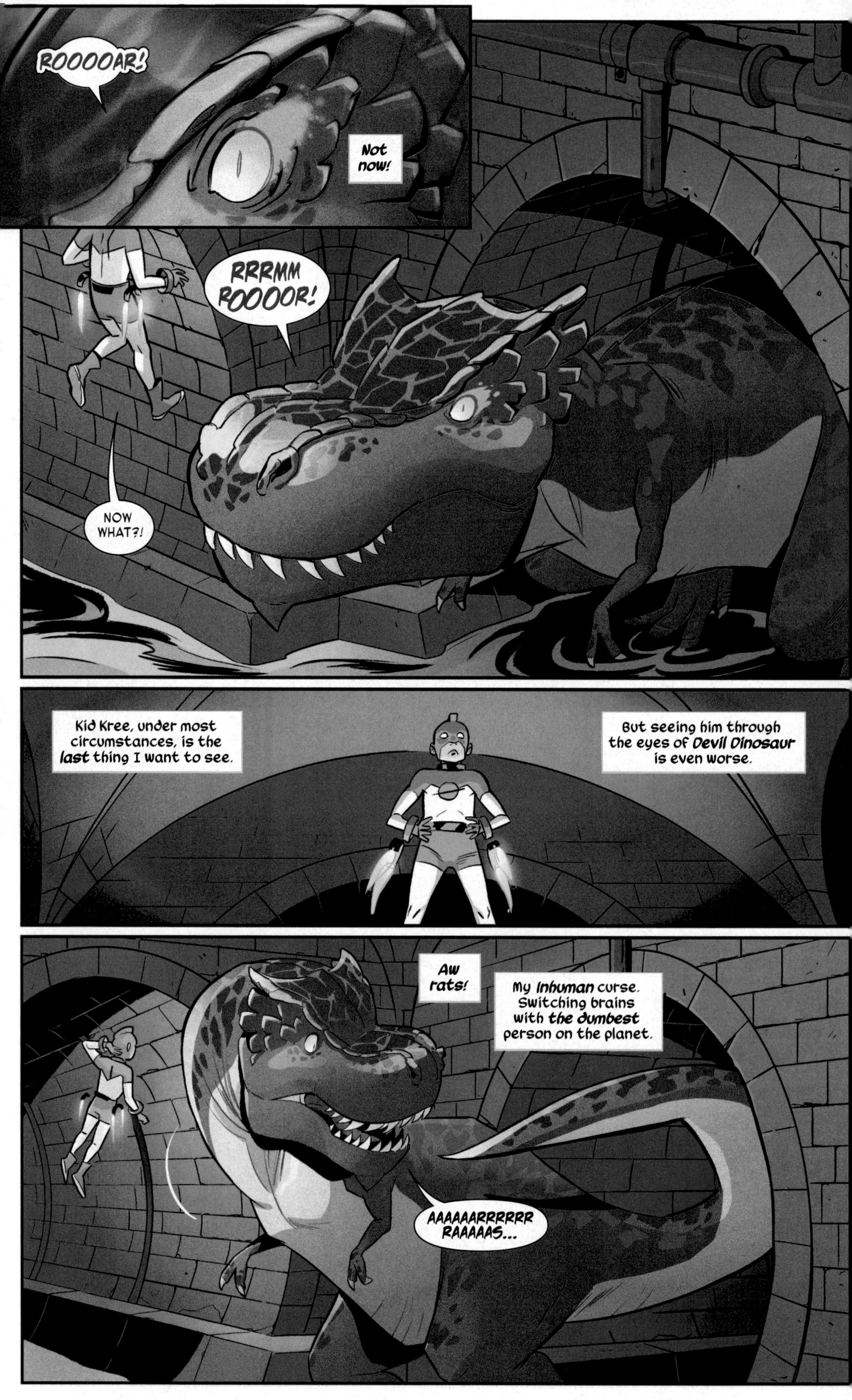
ROOOOAR!
Not now!
RRRMM ROOOOR!
NOW WHAT?!
Kid Kree, under most circumstances, is the last thing I want to see.
But seeing him through the eyes of Devil Dinosaur is even worse.
Aw rats!
My Inhuman curse. Switching brains with the dumbest person on the planet.
AAAAAARRRRRR RAAAAAS...

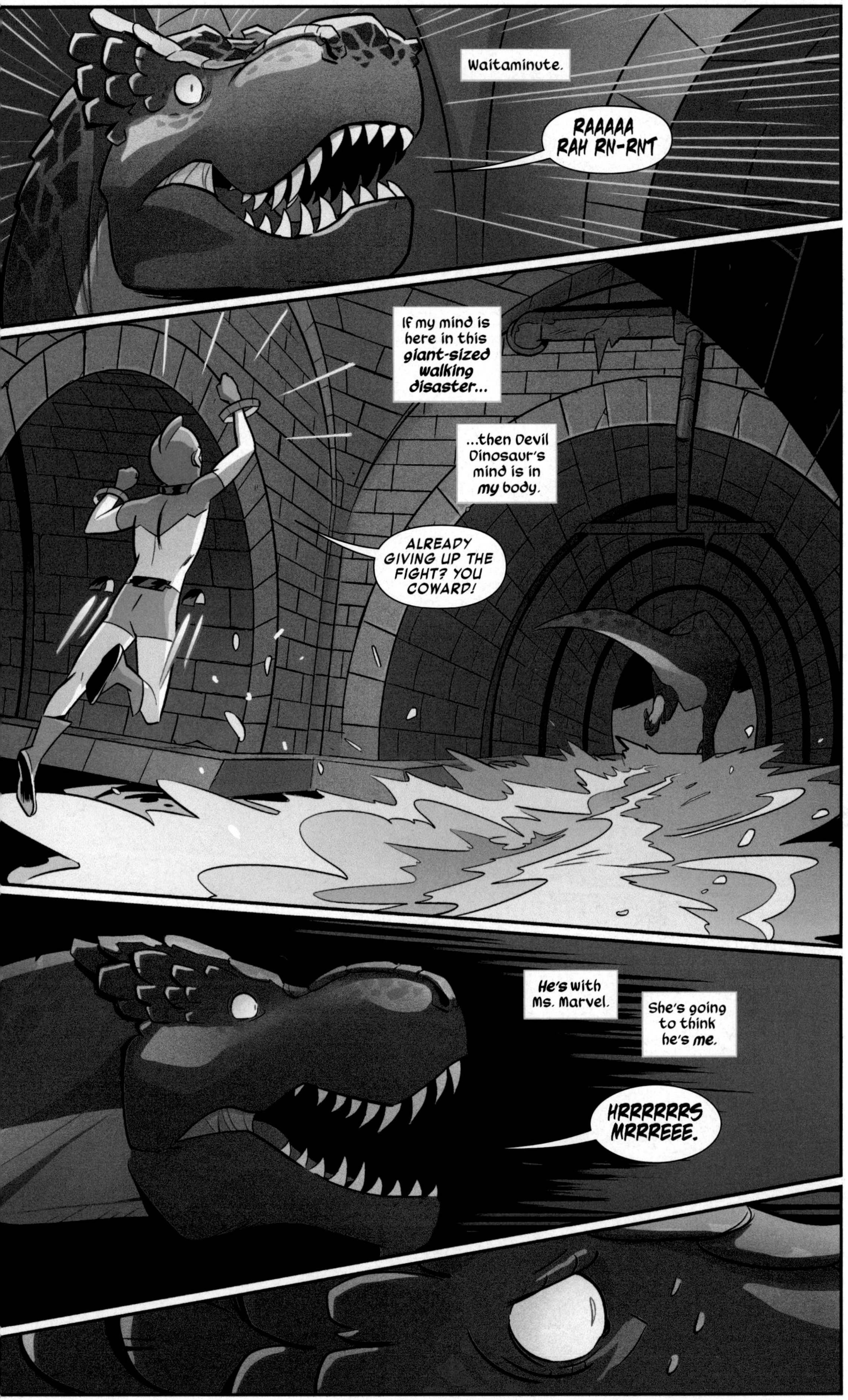
Waitaminute.
RAAAAAA RAH RN-RNT
If my mind is here in this giant-sized walking disaster...
...then Devil Dinosaur's mind is in my body.
ALREADY GIVING UP THE FIGHT? YOU COWARD!
He's with Ms. Marvel.
She's going to think he's me.
HRRRRRRS MRRREEE.

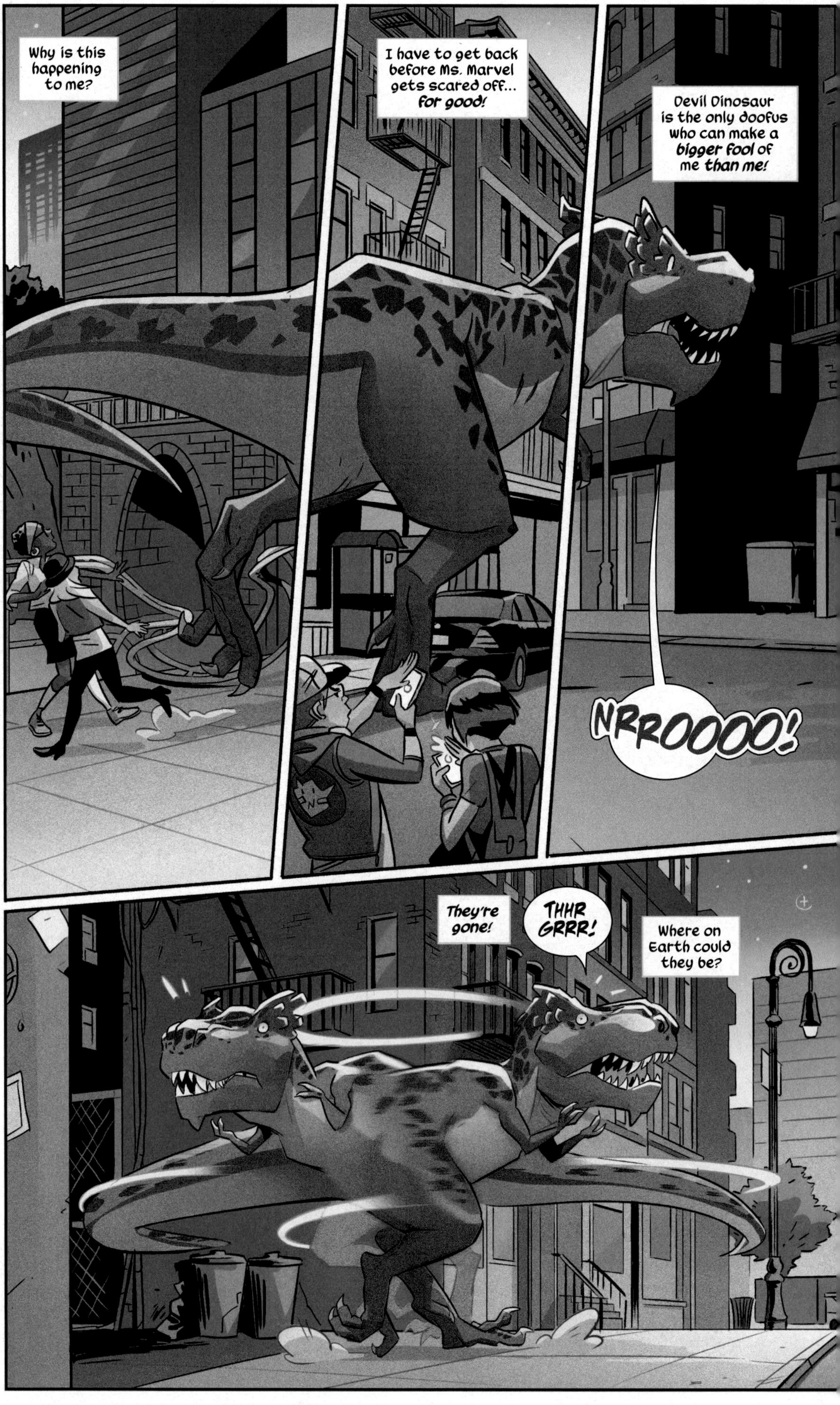

Why is this happening to me?
I have to get back before Ms. Marvel gets scared off... for good!
Devil Dinosaur is the only doofus who can make a bigger fool of me than me!
NRROOOO!
They're gone!
THHR GRRR!
Where on Earth could they be?

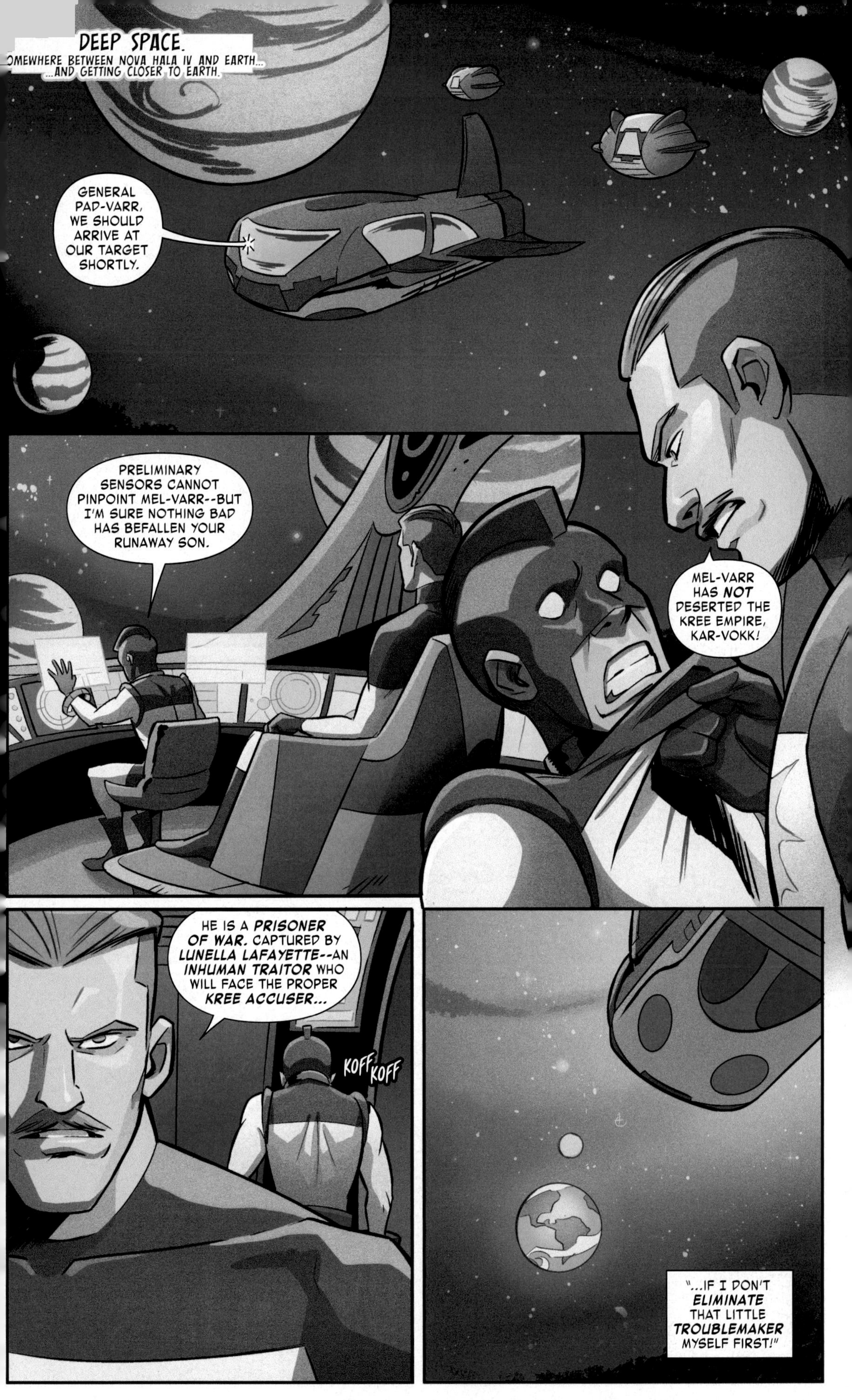

DEEP SPACE.
SOMEWHERE BETWEEN NOVA HALA IV AND EARTH...
...AND GETTING CLOSER TO EARTH.
GENERAL PAD-VARR, WE SHOULD ARRIVE AT OUR TARGET SHORTLY.
PRELIMINARY SENSORS CANNOT PINPOINT MEL-VARR--BUT I'M SURE NOTHING BAD HAS BEFALLEN YOUR RUNAWAY SON.
MEL-VARR HAS NOT DESERTED THE KREE EMPIRE, KAR-VOKK!
HE IS A PRISONER OF WAR. CAPTURED BY LUNELLA LAFAYETTE--AN INHUMAN TRAITOR WHO WILL FACE THE PROPER KREE ACCUSER...
KOFF KOFF
"...IF I DON'T ELIMINATE THAT LITTLE TROUBLEMAKER MYSELF FIRST!"

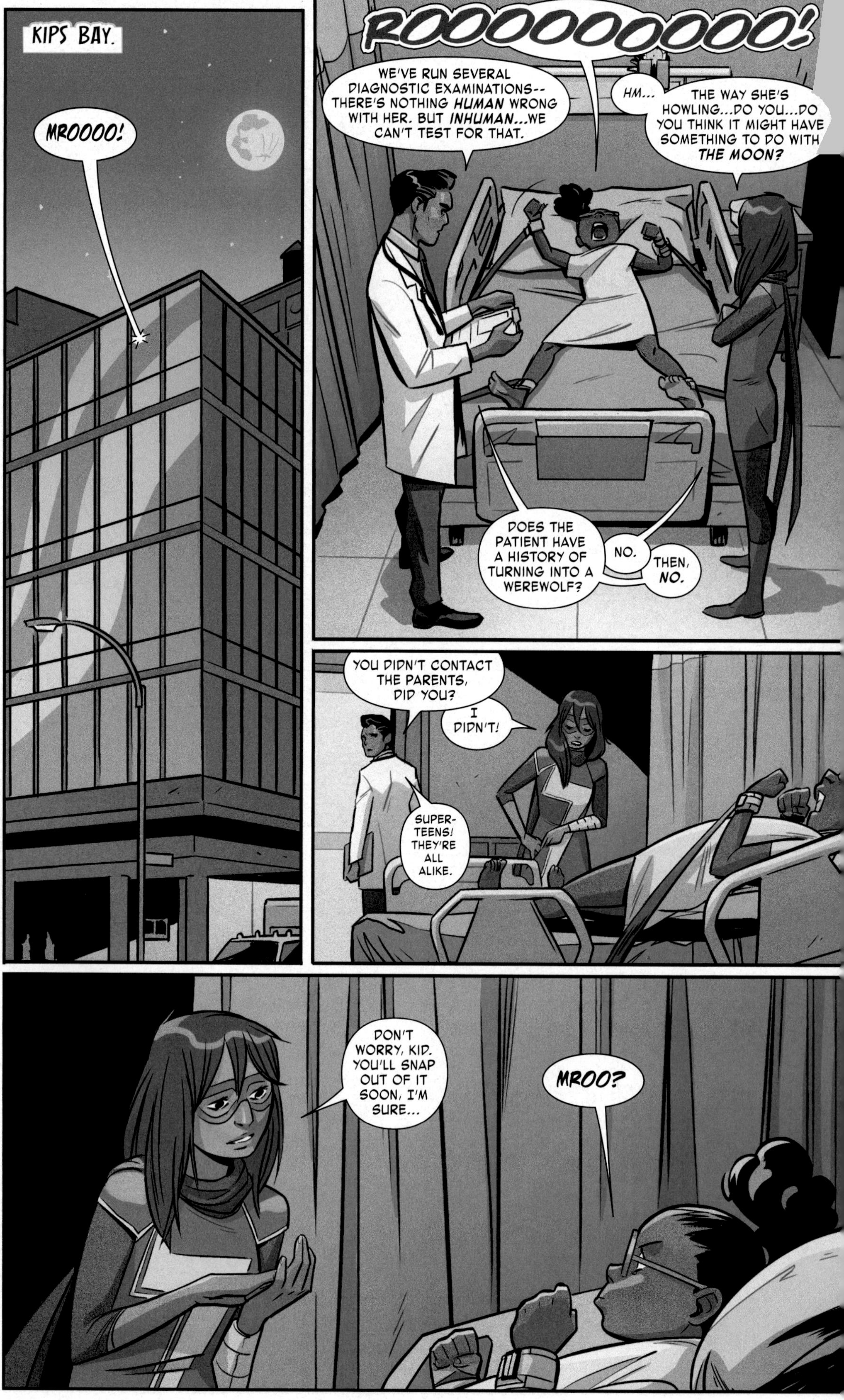
KIPS BAY.
MROOOO!
ROOOOOOOOO!
WE'VE RUN SEVERAL DIAGNOSTIC EXAMINATIONS-- THERE'S NOTHING HUMAN WRONG WITH HER. BUT INHUMAN...WE CAN'T TEST FOR THAT.
HM...
THE WAY SHE'S HOWLING...DO YOU...DO YOU THINK IT MIGHT HAVE SOMETHING TO DO WITH THE MOON?
DOES THE PATIENT HAVE A HISTORY OF TURNING INTO A WEREWOLF?
NO.
THEN, NO.
YOU DIDN'T CONTACT THE PARENTS, DID YOU?
I DIDN'T!
SUPER-TEENS! THEY'RE ALL ALIKE.
DON'T WORRY, KID. YOU'LL SNAP OUT OF IT SOON, I'M SURE...
MROO?

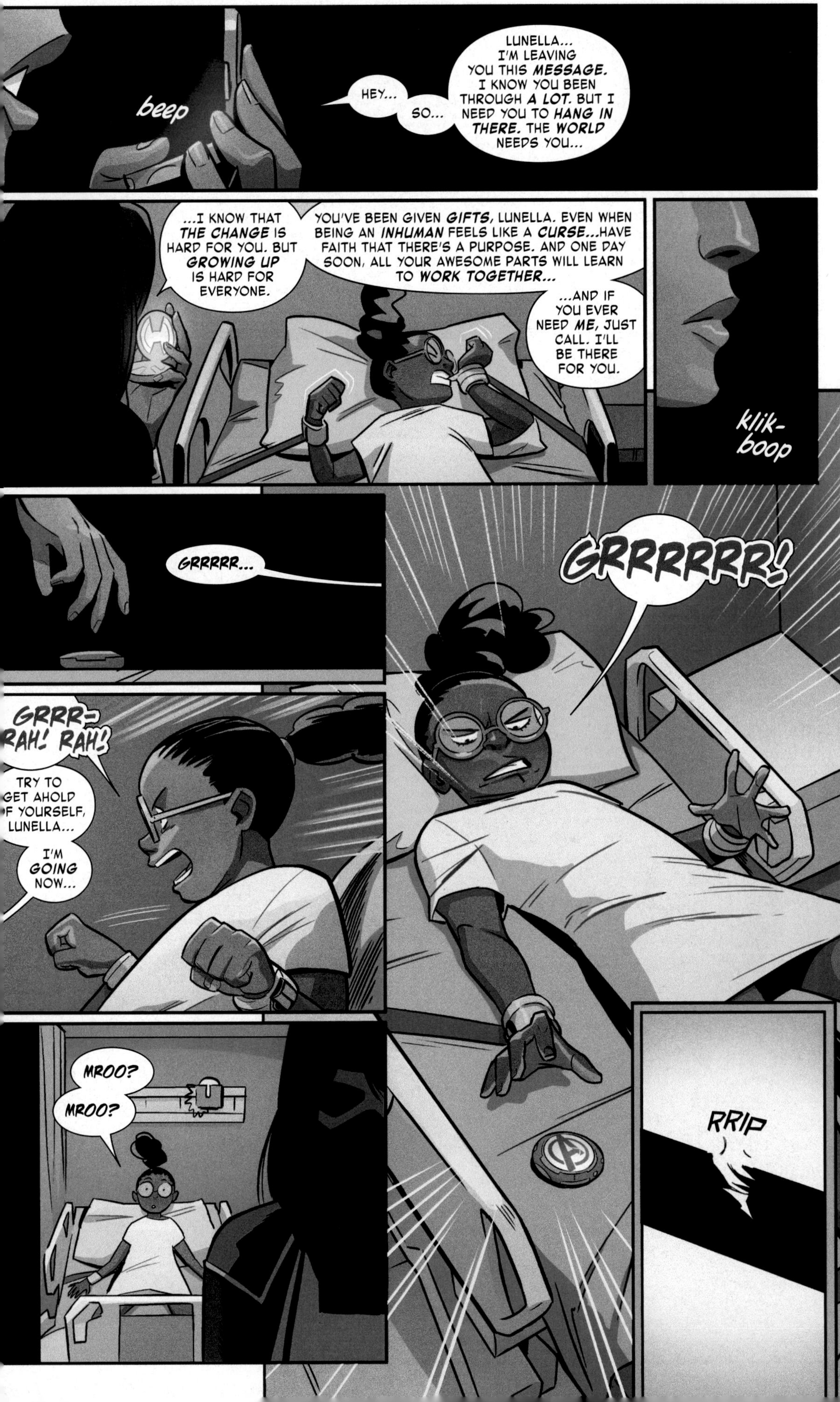
beep
HEY...
SO...
LUNELLA... I'M LEAVING YOU THIS MESSAGE. I KNOW YOU BEEN THROUGH A LOT. BUT I NEED YOU TO HANG IN THERE. THE WORLD NEEDS YOU...
...I KNOW THAT THE CHANGE IS HARD FOR YOU. BUT GROWING UP IS HARD FOR EVERYONE.
YOU'VE BEEN GIVEN GIFTS, LUNELLA. EVEN WHEN BEING AN INHUMAN FEELS LIKE A CURSE...HAVE FAITH THAT THERE'S A PURPOSE. AND ONE DAY SOON, ALL YOUR AWESOME PARTS WILL LEARN TO WORK TOGETHER...
...AND IF YOU EVER NEED ME, JUST CALL. I'LL BE THERE FOR YOU.
klik-boop
GRRRRR...
GRRRRRRR!
GRRR-RAH! RAH!
TRY TO GET AHOLD OF YOURSELF, LUNELLA...
I'M GOING NOW...
MROO?
MROO?
RRIP

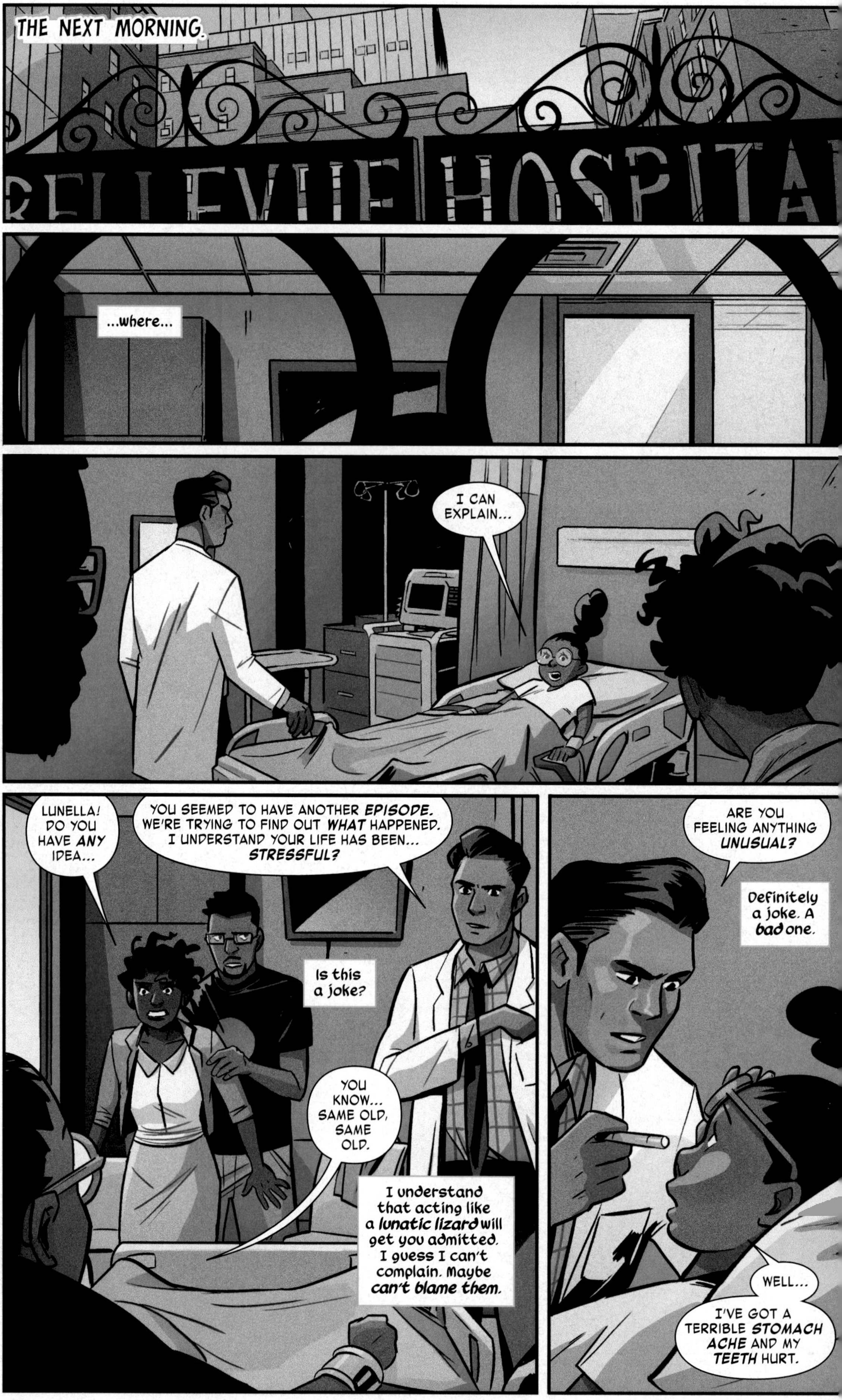
THE NEXT MORNING.
BELLEVUE HOSPITAL
...where...
I CAN EXPLAIN...
LUNELLA! DO YOU HAVE ANY IDEA...
YOU SEEMED TO HAVE ANOTHER EPISODE. WE'RE TRYING TO FIND OUT WHAT HAPPENED. I UNDERSTAND YOUR LIFE HAS BEEN... STRESSFUL?
Is this a joke?
YOU KNOW... SAME OLD, SAME OLD.
I understand that acting like a lunatic lizard will get you admitted. I guess I can't complain. Maybe can't blame them.
ARE YOU FEELING ANYTHING UNUSUAL?
Definitely a joke. A bad one.
WELL...
I'VE GOT A TERRIBLE STOMACH ACHE AND MY TEETH HURT.

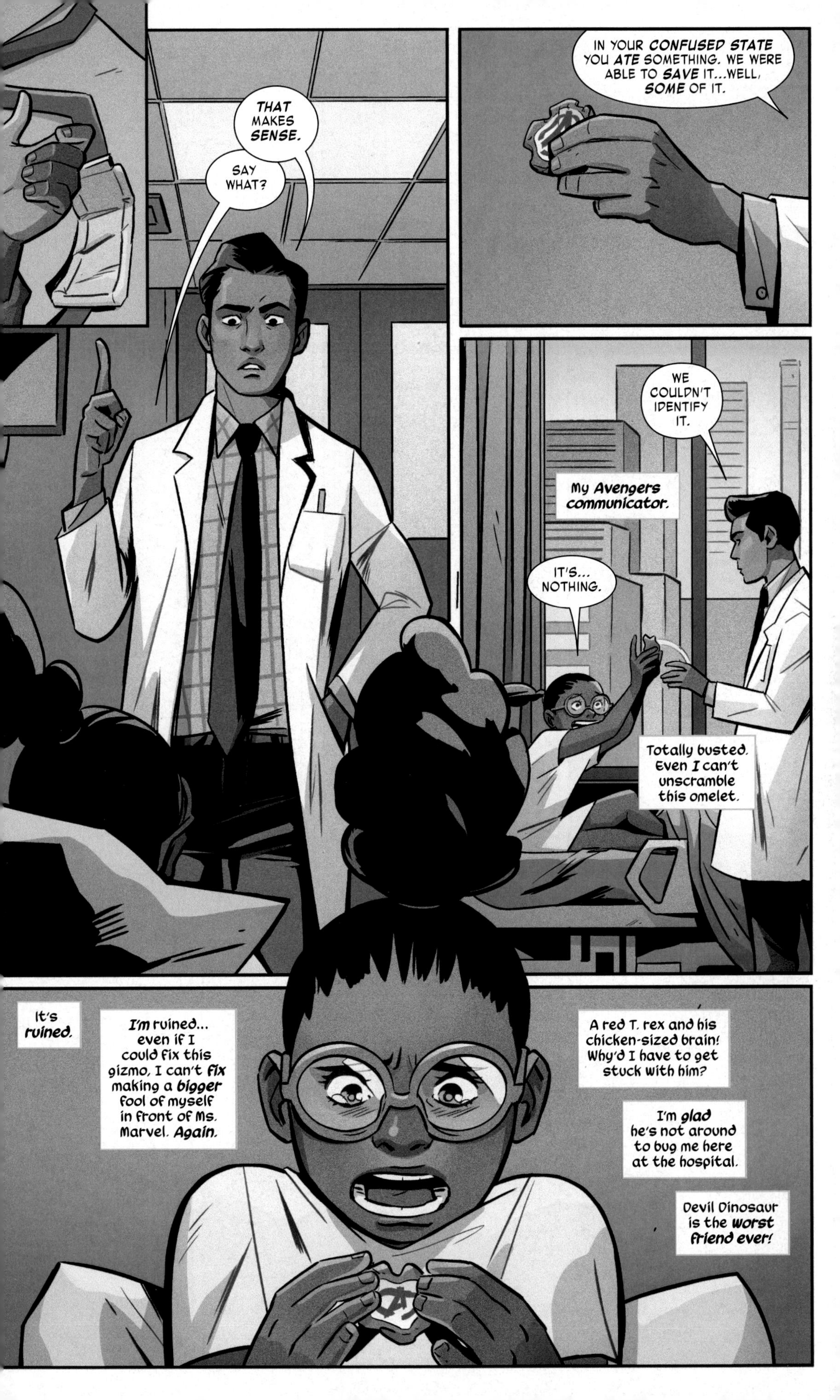

SAY WHAT?
THAT MAKES SENSE.
IN YOUR CONFUSED STATE YOU ATE SOMETHING. WE WERE ABLE TO SAVE IT...WELL, SOME OF IT.
WE COULDN'T IDENTIFY IT.
My Avengers communicator.
IT'S... NOTHING.
Totally busted. Even I can't unscramble this omelet.
It's ruined.
I'm ruined... even if I could fix this gizmo, I can't fix making a bigger fool of myself in front of Ms. Marvel. Again.
A red T. rex and his chicken-sized brain! Why'd I have to get stuck with him?
I'm glad he's not around to bug me here at the hospital.
Devil Dinosaur is the worst friend ever!

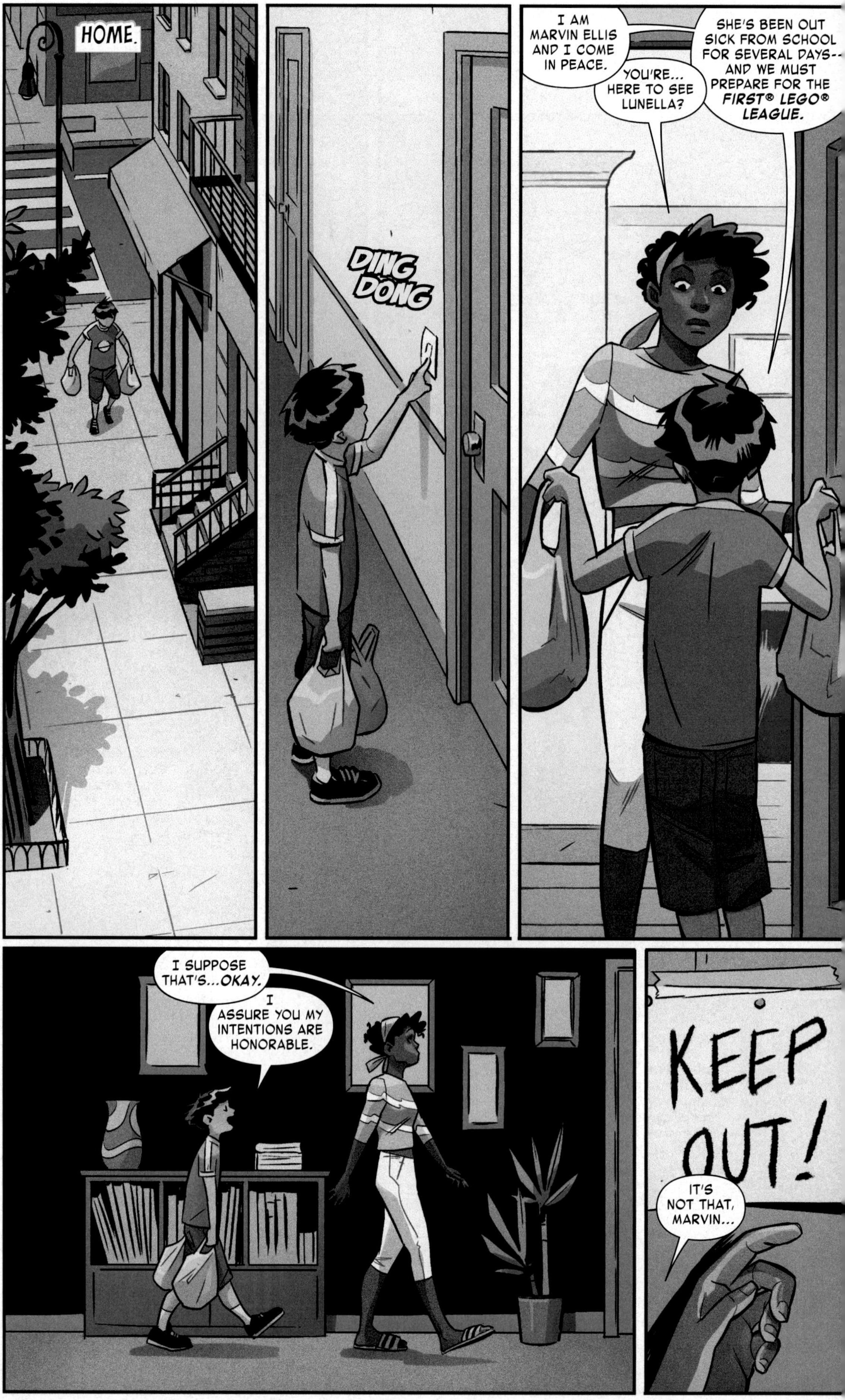
HOME.
DING DONG
I AM MARVIN ELLIS AND I COME IN PEACE.
YOU'RE... HERE TO SEE LUNELLA?
SHE'S BEEN OUT SICK FROM SCHOOL FOR SEVERAL DAYS-- AND WE MUST PREPARE FOR THE FIRST® LEGO® LEAGUE.
I SUPPOSE THAT'S...OKAY.
I ASSURE YOU MY INTENTIONS ARE HONORABLE.
KEEP OUT!
IT'S NOT THAT, MARVIN...

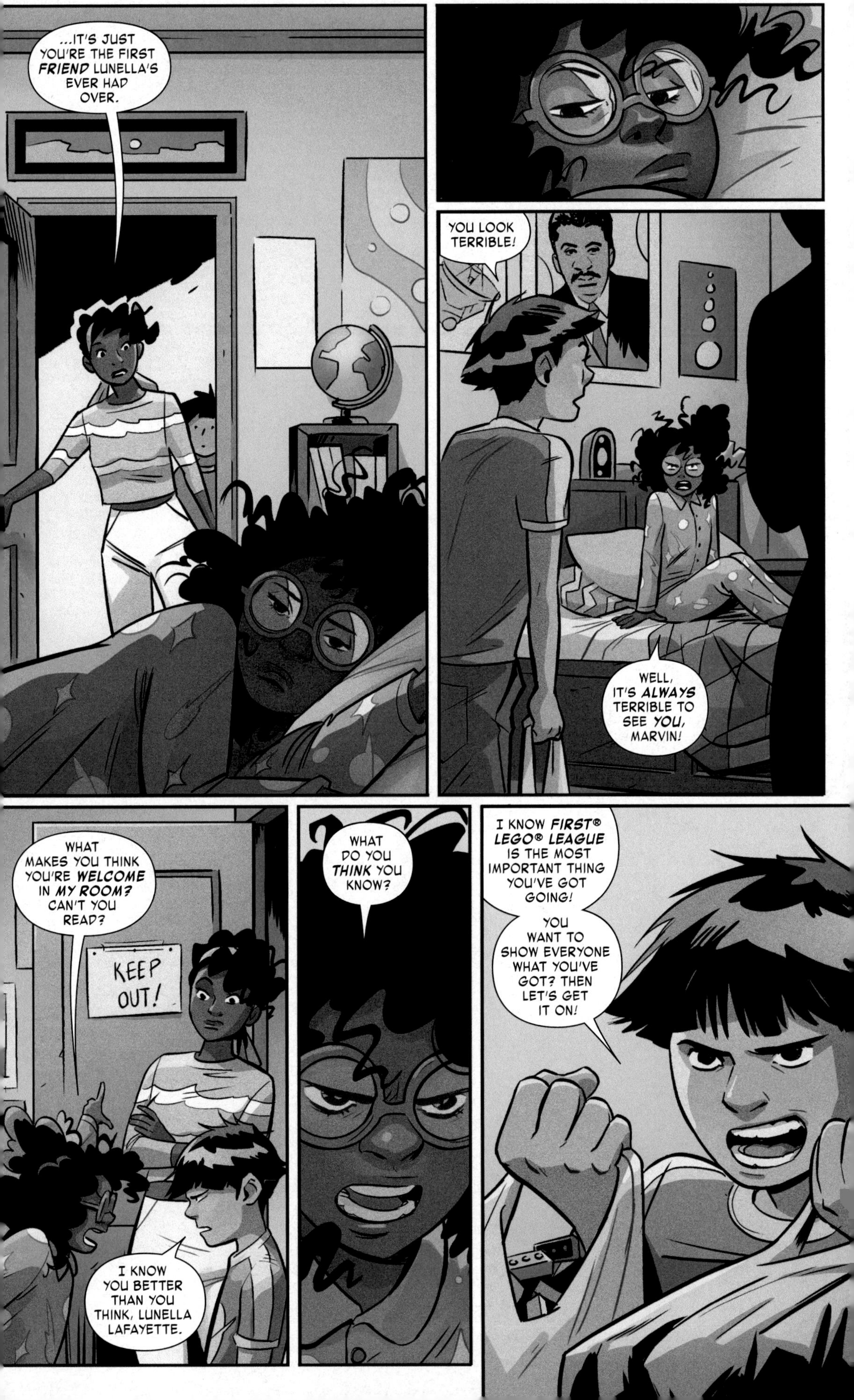
...IT'S JUST YOU'RE THE FIRST FRIEND LUNELLA'S EVER HAD OVER.
YOU LOOK TERRIBLE!
WELL, IT'S ALWAYS TERRIBLE TO SEE YOU, MARVIN!
WHAT MAKES YOU THINK YOU'RE WELCOME IN MY ROOM? CAN'T YOU READ?
KEEP OUT!
I KNOW YOU BETTER THAN YOU THINK, LUNELLA LAFAYETTE.
WHAT DO YOU THINK YOU KNOW?
I KNOW FIRST® LEGO® LEAGUE IS THE MOST IMPORTANT THING YOU'VE GOT GOING!
YOU WANT TO SHOW EVERYONE WHAT YOU'VE GOT? THEN LET'S GET IT ON!

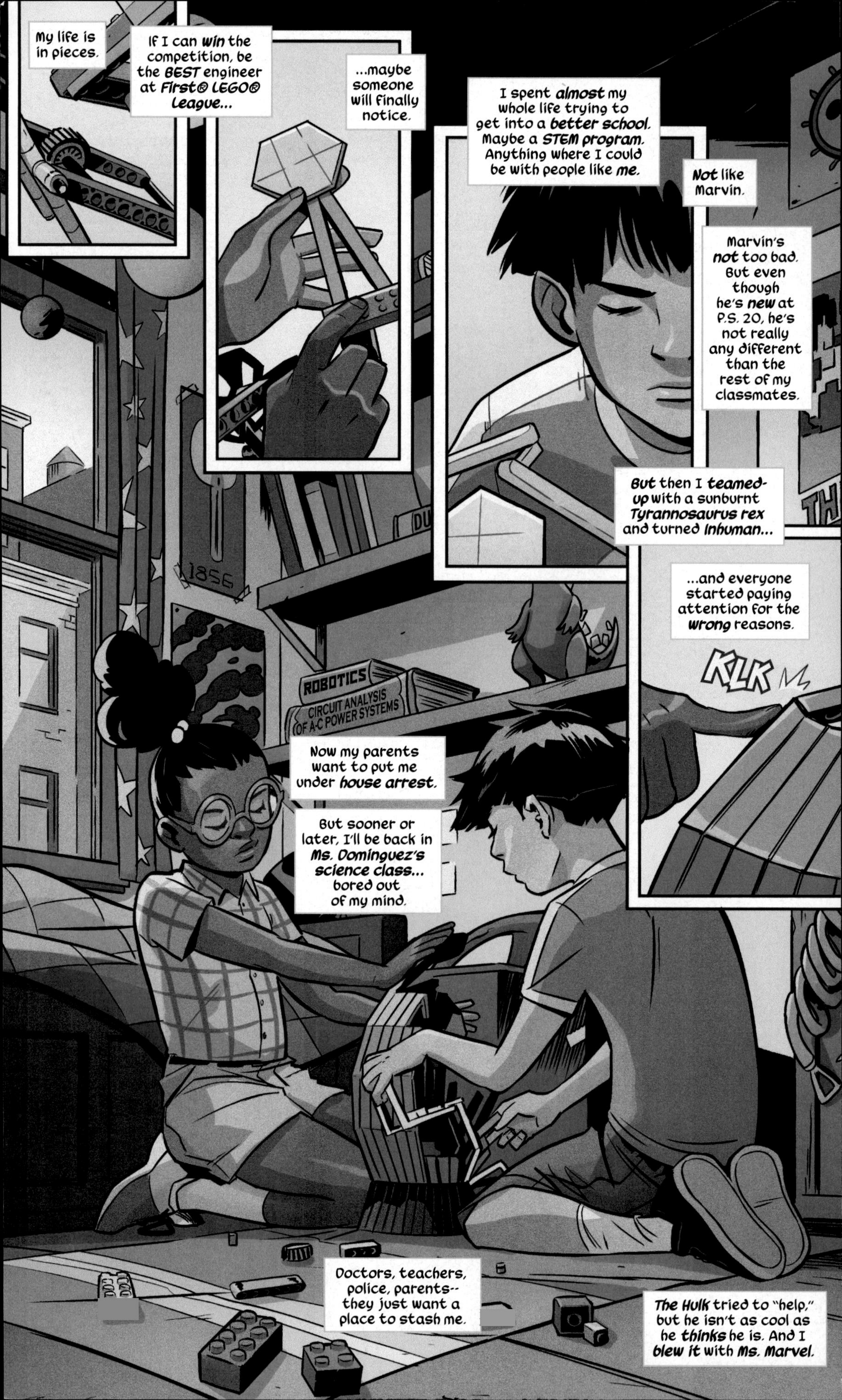
My life is in pieces.
If I can win the competition, be the BEST engineer at First® LEGO® League...
...maybe someone will finally notice.
I spent almost my whole life trying to get into a better school. Maybe a STEM program. Anything where I could be with people like me.
Not like Marvin.
Marvin's not too bad. But even though he's new at P.S. 20, he's not really any different than the rest of my classmates.
But then I teamed-up with a sunburnt Tyrannosaurus rex and turned Inhuman...
...and everyone started paying attention for the wrong reasons.
KLK
ROBOTICS
CIRCUIT ANALYSIS OF A-C POWER SYSTEMS
Now my parents want to put me under house arrest.
But sooner or later, I'll be back in Ms. Dominguez's science class... bored out of my mind.
Doctors, teachers, police, parents-- they just want a place to stash me.
The Hulk tried to "help," but he isn't as cool as he thinks he is. And I blew it with Ms. Marvel.

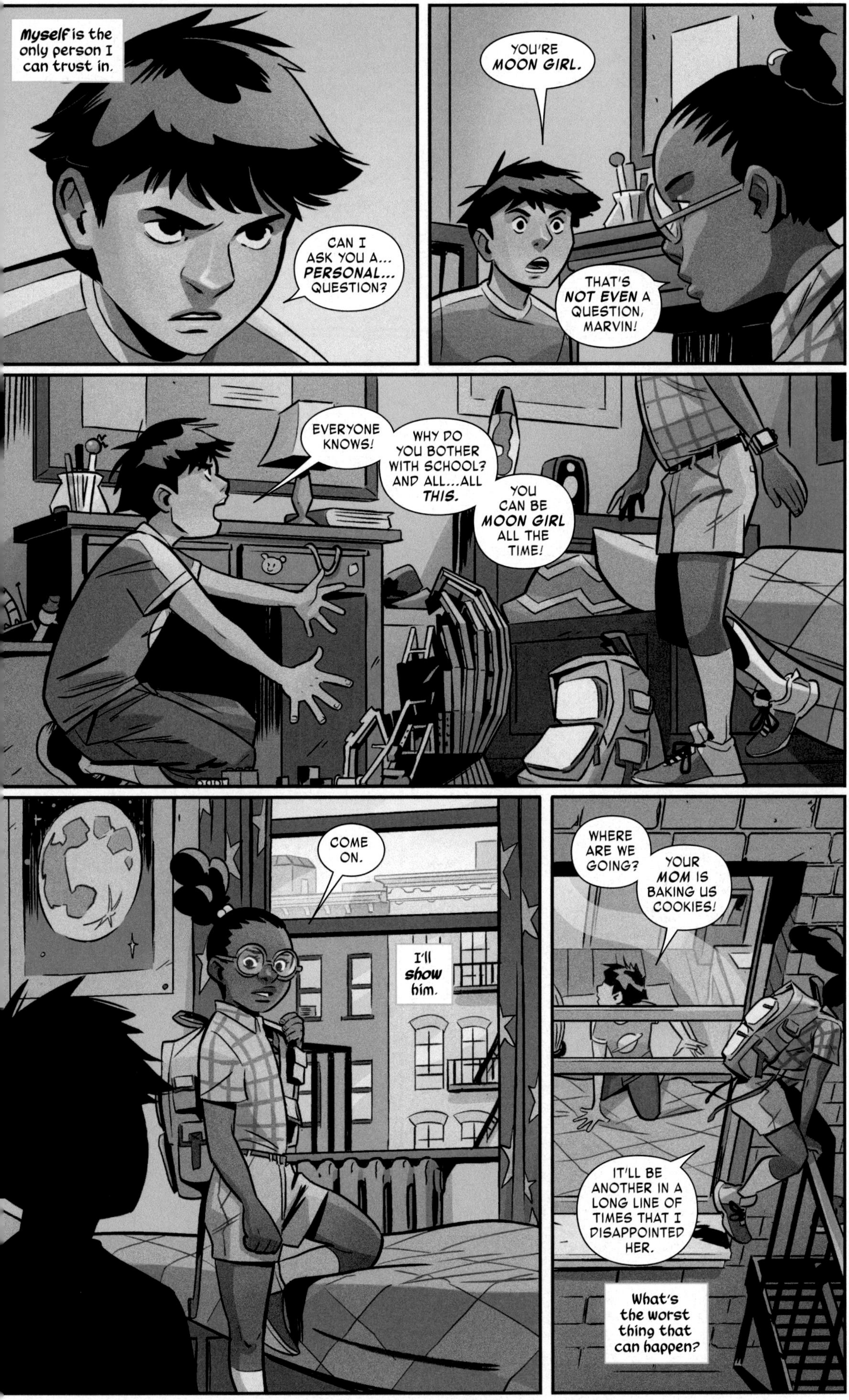
Myself is the only person I can trust in.
CAN I ASK YOU A... PERSONAL... QUESTION?
YOU'RE MOON GIRL.
THAT'S NOT EVEN A QUESTION, MARVIN!
EVERYONE KNOWS!
WHY DO YOU BOTHER WITH SCHOOL? AND ALL...ALL THIS.
YOU CAN BE MOON GIRL ALL THE TIME!
COME ON.
I'll show him.
WHERE ARE WE GOING?
YOUR MOM IS BAKING US COOKIES!
IT'LL BE ANOTHER IN A LONG LINE OF TIMES THAT I DISAPPOINTED HER.
What's the worst thing that can happen?

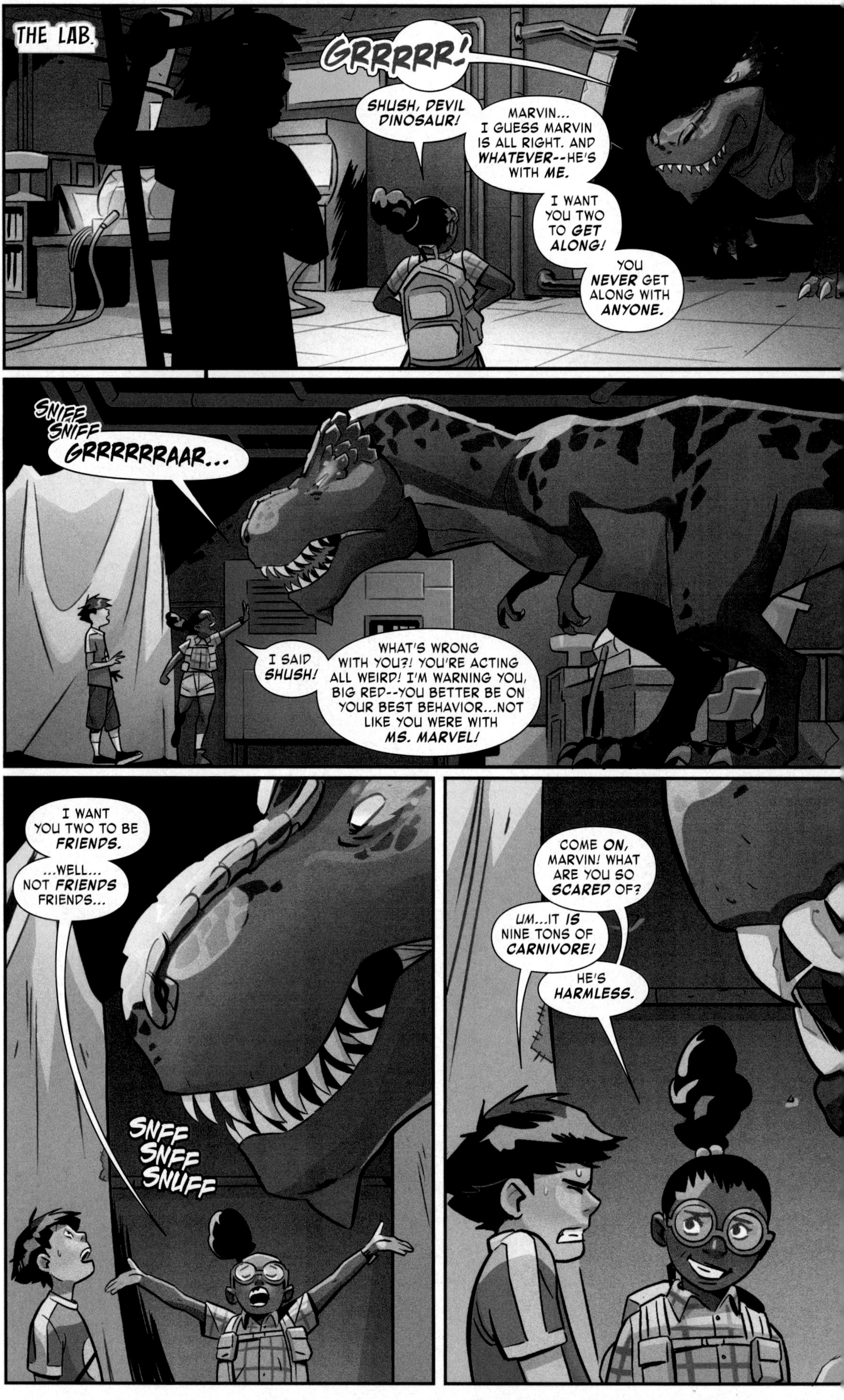
THE LAB.
GRRRRR!
SHUSH, DEVIL DINOSAUR!
MARVIN... I GUESS MARVIN IS ALL RIGHT. AND WHATEVER--HE'S WITH ME.
I WANT YOU TWO TO GET ALONG!
YOU NEVER GET ALONG WITH ANYONE.
SNIFF SNIFF
GRRRRRRAAR...
I SAID SHUSH!
WHAT'S WRONG WITH YOU?! YOU'RE ACTING ALL WEIRD! I'M WARNING YOU, BIG RED--YOU BETTER BE ON YOUR BEST BEHAVIOR...NOT LIKE YOU WERE WITH MS. MARVEL!
I WANT YOU TWO TO BE FRIENDS.
...WELL... NOT FRIENDS FRIENDS...
SNFF SNFF SNUFF
COME ON, MARVIN! WHAT ARE YOU SO SCARED OF?
UM...IT IS NINE TONS OF CARNIVORE!
HE'S HARMLESS.

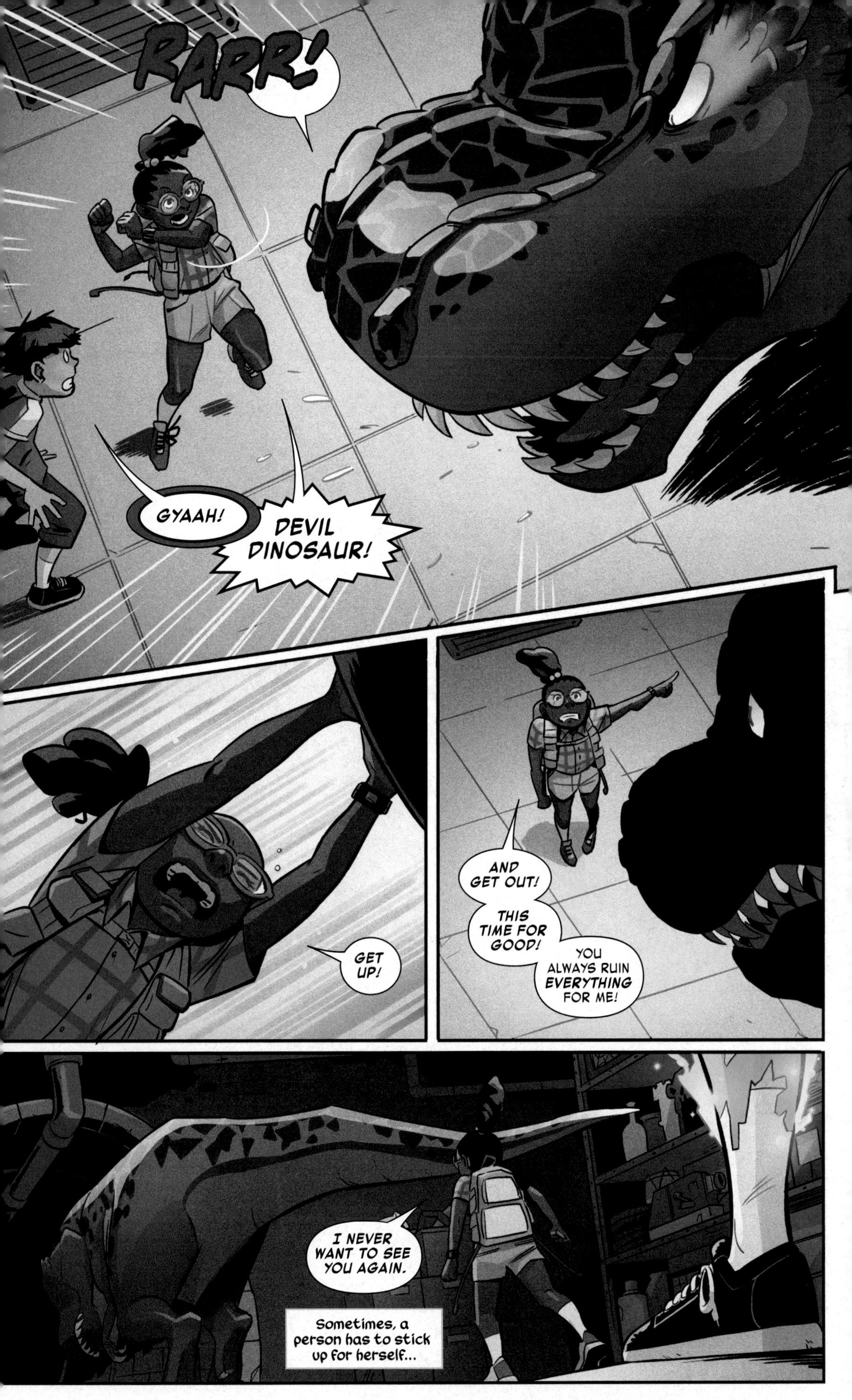
RARR!
GYAAH!
DEVIL DINOSAUR!
GET UP!
AND GET OUT!
THIS TIME FOR GOOD!
YOU ALWAYS RUIN EVERYTHING FOR ME!
I NEVER WANT TO SEE YOU AGAIN.
Sometimes, a person has to stick up for herself...

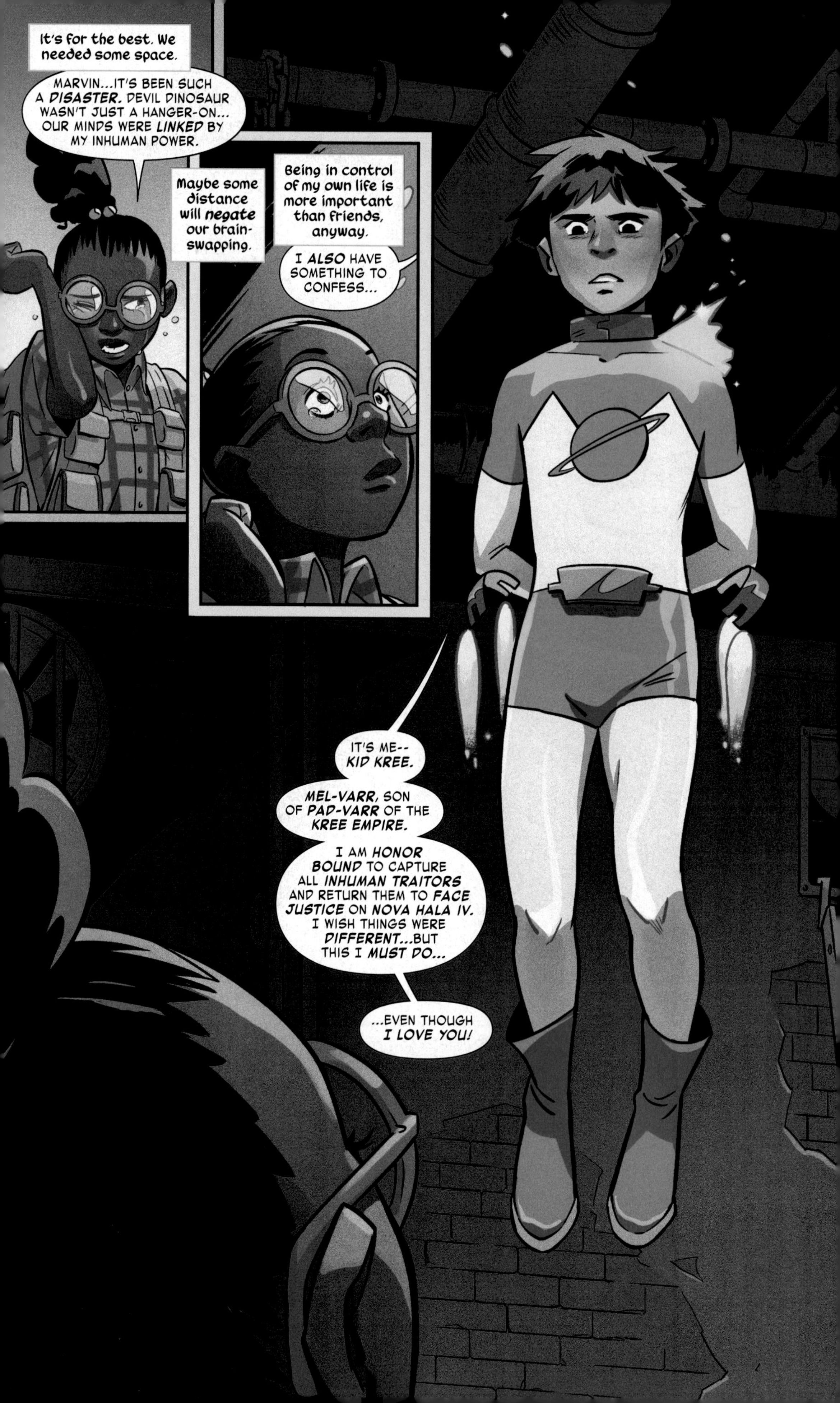

It's for the best. We needed some space.
MARVIN...IT'S BEEN SUCH A DISASTER. DEVIL DINOSAUR WASN'T JUST A HANGER-ON... OUR MINDS WERE LINKED BY MY INHUMAN POWER.
Maybe some distance will negate our brain-swapping.
Being in control of my own life is more important than friends, anyway.
I ALSO HAVE SOMETHING TO CONFESS...
IT'S ME--KID KREE.
MEL-VARR, SON OF PAD-VARR OF THE KREE EMPIRE.
I AM HONOR BOUND TO CAPTURE ALL INHUMAN TRAITORS AND RETURN THEM TO FACE JUSTICE ON NOVA HALA IV. I WISH THINGS WERE DIFFERENT...BUT THIS I MUST DO...
...EVEN THOUGH I LOVE YOU!

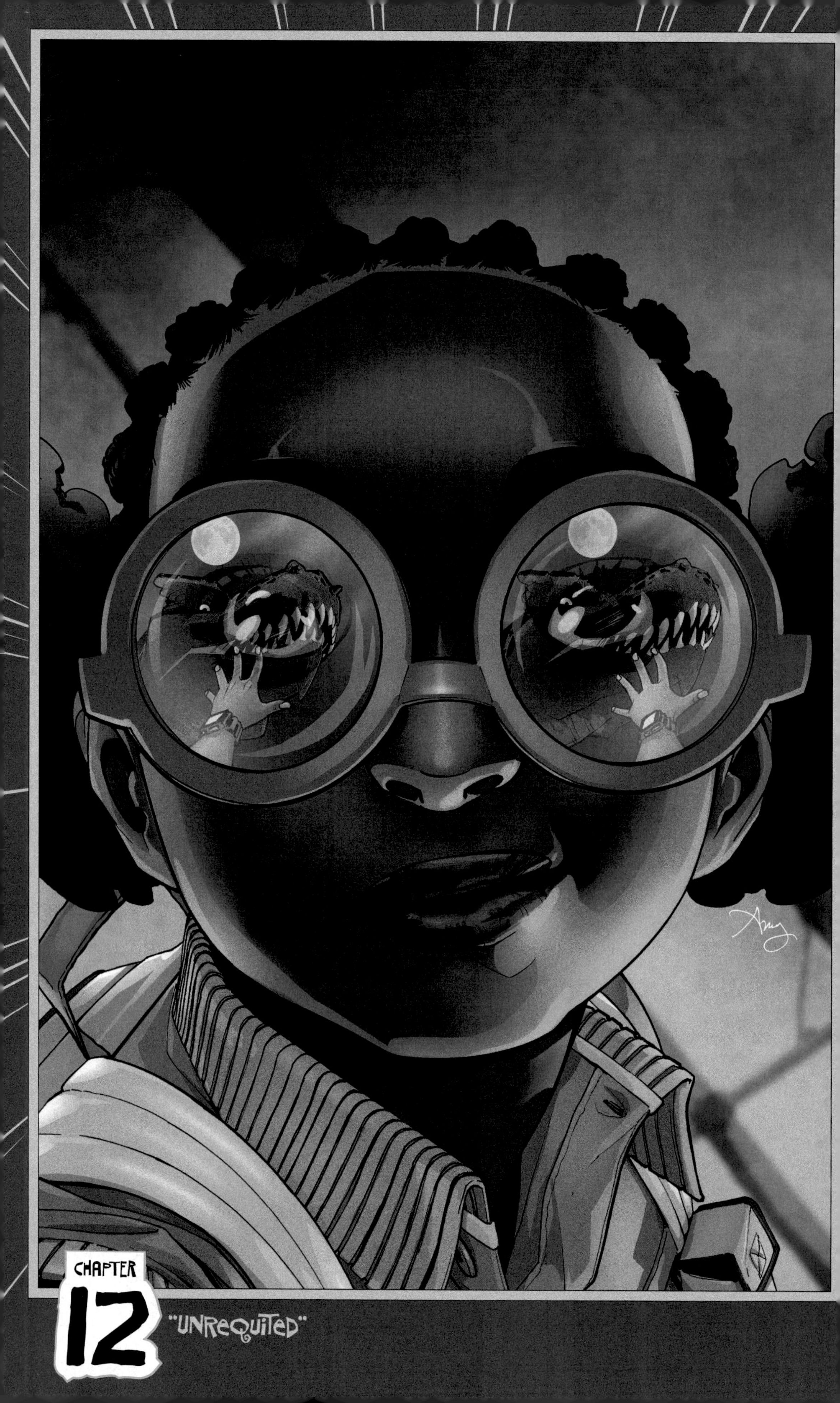

CHAPTER
12
"UNREQUITED"

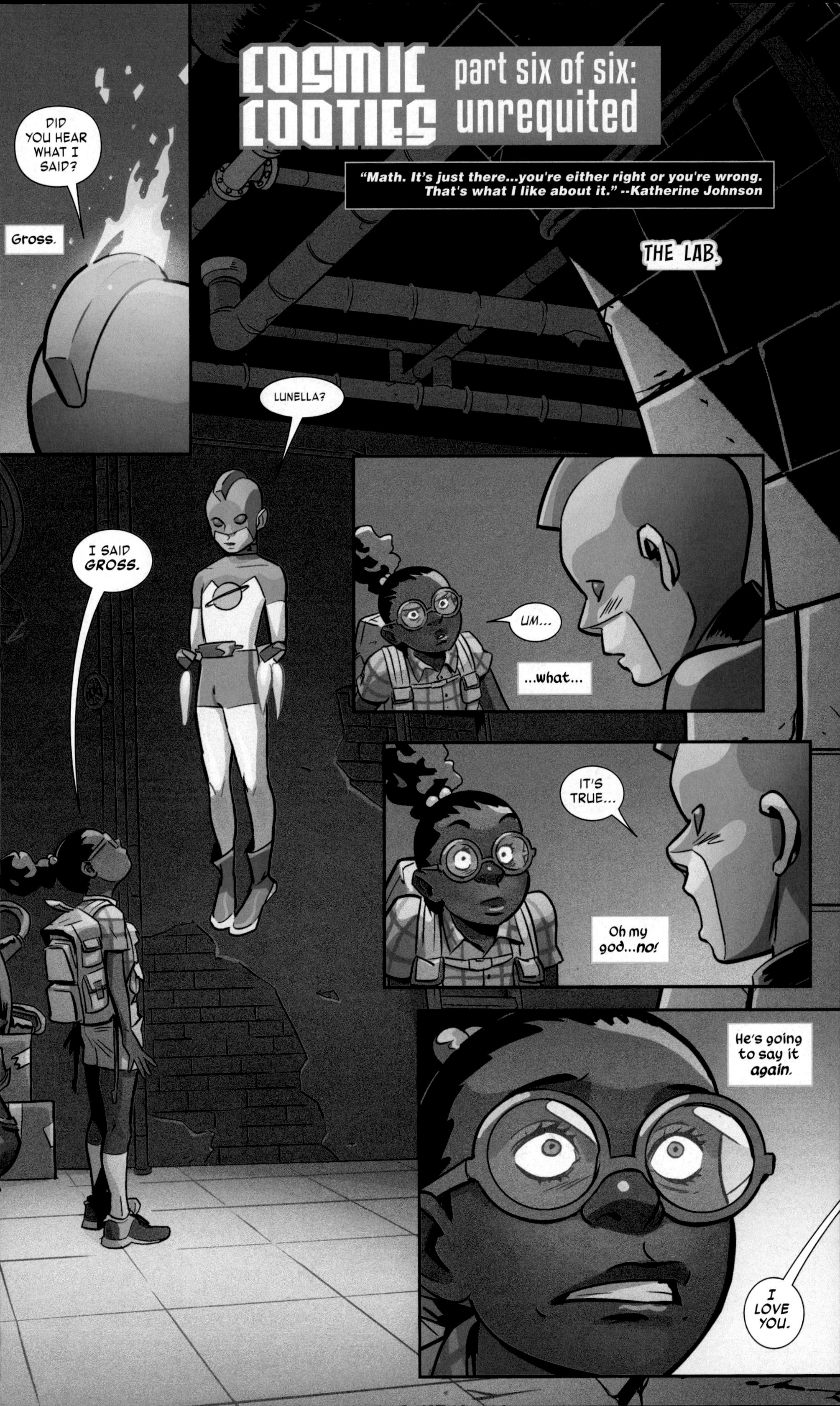
COSMIC COOTIES
part six of six: unrequited
"Math. It's just there...you're either right or you're wrong. That's what I like about it." --Katherine Johnson
DID YOU HEAR WHAT I SAID?
Gross.
THE LAB.
LUNELLA?
I SAID GROSS.
UM...
...what...
IT'S TRUE...
Oh my god...no!
He's going to say it again.
I LOVE YOU.

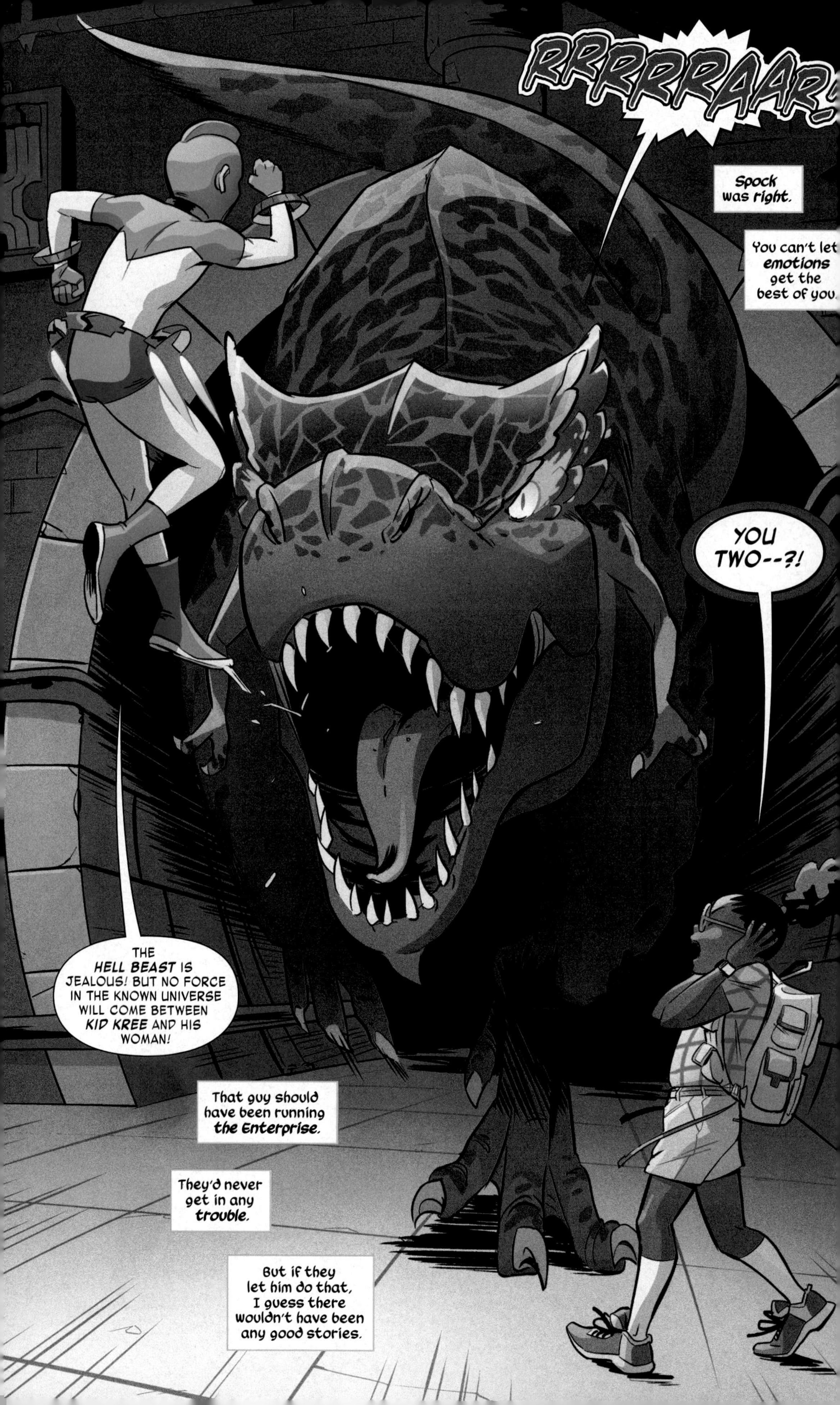
RRRRRAAR!
Spock was right.
You can't let emotions get the best of you.
YOU TWO--?!
THE HELL BEAST IS JEALOUS! BUT NO FORCE IN THE KNOWN UNIVERSE WILL COME BETWEEN KID KREE AND HIS WOMAN!
That guy should have been running the Enterprise.
They'd never get in any trouble.
But if they let him do that, I guess there wouldn't have been any good stories.

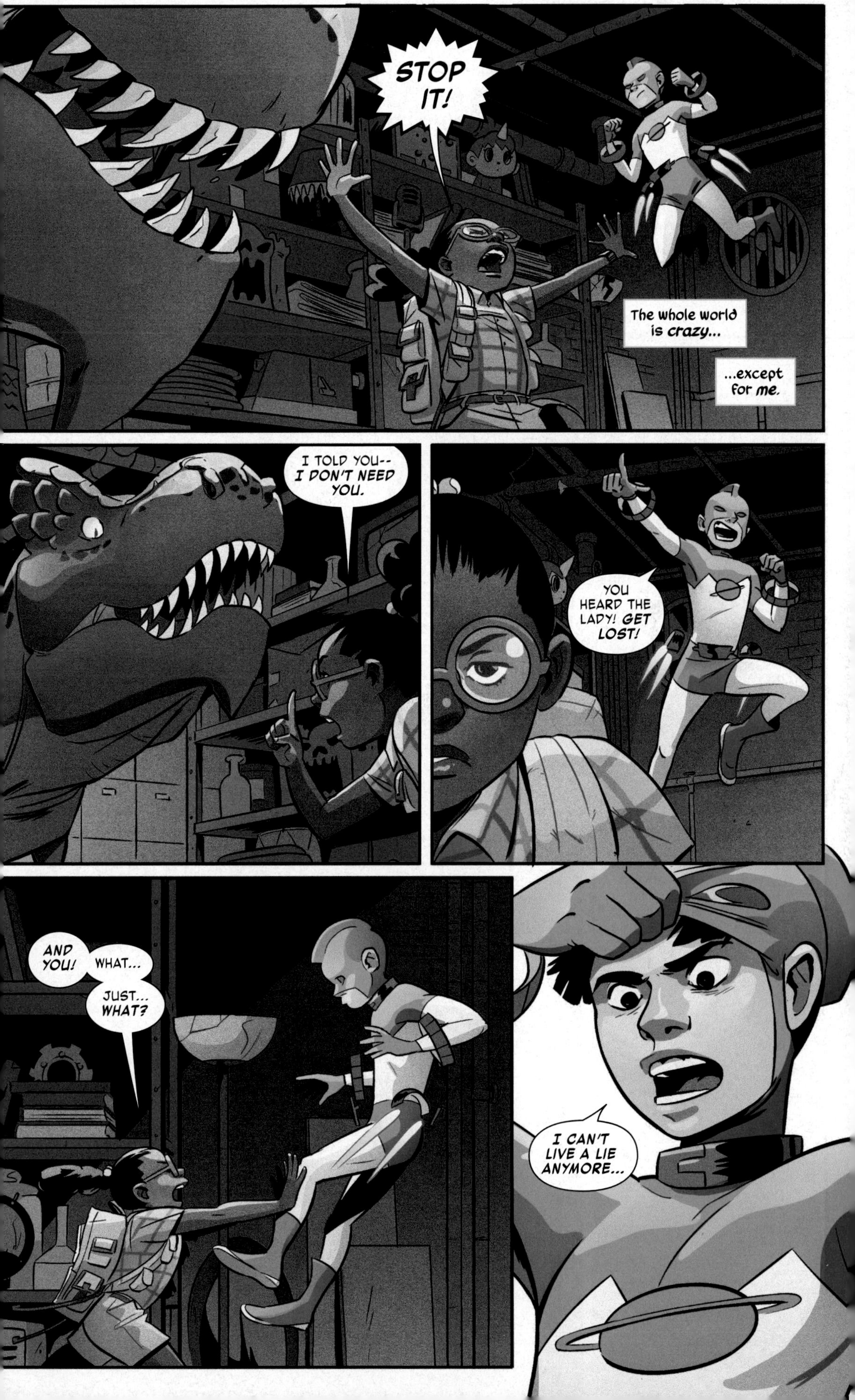

STOP IT!
The whole world is crazy...
...except for me.
I TOLD YOU-- I DON'T NEED YOU.
YOU HEARD THE LADY! GET LOST!
AND YOU!
WHAT...
JUST... WHAT?
I CAN'T LIVE A LIE ANYMORE...

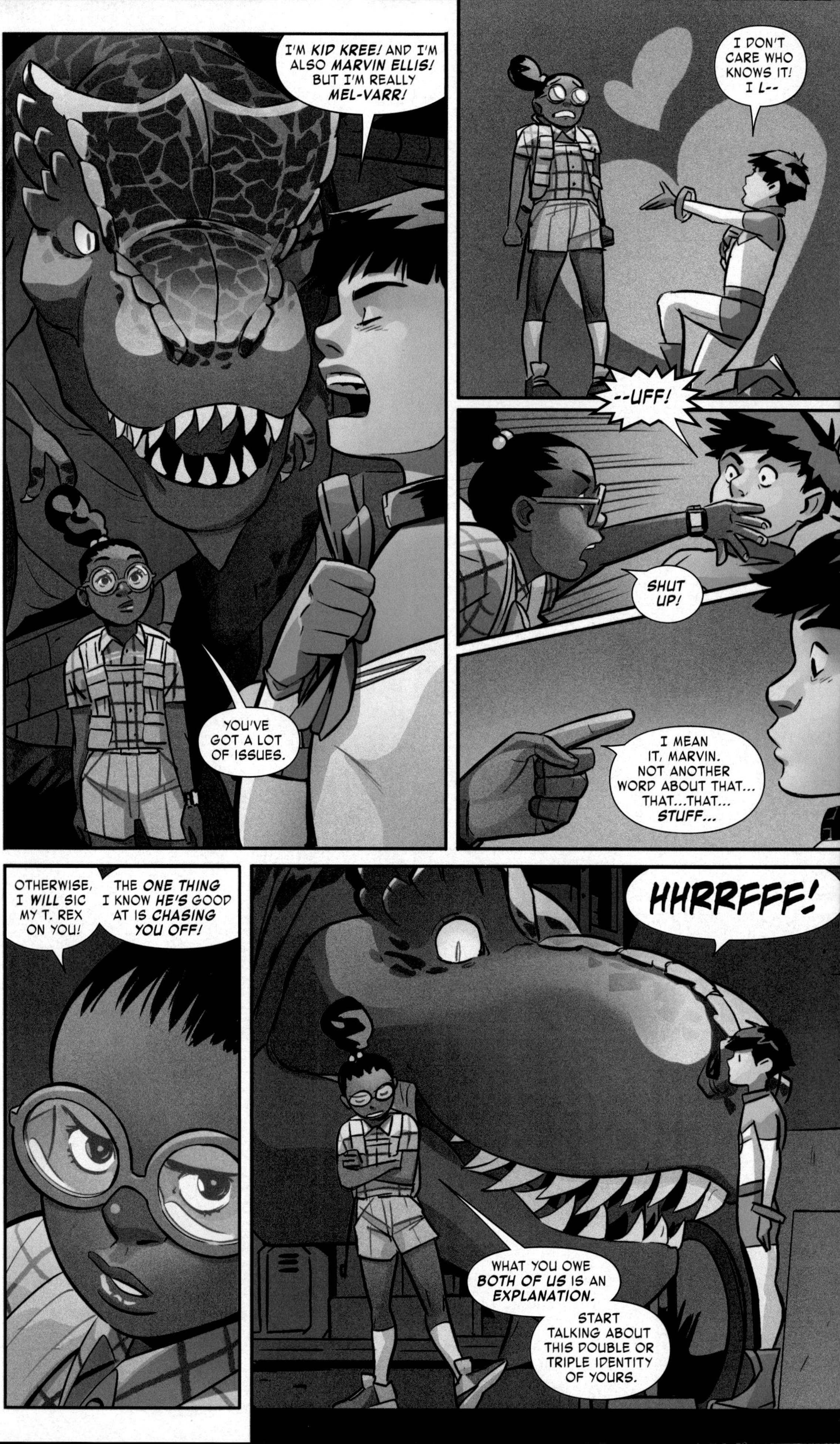

I'M KID KREE! AND I'M ALSO MARVIN ELLIS! BUT I'M REALLY MEL-VARR!
YOU'VE GOT A LOT OF ISSUES.
I DON'T CARE WHO KNOWS IT! I L--
--UFF!
SHUT UP!
I MEAN IT, MARVIN. NOT ANOTHER WORD ABOUT THAT... THAT...THAT... STUFF...
OTHERWISE, I WILL SIC MY T. REX ON YOU!
THE ONE THING I KNOW HE'S GOOD AT IS CHASING YOU OFF!
HHRRFFF!
WHAT YOU OWE BOTH OF US IS AN EXPLANATION.
START TALKING ABOUT THIS DOUBLE OR TRIPLE IDENTITY OF YOURS.

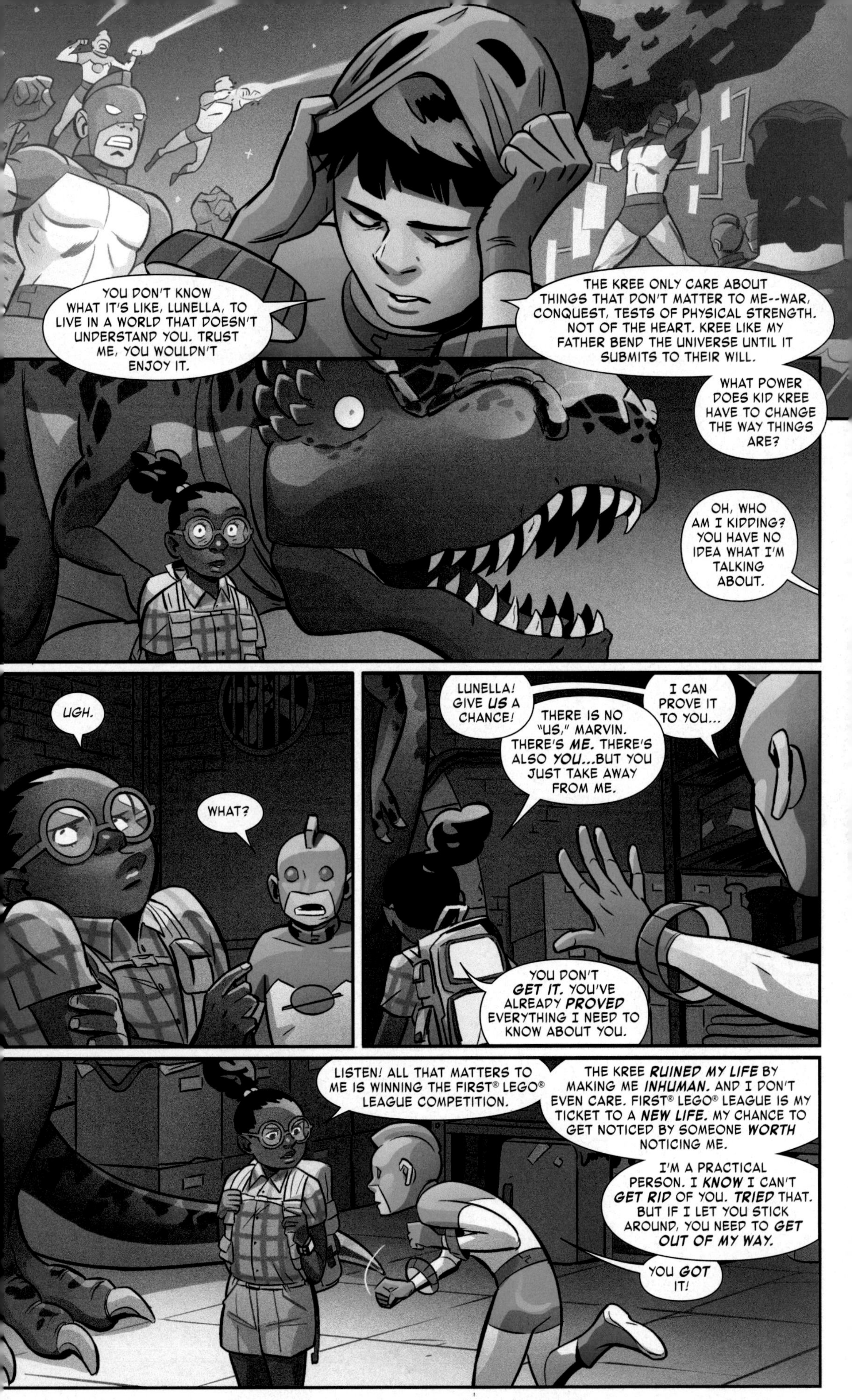

YOU DON'T KNOW WHAT IT'S LIKE, LUNELLA, TO LIVE IN A WORLD THAT DOESN'T UNDERSTAND YOU. TRUST ME, YOU WOULDN'T ENJOY IT.
THE KREE ONLY CARE ABOUT THINGS THAT DON'T MATTER TO ME--WAR, CONQUEST, TESTS OF PHYSICAL STRENGTH. NOT OF THE HEART. KREE LIKE MY FATHER BEND THE UNIVERSE UNTIL IT SUBMITS TO THEIR WILL.
WHAT POWER DOES KID KREE HAVE TO CHANGE THE WAY THINGS ARE?
OH, WHO AM I KIDDING? YOU HAVE NO IDEA WHAT I'M TALKING ABOUT.
UGH.
WHAT?
LUNELLA! GIVE US A CHANCE!
I CAN PROVE IT TO YOU...
THERE IS NO "US," MARVIN. THERE'S ME. THERE'S ALSO YOU...BUT YOU JUST TAKE AWAY FROM ME.
YOU DON'T GET IT. YOU'VE ALREADY PROVED EVERYTHING I NEED TO KNOW ABOUT YOU.
LISTEN! ALL THAT MATTERS TO ME IS WINNING THE FIRST® LEGO® LEAGUE COMPETITION.
THE KREE RUINED MY LIFE BY MAKING ME INHUMAN. AND I DON'T EVEN CARE. FIRST® LEGO® LEAGUE IS MY TICKET TO A NEW LIFE. MY CHANCE TO GET NOTICED BY SOMEONE WORTH NOTICING ME.
I'M A PRACTICAL PERSON. I KNOW I CAN'T GET RID OF YOU. TRIED THAT. BUT IF I LET YOU STICK AROUND, YOU NEED TO GET OUT OF MY WAY.
YOU GOT IT!

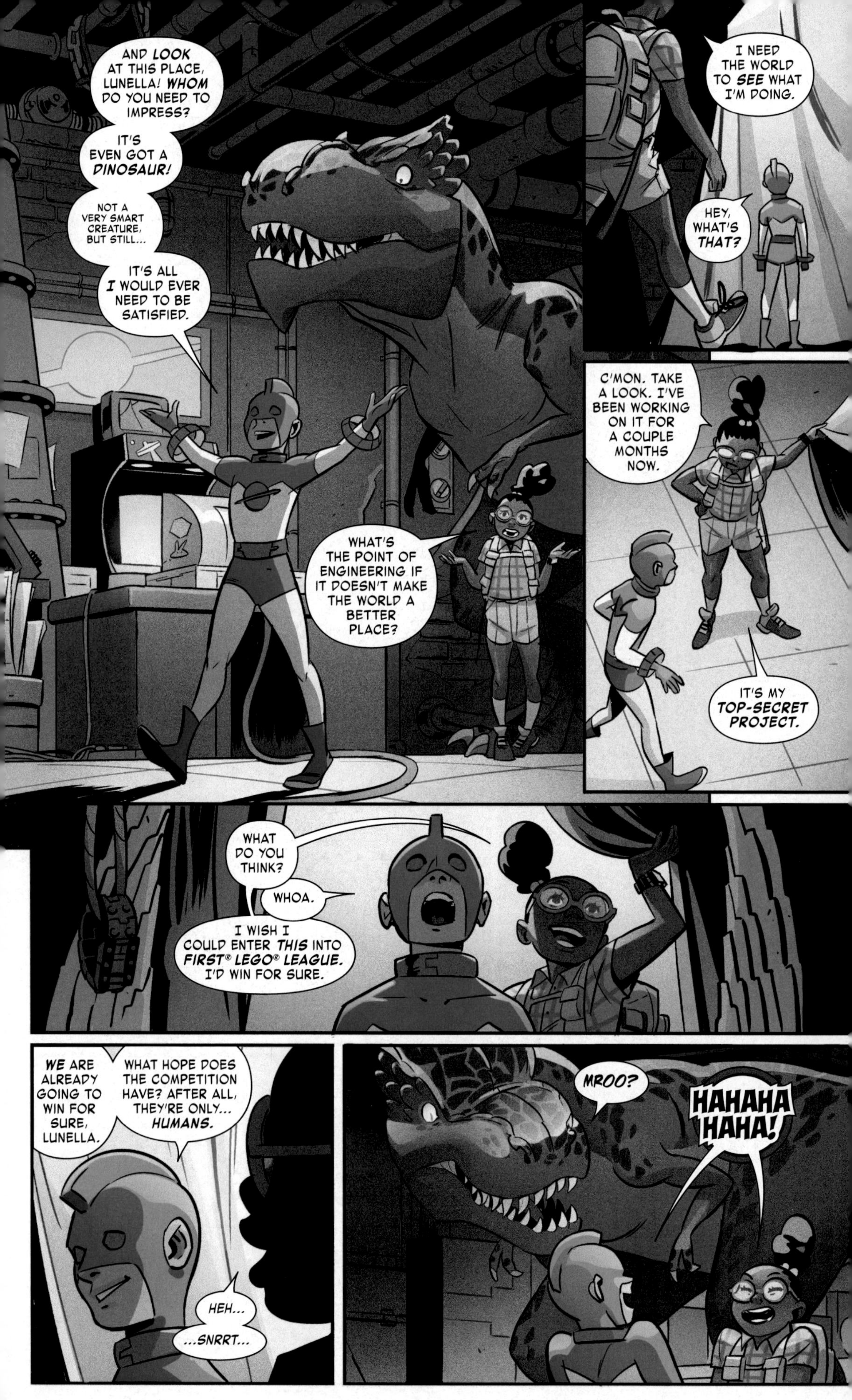

AND LOOK AT THIS PLACE, LUNELLA! WHOM DO YOU NEED TO IMPRESS?
IT'S EVEN GOT A DINOSAUR!
NOT A VERY SMART CREATURE, BUT STILL...
IT'S ALL I WOULD EVER NEED TO BE SATISFIED.
WHAT'S THE POINT OF ENGINEERING IF IT DOESN'T MAKE THE WORLD A BETTER PLACE?
I NEED THE WORLD TO SEE WHAT I'M DOING.
HEY, WHAT'S THAT?
C'MON. TAKE A LOOK. I'VE BEEN WORKING ON IT FOR A COUPLE MONTHS NOW.
IT'S MY TOP-SECRET PROJECT.
WHAT DO YOU THINK?
WHOA.
I WISH I COULD ENTER THIS INTO FIRST® LEGO® LEAGUE. I'D WIN FOR SURE.
WE ARE ALREADY GOING TO WIN FOR SURE, LUNELLA.
WHAT HOPE DOES THE COMPETITION HAVE? AFTER ALL, THEY'RE ONLY... HUMANS.
HEH...
...SNRRT...
MROO?
HAHAHA HAHA!

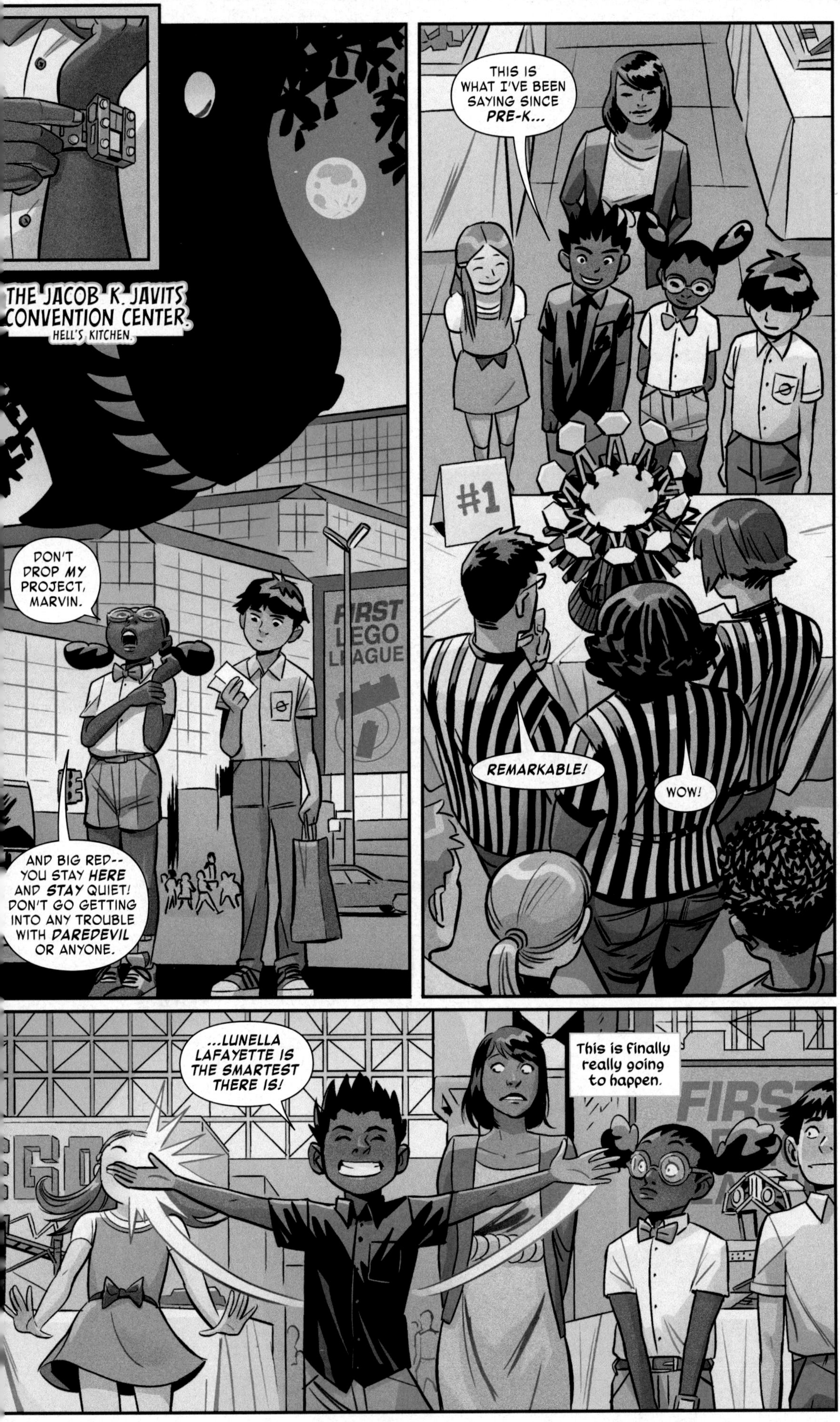
THE JACOB K. JAVITS CONVENTION CENTER.
HELL'S KITCHEN.
DON'T DROP MY PROJECT, MARVIN.
FIRST LEGO LEAGUE
AND BIG RED-- YOU STAY HERE AND STAY QUIET! DON'T GO GETTING INTO ANY TROUBLE WITH DAREDEVIL OR ANYONE.
THIS IS WHAT I'VE BEEN SAYING SINCE PRE-K...
#1
REMARKABLE!
WOW!
...LUNELLA LAFAYETTE IS THE SMARTEST THERE IS!
This is finally really going to happen.

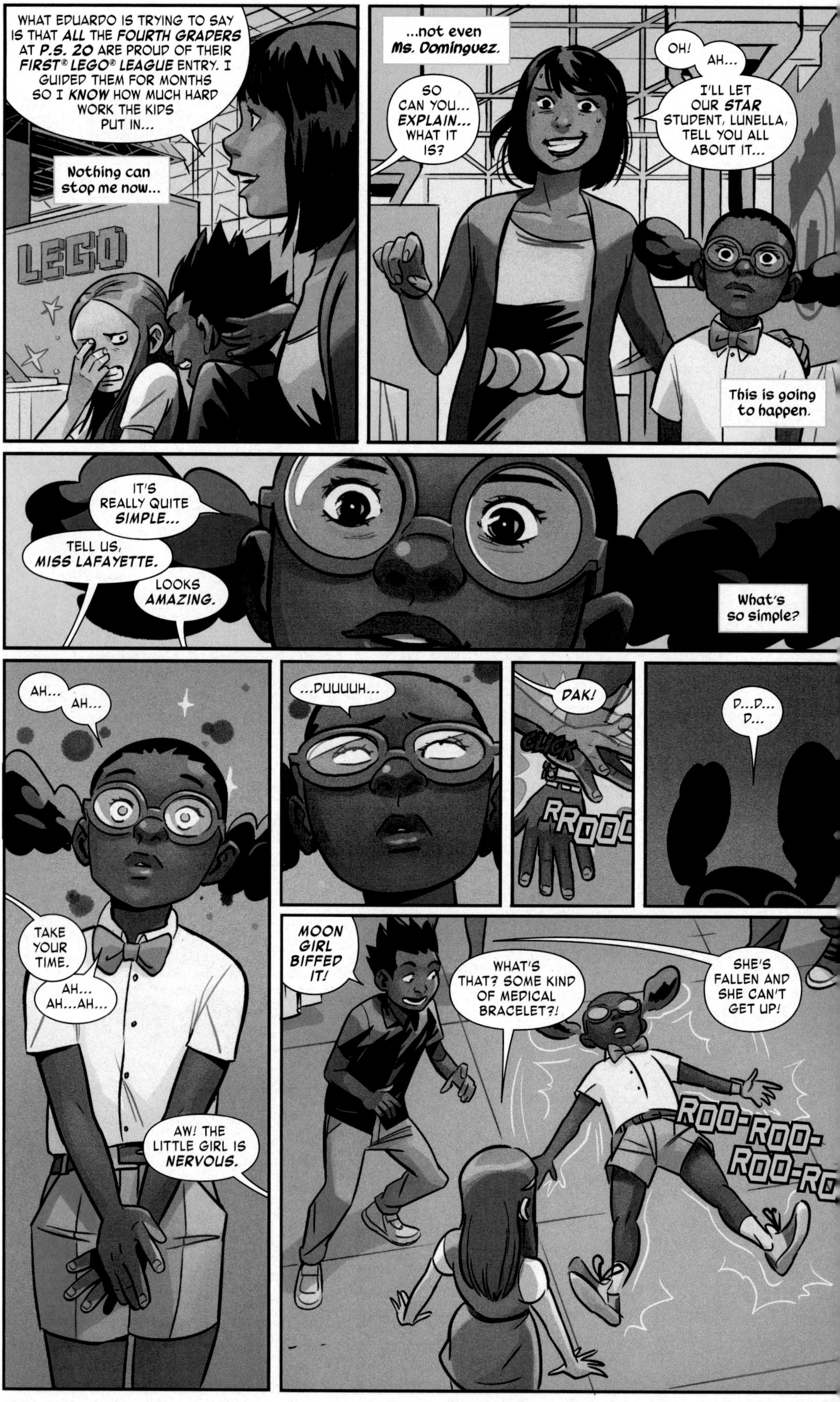
WHAT EDUARDO IS TRYING TO SAY IS THAT ALL THE FOURTH GRADERS AT P.S. 20 ARE PROUD OF THEIR FIRST® LEGO® LEAGUE ENTRY. I GUIDED THEM FOR MONTHS SO I KNOW HOW MUCH HARD WORK THE KIDS PUT IN...
Nothing can stop me now...
LEGO
...not even Ms. Dominguez.
SO CAN YOU... EXPLAIN... WHAT IT IS?
OH!
AH...
I'LL LET OUR STAR STUDENT, LUNELLA, TELL YOU ALL ABOUT IT...
This is going to happen.
IT'S REALLY QUITE SIMPLE...
TELL US, MISS LAFAYETTE.
LOOKS AMAZING.
What's so simple?
AH...
AH...
TAKE YOUR TIME.
AH... AH...AH...
AW! THE LITTLE GIRL IS NERVOUS.
...DUUUUH...
DAK!
CLICK
RROOO
D...D... D...
MOON GIRL BIFFED IT!
WHAT'S THAT? SOME KIND OF MEDICAL BRACELET?!
SHE'S FALLEN AND SHE CAN'T GET UP!
ROO-ROO-ROO-RO

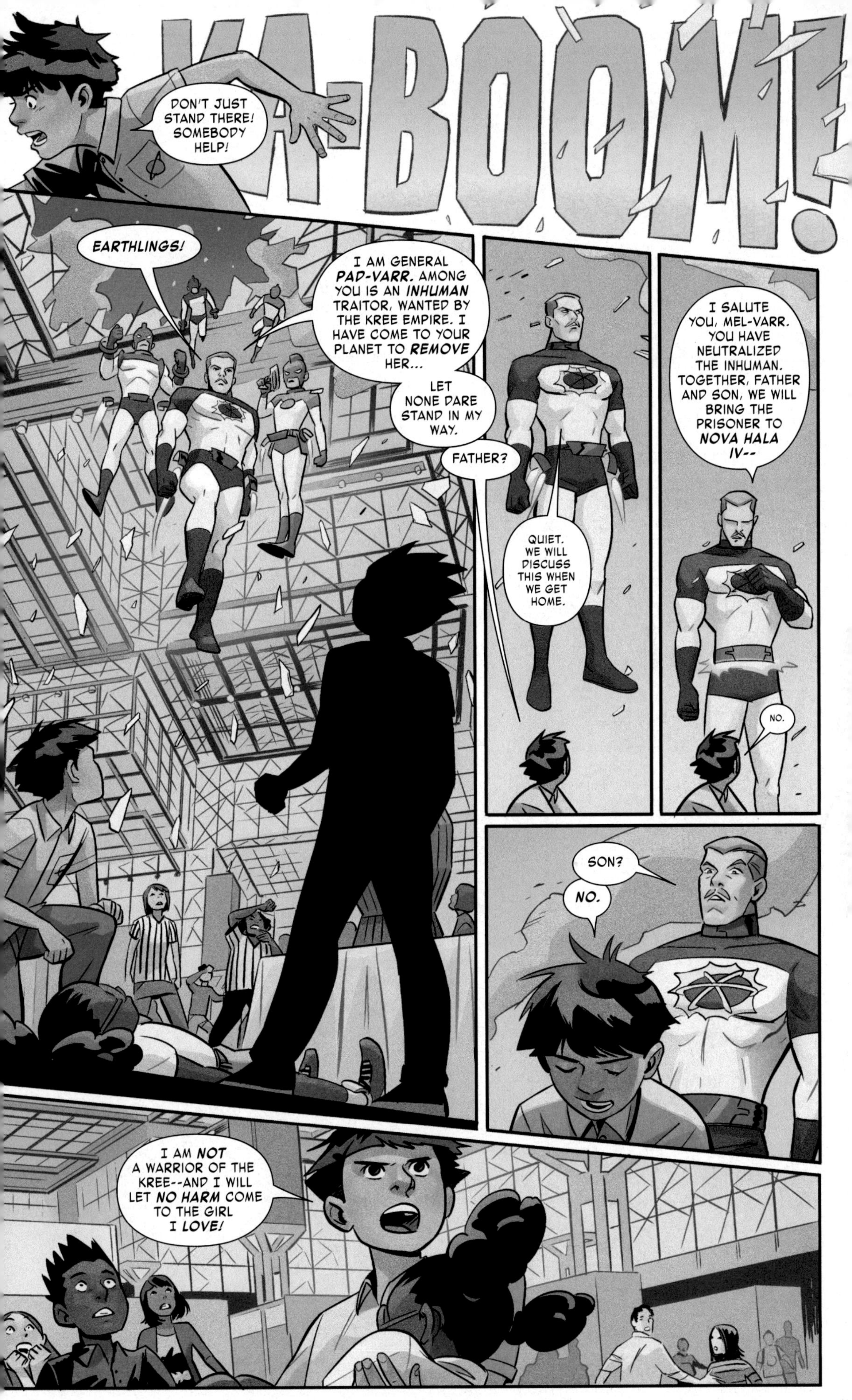
KA-BOOM!
DON'T JUST STAND THERE! SOMEBODY HELP!
EARTHLINGS!
I AM GENERAL PAD-VARR. AMONG YOU IS AN INHUMAN TRAITOR, WANTED BY THE KREE EMPIRE. I HAVE COME TO YOUR PLANET TO REMOVE HER...
LET NONE DARE STAND IN MY WAY.
FATHER?
QUIET. WE WILL DISCUSS THIS WHEN WE GET HOME.
I SALUTE YOU, MEL-VARR. YOU HAVE NEUTRALIZED THE INHUMAN. TOGETHER, FATHER AND SON, WE WILL BRING THE PRISONER TO NOVA HALA IV--
NO.
SON?
NO.
I AM NOT A WARRIOR OF THE KREE--AND I WILL LET NO HARM COME TO THE GIRL I LOVE!

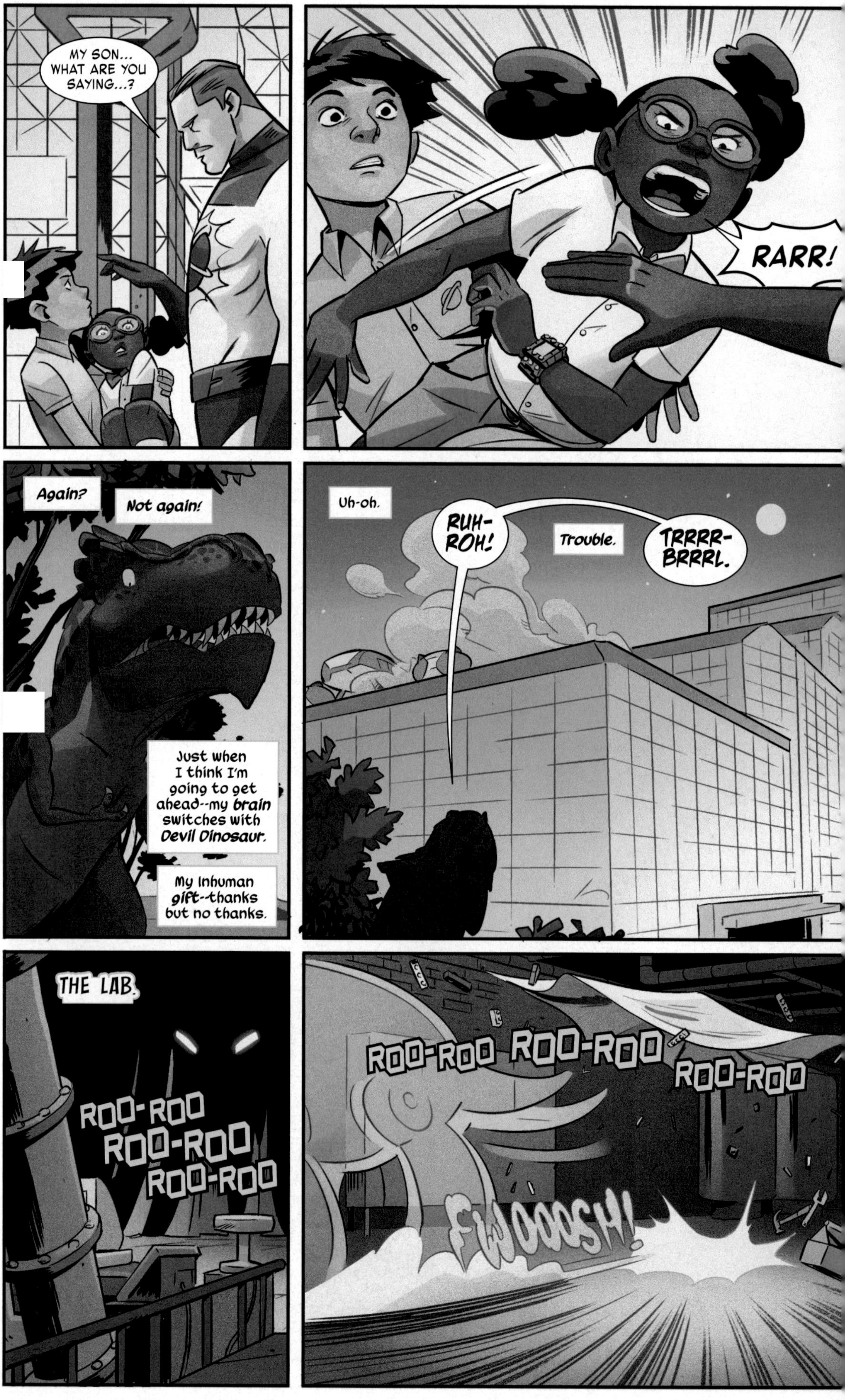
MY SON... WHAT ARE YOU SAYING...?
RARR!
Again?
Not again!
Just when I think I'm going to get ahead--my brain switches with Devil Dinosaur.
My Inhuman gift--thanks but no thanks.
Uh-oh.
RUH-ROH!
Trouble.
TRRRR-BRRRL.
THE LAB.
ROO-ROO
ROO-ROO
ROO-ROO
ROO-ROO ROO-ROO
ROO-ROO
FWOOOSH!

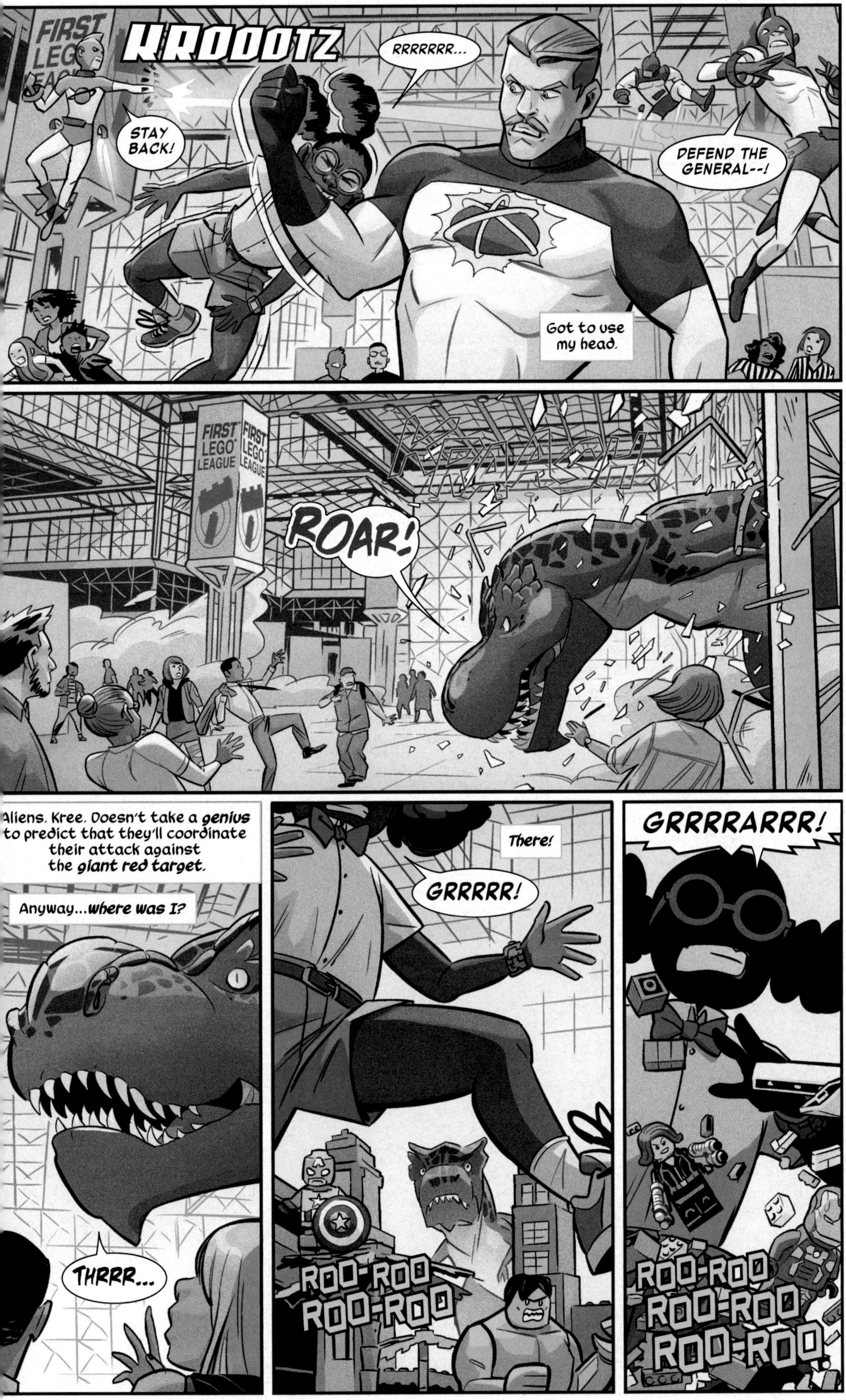
KROOOTZ
STAY BACK!
RRRRRRR...
DEFEND THE GENERAL--!
Got to use my head.
FIRST LEGO LEAGUE
ROAR!
Aliens. Kree. Doesn't take a *genius* to predict that they'll coordinate their attack against the *giant red target*.
Anyway...*where was I?*
THRRR...
There!
GRRRRR!
ROO-ROO ROO-ROO
GRRRRARRR!
ROO-ROO ROO-ROO ROO-ROO

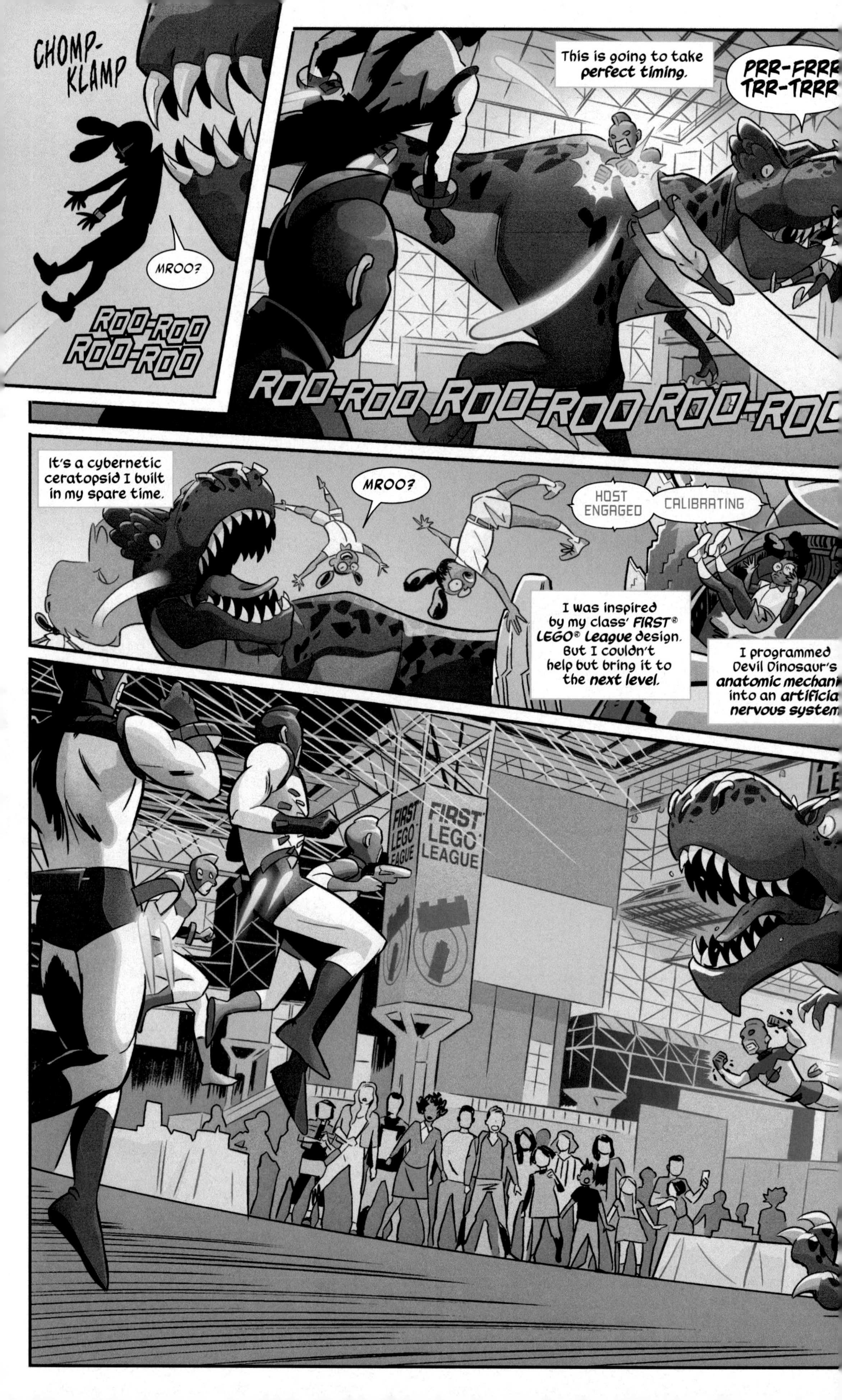

CHOMP-KLAMP
MROO?
ROO-ROO ROO-ROO
This is going to take perfect timing.
PRR-FRRR TRR-TRRR
ROO-ROO ROO-ROO ROO-ROO
It's a cybernetic ceratopsid I built in my spare time.
MROO?
HOST ENGAGED
CALIBRATING
I was inspired by my class' FIRST® LEGO® League design. But I couldn't help but bring it to the next level.
I programmed Devil Dinosaur's anatomic mechani into an artificia nervous system
FIRST LEGO LEAGUE
FIRST LEGO LEAGUE

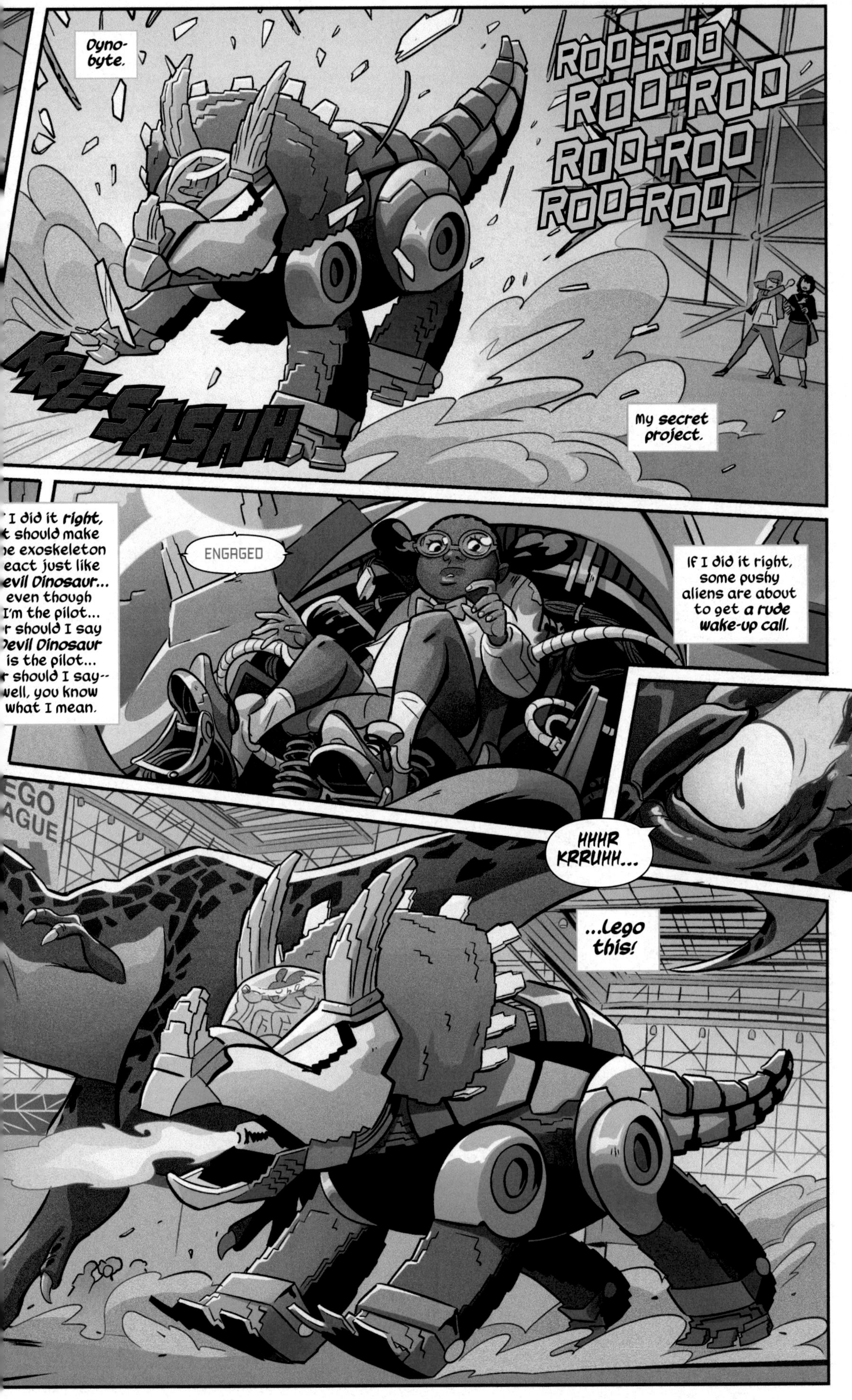
Dyno-byte.
ROO-ROO ROO-ROO ROO-ROO ROO-ROO
KRE-SASHH
My secret project.
I did it right, t should make e exoskeleton eact just like evil Dinosaur... even though I'm the pilot... r should I say evil Dinosaur is the pilot... r should I say-- well, you know what I mean.
ENGAGED
If I did it right, some pushy aliens are about to get a rude wake-up call.
HHHR KRRUHH...
...Lego this!

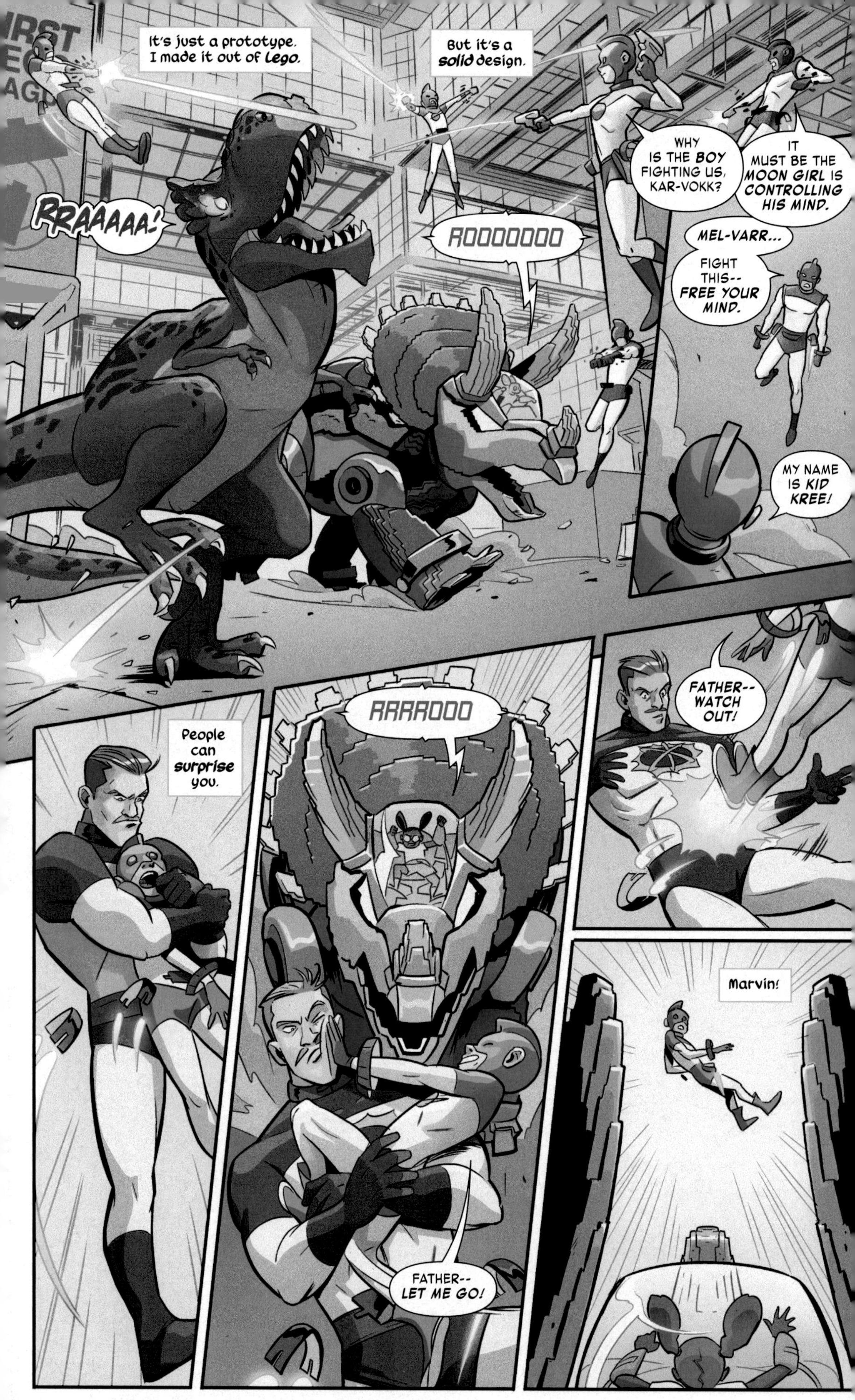

It's just a prototype. I made it out of Lego.
But it's a solid design.
WHY IS THE BOY FIGHTING US, KAR-VOKK?
IT MUST BE THE MOON GIRL IS CONTROLLING HIS MIND.
RRAAAAA!
ROOOOOOO
MEL-VARR...
FIGHT THIS-- FREE YOUR MIND.
MY NAME IS KID KREE!
People can surprise you.
RRRROOO
FATHER-- LET ME GO!
FATHER-- WATCH OUT!
Marvin!

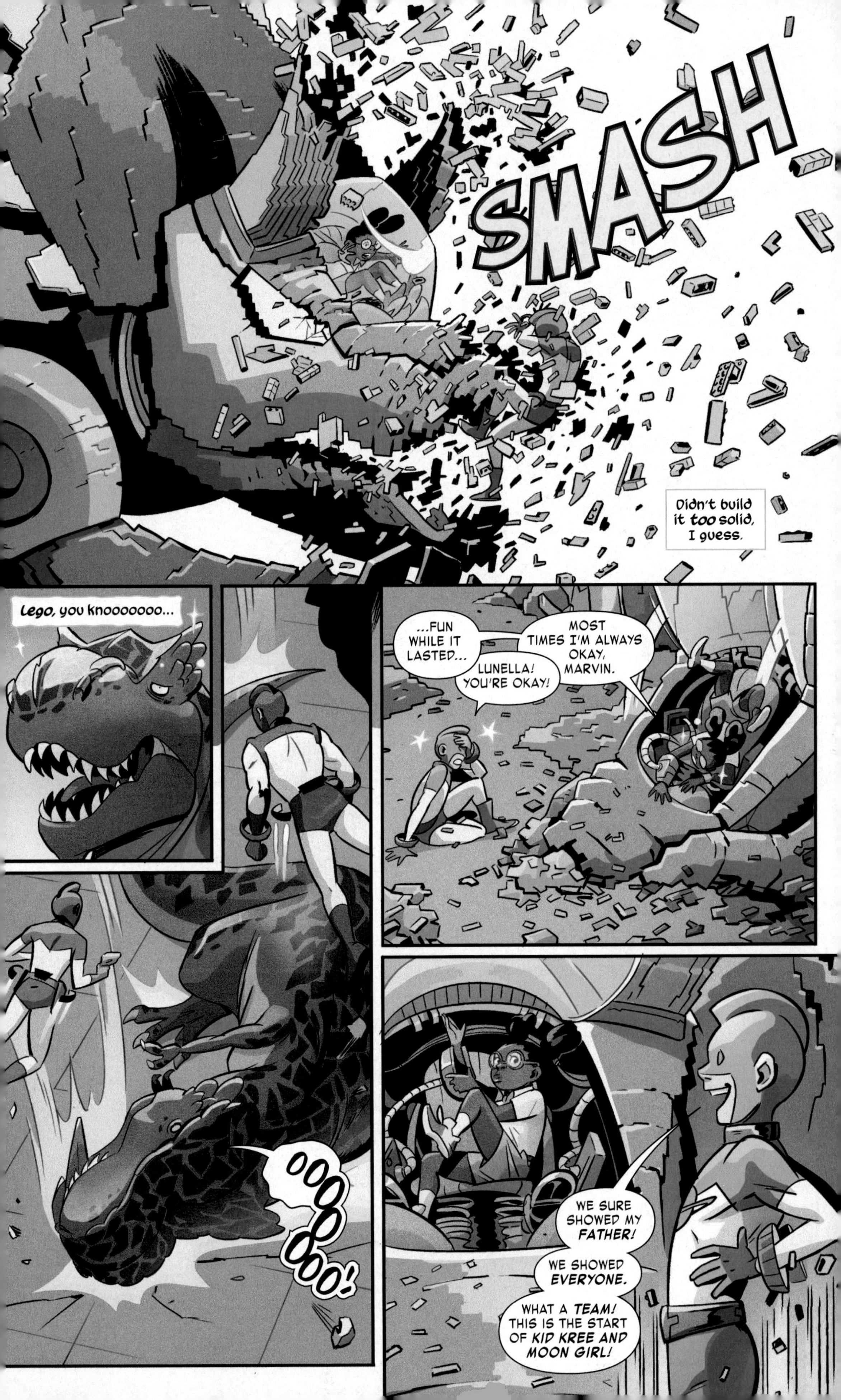
SMASH
Didn't build it too solid, I guess.
Lego, you knooooooo...
OOOOOOO!
...FUN WHILE IT LASTED...
LUNELLA! YOU'RE OKAY!
MOST TIMES I'M ALWAYS OKAY, MARVIN.
WE SURE SHOWED MY FATHER!
WE SHOWED EVERYONE.
WHAT A TEAM! THIS IS THE START OF KID KREE AND MOON GIRL!

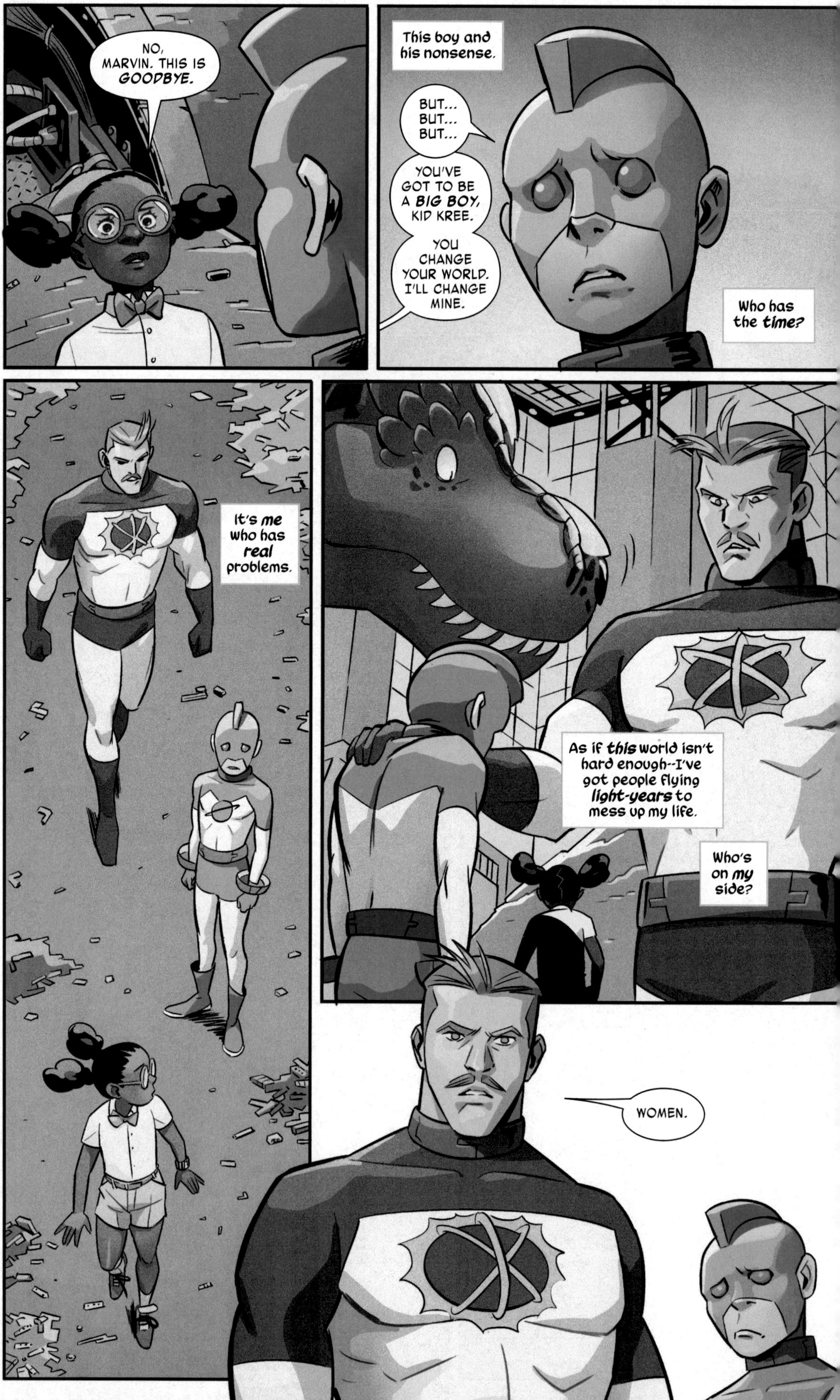

NO, MARVIN. THIS IS GOODBYE.
This boy and his nonsense.
BUT... BUT... BUT...
YOU'VE GOT TO BE A BIG BOY, KID KREE.
YOU CHANGE YOUR WORLD. I'LL CHANGE MINE.
Who has the time?
It's me who has real problems.
As if this world isn't hard enough--I've got people flying light-years to mess up my life.
Who's on my side?
WOMEN.

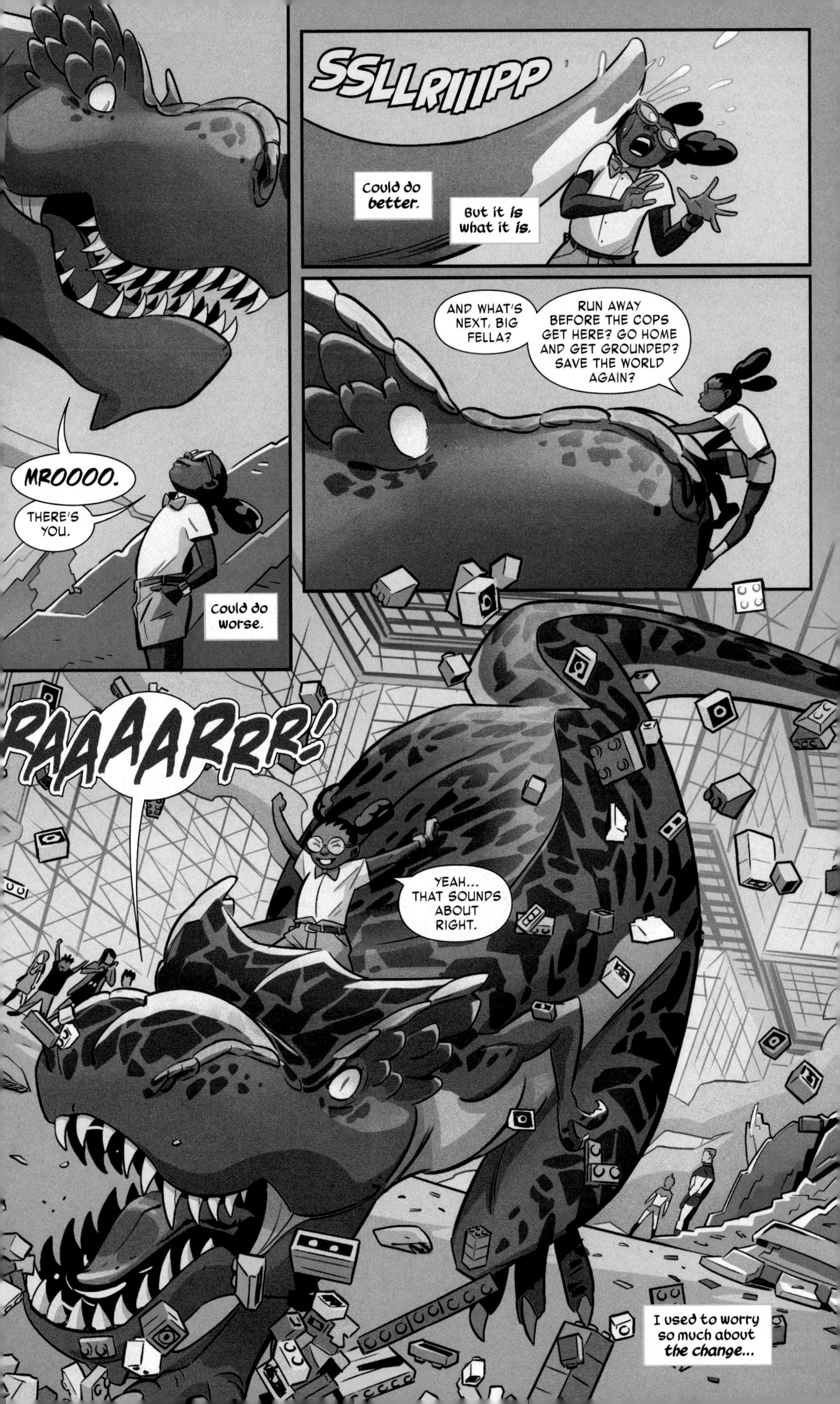
MROOOO.
THERE'S YOU.
Could do worse.
SSLLRIIIPP
Could do better.
But it is what it is.
AND WHAT'S NEXT, BIG FELLA?
RUN AWAY BEFORE THE COPS GET HERE? GO HOME AND GET GROUNDED? SAVE THE WORLD AGAIN?
RAAAAARRRR!
YEAH... THAT SOUNDS ABOUT RIGHT.
I used to worry so much about the change...

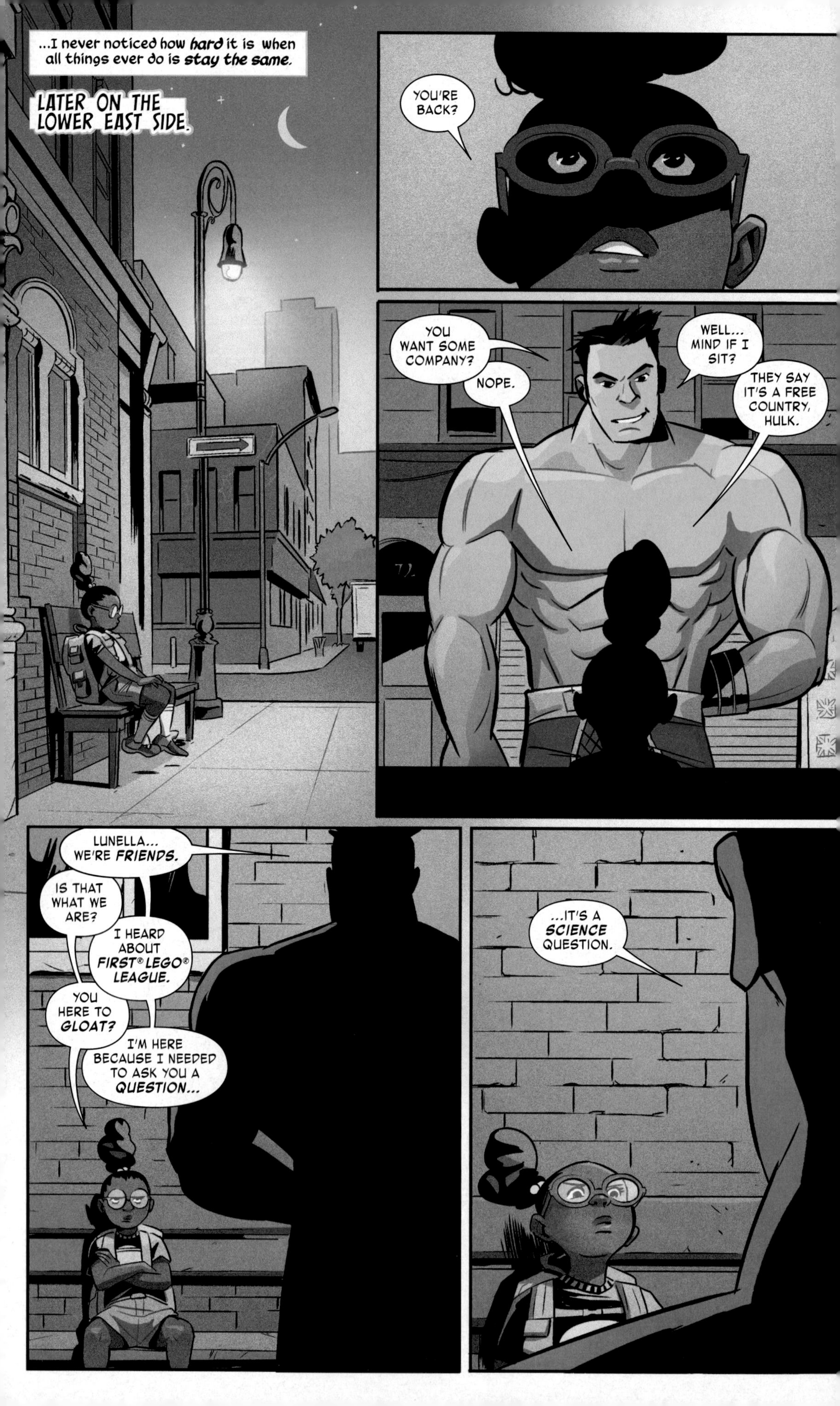
...I never noticed how hard it is when all things ever do is stay the same.
LATER ON THE LOWER EAST SIDE.
YOU'RE BACK?
YOU WANT SOME COMPANY?
NOPE.
WELL... MIND IF I SIT?
THEY SAY IT'S A FREE COUNTRY, HULK.
LUNELLA... WE'RE FRIENDS.
IS THAT WHAT WE ARE?
I HEARD ABOUT FIRST® LEGO® LEAGUE.
YOU HERE TO GLOAT?
I'M HERE BECAUSE I NEEDED TO ASK YOU A QUESTION...
...IT'S A SCIENCE QUESTION.

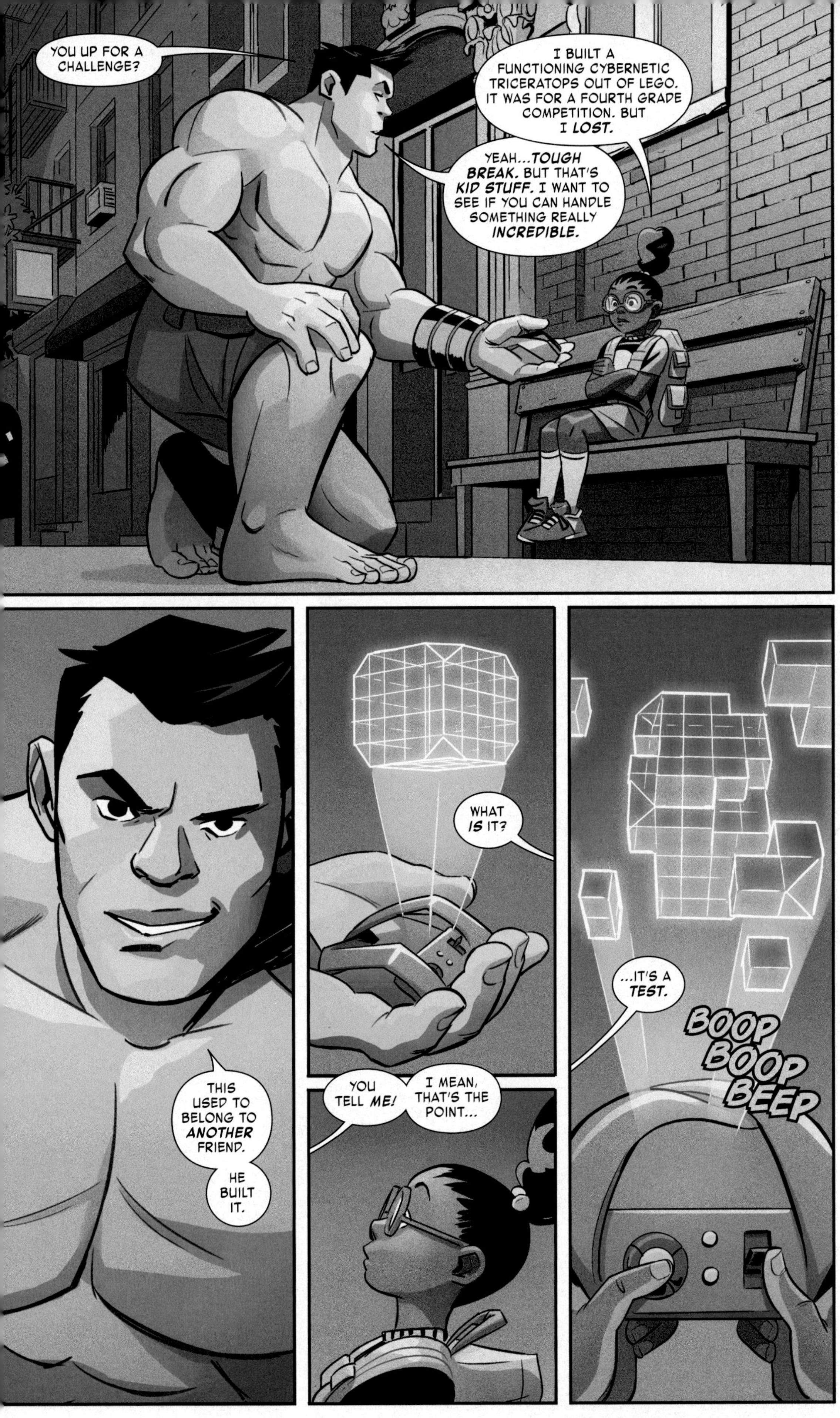

YOU UP FOR A CHALLENGE?
I BUILT A FUNCTIONING CYBERNETIC TRICERATOPS OUT OF LEGO. IT WAS FOR A FOURTH GRADE COMPETITION. BUT I LOST.
YEAH...TOUGH BREAK. BUT THAT'S KID STUFF. I WANT TO SEE IF YOU CAN HANDLE SOMETHING REALLY INCREDIBLE.
THIS USED TO BELONG TO ANOTHER FRIEND.
HE BUILT IT.
WHAT IS IT?
YOU TELL ME!
I MEAN, THAT'S THE POINT...
...IT'S A TEST.
BOOP BOOP BEEP

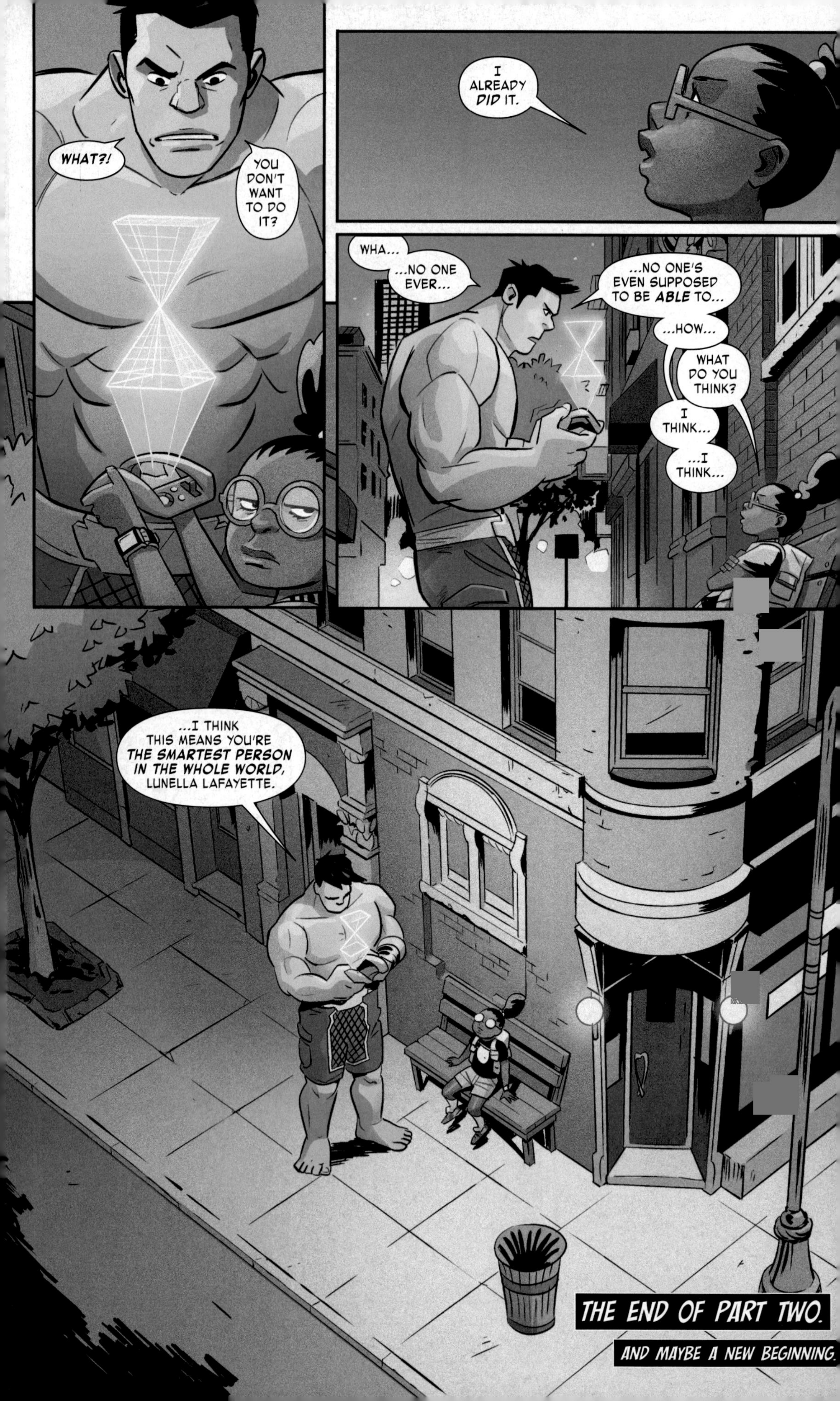
WHAT?!
YOU DON'T WANT TO DO IT?
I ALREADY DID IT.
WHA...
...NO ONE EVER...
...NO ONE'S EVEN SUPPOSED TO BE ABLE TO...
...HOW...
WHAT DO YOU THINK?
I THINK...
...I THINK...
...I THINK THIS MEANS YOU'RE THE SMARTEST PERSON IN THE WHOLE WORLD, LUNELLA LAFAYETTE.
THE END OF PART TWO.
AND MAYBE A NEW BEGINNING.

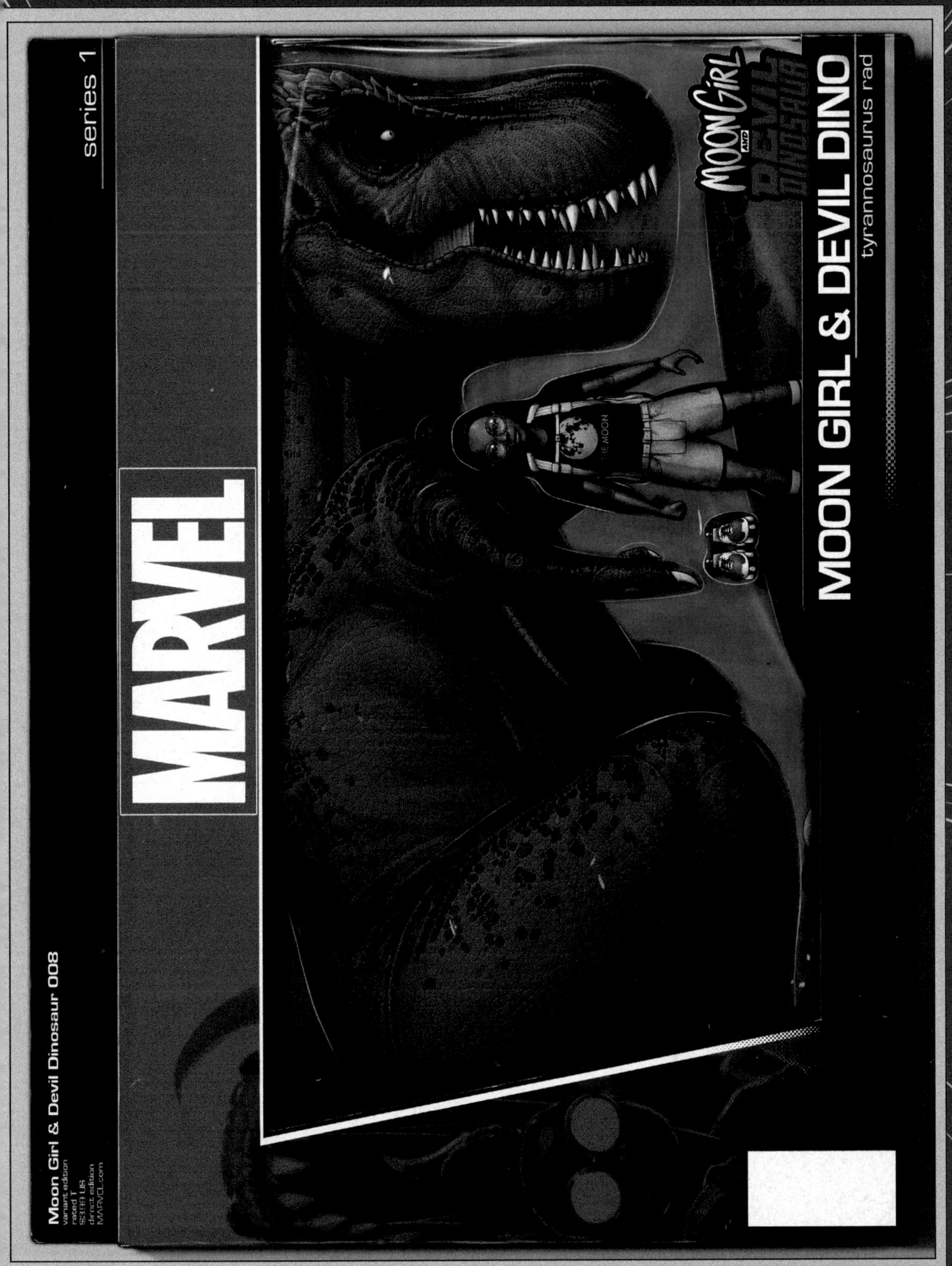
series 1
MARVEL
MOON GIRL AND DEVIL DINOSAUR
MOON GIRL & DEVIL DINO
tyrannosaurus rad
Moon Girl & Devil Dinosaur 008

#8 ACTION FIGURE VARIANT BY JOHN TYLER CHIRSTOPHER

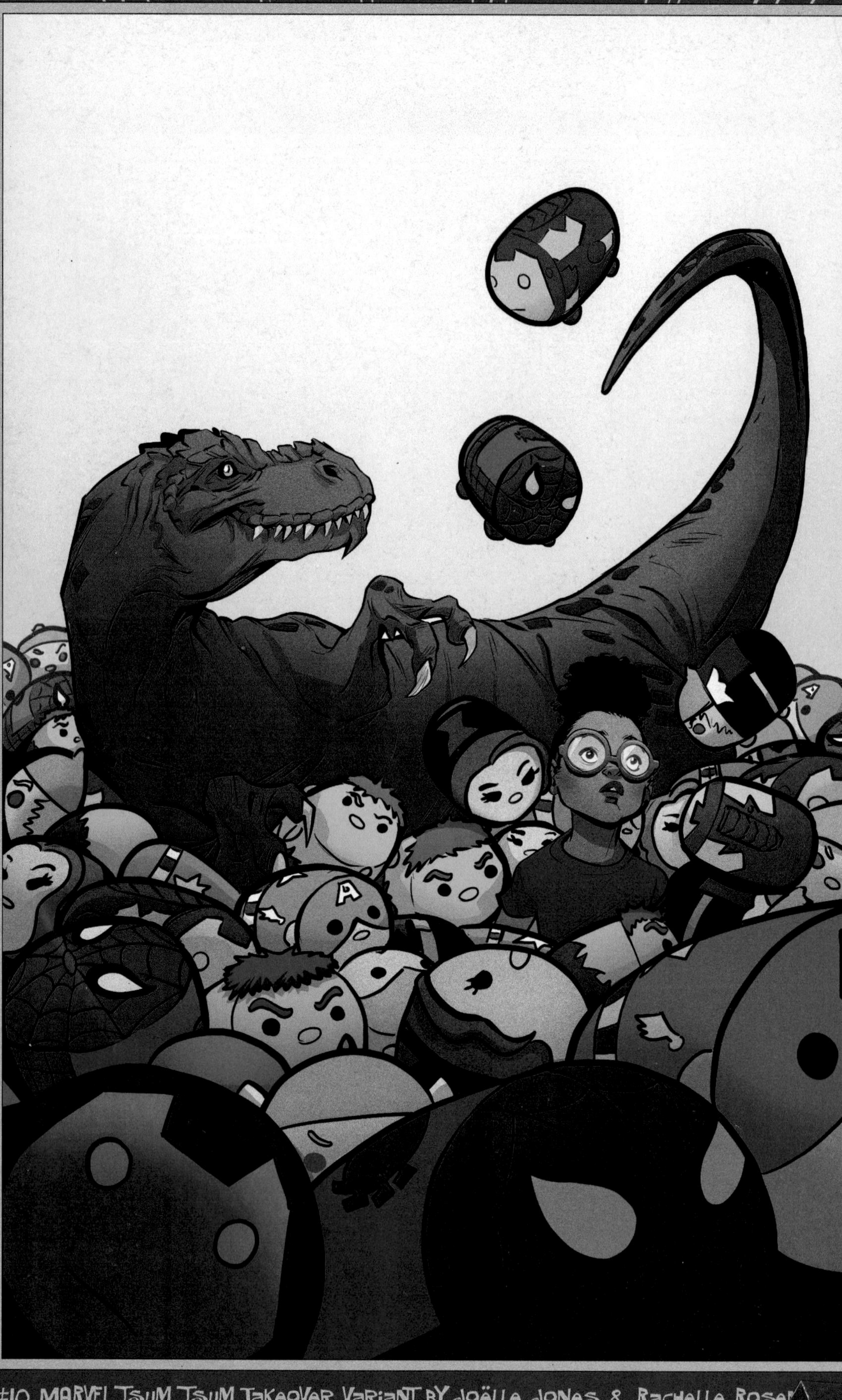

#10 MARVEL TSUM TSUM TAKEOVER VARIANT BY JOËLLE JONES & RACHELLE ROSEN